ENGRAVEN UPON PLATES, PRINTED UPON PAPER

ENGRAVEN UPON PLATES, PRINTED UPON PAPER

Textual and Narrative Structures of the Book of Mormon

BRANT A. GARDNER

Greg Kofford Books
Salt Lake City, 2023

Copyright © 2023 Brant A. Gardner
Cover design copyright © 2023 Greg Kofford Books, Inc.
Cover design by Loyd Isao Ericson

Published in the USA.

All rights reserved. No part of this volume may be reproduced in any form without written permission from the publisher, Greg Kofford Books. The views expressed herein are the responsibility of the author and do not necessarily represent the position of Greg Kofford Books.

ISBN: 978-1-58958-800-4
Also available in ebook.

Greg Kofford Books
P.O. Box 1362
Draper, UT 84020
www.gregkofford.com
facebook.com/gkbooks
twitter.com/gkbooks

Library of Congress Control Number: 2023949895

For Mark A. Wright and his inspiration on so many fronts.

Contents

Introduction ix

Section I: The Nineteenth-Century Text

1. Joseph and Translation 3
2. Nineteenth-Century Influence on the Text 17
3. Translation Artifacts in the English Text 35
4. Ancient and Modern Elements in a Divinely Translated Text 61

Section II: The Nephite Book of Mormon

5. A Written Original Behind the Translation 71
6. Structuring the Text 79
7. Influence of the Assumed Audience 103
8. Interweaving Names and Narrative 113
9. Preserved Orality in Nephite Literature 123
10. Blocks of Time 155

Section III: Nephite Writers and Their Sources

11. Reconstructing the Final Nephite Archive 167
12. The Structure of the Large Plates 173
13. Nephi's and Jacob's Use of Source Texts 185
14. Mormon's Use of Source Texts 195
15. Mormon's Appendix 215
    Bibliography 221
    Scripture Index 231
    Subject Index 235

Introduction

For Latter-day Saints in the last hundred years, the official story of Joseph Smith's prophetic ministry begins with what is called the First Vision, a vision of the Father and Jesus Christ who forbade him joining any of the churches in his region. However, in the decade from 1820 to 1830, he only told one person, a minister. The experience was sufficiently negative that Joseph declined to tell the story again until a decade or more later.[1]

Instead, the story the earliest Saints heard, and for whom it formed the foundation of their belief in the new religion, was the story of golden plates:

> When I was seventeen years of age I called again upon the Lord and he shewed unto me a heavenly vision for behold an angel of the Lord came and stood before me and it was by night and he called me by name and he said the Lord had forgiven me my sins and he revealed unto me that in the Town of Manchester Ontario County N.Y. there was plates of gold upon which there was engravings which was engraven by Maroni & his fathers the servants of the living God in ancient days and deposited by th[e] commandments of God and kept by the power thereof and that I should go and get them and he revealed unto me many things concerning the inhabitents of the earth which since have been revealed in commandments & revelations and it was on the 22d day of Sept. AD 1822.[2]

Joseph declared that his personal failings prevented him from receiving those plates for four years. After that time, he recounted:

> I was chastened and saught diligently to obtain the plates and obtained them not untill I was twenty one years of age and in this year I was married to Emma Hale Daughtr of Isaach [Isaac] Hale who lived in Harmony Susquehan[n]a County Pensylvania on the 18th January AD, 1827, on the 22d day of Sept of this same year I obtained the plat[e]s.[3]

In between that visit where the angel declared that ancient writers had engraven on plates and the printing of the Book of Mormon in 1830 is

---

1. Steven C. Harper, *First Vision: Memory and Mormon Origins*, 9–11.
2. "History, circa Summer 1832," The Joseph Smith Papers, 4. This version is the only one of Joseph's histories that contains some of his own handwriting. One minor repetition and a cross-out silently removed.
3. "History, circa Summer 1832," 5.

the story of the translation itself and the production of the Original and Printer's Manuscripts. This book focuses on what may be learned from the manuscripts about the translation, and what may be discerned from the translation of how those ancient writers composed their intended stories. This book examines the English translation for information about which elements of the text correspond to the act of translation, and which elements were present in the Nephite original prior to its translation.

The analysis covers three compositional layers that are explicit and implicit in the text of the Book of Mormon.

1. The Nineteenth-Century Text

The modern historical record makes it clear that Joseph Smith and various scribes were involved in producing the 1829 English language text that became known as the "Original Manuscript." Because the first 116 dictated pages by Martin Harris were lost, a copy of the subsequent translation was made for the compositor to avoid a similar fate.[4] That manuscript is known as the "Printer's Manuscript," the majority of which was used to typeset the first printing of the Book of Mormon. Were it complete, the Original Manuscript would have been the most important source for understanding the dictated text prior to the compositor's paratextual additions, but much more is missing than remains.[5] Fortunately, the Printer's Manuscript remains mostly intact, missing only three lines of text.[6]

A comparison of the Printer's Manuscript with the extant portions of the Original Manuscript shows that while there were some scribal errors introduced in the creation of the Printer's Manuscript, there are no signs of editing.[7] This means that while we cannot compare the Printer's Manuscript

---

4. According to research done by Don Bradley, the number of pages dictated to and lost by Martin Harris may have actually been as high as 300 pages, with the number 116 being instead the page count of the small plates translation contained in the Printer's Manuscript. See Don Bradley, *The Lost 116 Pages: Reconstructing the Book of Mormon's Missing Stories*, 92–103.

5. In the introduction to the Joseph Smith Papers' publication of the remaining Original Manuscript, the editors note: "Of the nearly 500 pages that were placed in the Nauvoo House cornerstone, portions of 232 pages survive, amounting to roughly 28 percent of the text. Some of what remains is badly faded, obscured, or otherwise damaged." Royal Skousen and Robin Scott Jensen, eds., *Revelations and Translations, Volume 5: Original Manuscript of the Book of Mormon*, xi.

6. Royal Skousen and Robin Scott Jensen, eds., *Revelations and Translations, Volume 3: Printer's Manuscript of the Book of Mormon*, xii.

7. Skousen and Jensen, *Original Manuscript*, xxv.

to the Original, there is yet confidence that the Printer's Manuscript is reasonably faithful to the Original.

These two manuscripts were unquestionably produced in the nineteenth century and dictated in an English translation. They establish the most recent composition layer of the Book of Mormon. Section I examines the question of whether Joseph's mind was an active presence in the creation of the English text and explores elements that may be ascribed to its nineteenth-century composition.

2. The Nephite Book of Mormon

Section II begins to look at the text that was engraved on the plates. As the only way to examine this earlier composition layer is through the analysis of the translation layer, this section examines the evidence for a written text that underlies the dictated English text; it also explores elements of the text that fit better with the ancient compositional layer.

3. Nephite Writers and Their Sources

Section III looks to an even earlier compositional layer. The Nephite writers Nephi$_1$, Jacob, Mormon, and Moroni all indicate that they used previously written sources as they crafted their own stories. This section looks to understand those sources, how they were constructed, what they contained, and how they were used.

The perspective of this book is that of a believer in the claims the Book of Mormon makes to its provenance. Nevertheless, it should not be seen as an apologetic work, at least in the sense of an apologetic defense of the truth claims of the text. Those claims are simply accepted so that the analysis of the different compositional layers can be made to see which elements reasonably belong to each of the three creative layers claimed by the final publication. It is hoped that even those not of the faith might gain insight into the multiple dimensions represented by those compositional categories.

Much of the analyses of ancient textual flow elements resulted from a project where I took the bare, punctuation-free Printer's Manuscript and, just as John H. Gilbert did for the 1830 edition, added my own punctuation and paragraphing to format the text into a readable published version. Although the sentence and paragraph structure often parallel those of Gilbert's, the logic for the creation of paragraphs differs significantly from all other publications. This text is available as *The Plates of Mormon:*

A Book of Mormon Study Edition Based on Textual and Narrative Structures in the English Translation, also available from Greg Kofford Books. In some ways, this book serves as an introduction to the editing decisions made in that work. Nevertheless, the two can stand on their own. I express my thanks to Loyd Ericson of Kofford Books for his hard work in making these books happen. A very different book entered his editing grinder. It fought both of us, but through his efforts a much better book emerged from the process.

Finally, a note on the use of subscripts with some Book of Mormon names: There are often two or more people who share the same name. These are designated as, for example, $Nephi_1$, $Nephi_2$, and $Nephi_3$. There are more duplicated names than are indicated in this book. The only Book of Mormon names receiving subscripts are those where at least two different men (and they are always men) have the same name and both are mentioned in this book. For example, Captain Moroni and Moroni the son of Mormon share the same name, but Moroni is not indicated with a subscript as Captain Moroni does not appear in this book.

The following is a short biography of the men carrying the same name who appear in this book:

$Alma_1$, father of $Alma_2$

$Alma_1$ was a descendant of $Nephi_1$ and lived in the land of Nephi after the people of Zeniff returned to that land from Zarahemla (born ca. 173 BC). He was a priest of the wicked king Noah and is described as "a young man" (Mosiah 17:2). He was sitting in king Noah's court when Abinadi was brought to trial and became Abinadi's only convert.

As an exile, $Alma_1$ began to gather those who were willing to listen to the gospel as Abinadi had preached it. So many people believed $Alma_1$'s preaching of the gospel that they began to form a large enough body that king Noah became aware of their meetings and meeting place. Warned to flee, $Alma_1$ and his followers left the land of Nephi and headed north, where they found a place to live which they called Helam (Mosiah 23:19–20). Eventually, they made their way to Zarahemla (Mosiah 25:5–6).

$Alma_1$ himself does not appear to have held any particular named position, although he was clearly influential. His son, also named Alma, became the first chief judge as well as the designated leader of all of the Nephite churches.

Alma$_2$, son of Alma$_1$

While Alma$_1$ was a confidant of king Mosiah$_2$, Alma$_2$ (ca. 100–73 BC) and his close friends, king Mosiah$_2$'s sons, rebelled against their fathers' religious teachings. In an event with some parallels to Saul's vision of Christ on the road to Damascus (Acts 9), Alma$_2$ was traveling with the sons of Mosiah$_2$, "going about rebelling against God" (Mosiah 27:11), when an angel appeared to them. Alma$_2$ was the focus of the angel's message, and the spiritual power of that event was "so great that [Alma] became dumb, that he could not open his mouth; yea, and he became weak, even that he could not move his hands" (Mosiah 27:19).

When Mosiah$_2$ dissolved the monarchy, Alma$_2$ was made the first chief judge, as well as the leader of the churches in the land of Zarahemla. In addition to keeping the large-plate record of the Nephites, Alma$_2$ kept a personal record that was available to Mormon, of which Mormon used to enter most of the material from Alma 7 through 42. Those chapters contain some of the most important sermons recorded in the Book of Mormon.

Helaman1, son of Alma2

Nephite recordkeeper and military leader (ca. 74–52 BC). After his father's passing, he also became the chief High Priest of the church, building it up (Alma 45:22–23). His military career was intertwined with the story of the two thousand stripling warriors. It was Helaman who convinced their parents (formerly known as the Anti-Nephi-Lehies) not to pick up arms and therefore break their oath (Alma 53:13).

Helaman2, son of Helaman2

He became the Nephite record keeper. His father, Helaman, had given charge of the records to Helaman's brother Shiblon, and Shiblon passed that responsibility to Helaman's son (Alma 63:11; 53 BC). In 50 BC he was elevated to chief judge, and the book of Helaman is named for him.

He ruled at a time when the ancient secret combinations were reborn. Kishkumen, leader of the group that would become known as the Gadianton robbers, attempted to assassinate Helaman, but was himself killed before he could succeed.

Helaman ruled righteously (Hel. 3:20) and died in 39 B.C. (Hel. 3:37).

Lehi$_1$ of Jerusalem

Lehi$_1$ was called as a prophet of the coming Babylonian destruction of Jerusalem around 600 BC and was contemporary with Jeremiah,

Zephaniah, Habakkuk, Obadiah, and Ezekiel. He faithfully fulfilled his call as a prophet to Jerusalem but was rejected by the people there. The Lord commanded that he take his family and flee. He was to be guided to a new land of promise for his family.

Lehi$_1$ continued to be the family prophet as well as patriarch in the Old World. In the New World, he is known for his blessings to his sons in 2 Nephi, and particularly his powerful teachings about agency found in 2 Nephi 2. The separation of his children into two groups appears to have occurred after his death.

Lehi$_2$, son of Helaman$_2$

Lehi$_2$ is known as the missionary companion to his brother Nephi (ca. 45 BC). He and his brother served among the Lamanites and converted eight thousand (Alma 5:16–20). Mormon was more interested in his brother Nephi, and we know of Lehi only as part of Nephi's missionary labors.

Mosiah$_1$, father of Benjamin

Born and raised in the land of Nephi, the Lord told Mosiah$_1$ to flee the land of Nephi with all those who would go with him (ca. 200 BC; Omni 1:12). They were led to the city of Zarahemla where they met the people who were descended from Mulek of Jerusalem. Mosiah$_1$ was made king over the united peoples, perhaps due to the brass plates which lent authority to his claim to divinely sanctioned rulership.

He used the interpreters to translate a large stone that the people of Zarahemla brought to him (Omni 1:20). That stone recorded some of the history of the Jaredites. Much of what might have been known of his reign was lost with the 116 pages.

Mosiah$_2$, son of Benjamin

Mosiah$_2$ was installed as king when his father, Benjamin, called a special gathering of the combined peoples of Zarahemla following a terrible civil war. He was king from about 124 to 91 BC. At the end of his reign, his sons refused to become king. Therefore, to forestall potential political divisions, Mosiah$_2$ altered the nature of Nephite government, moving from a king to the reign of judges (Mosiah 29:6–11). Part of that change included the establishment of laws that would be used to judge rather than simply follow the will of the king.

Nephi$_1$, son of Lehi$_1$

Nephi$_1$ was the youngest of the four sons of Lehi$_1$, born in Jerusalem (ca. 615–544 BC). He was favored of the Lord and prophesied to be a leader and teacher over his brothers (1 Ne. 2:22). After Lehi$_1$'s death, the Lord told Nephi$_1$ to flee as his brothers desired to kill him (2 Ne. 5:4–6). Nephi$_1$ became the leader of a new people who eventually took his name and elevated him as king. This fulfilled the prophecy of becoming a ruler, although it was over his brothers Sam, Jacob, and Joseph. Nephi$_1$ never ruled over Laman and Lemuel.

Nephi$_1$ was the original Nephite recordkeeper, creating two sets of plates on which different types of history were to be recorded. The official record has been called the large plates of Nephi, and the second set, which the Lord commanded Nephi$_1$ to create, has been called the small plates of Nephi. The adjectives large and small refer to quantity of plates rather than size.

Nephi$_1$ ruled righteously, although not without difficulty. In his farewell words he noted that there were "many that harden their hearts against the Holy Spirit, that it hath no place in them" (2 Ne. 33:2).

Nephi$_2$, son of Helaman$_2$

Nephi$_2$ was an important prophet and leader, filling the role of chief judge after his father's death (Hel. 3:37). He eventually abdicated to concentrate on the ministry (Hel. 5:1–5). His ministry spanned from approximately 39 BC to AD 1. He was joined in his missionary service by his brother, Lehi$_2$, and they had much success. First, they went to the people of Nephi in the land southward (Hel. 5:16) and then on to the Lamanites. There they were imprisoned but miraculously freed (Hel. 5:49). They were successful among the Lamanites, sufficiently so that eventually the Lamanites would send Samuel as a prophet to declare repentance to the Nephites (Hel. 13:1–2).

During Nephi$_2$'s lifetime, the Gadiantons gained control of the Nephite government (Hel. 7:4). Nephi$_2$ called upon God to seal the heavens, which resulted in a drought. Eventually, enough people repented that the drought was lifted.

Nephi$_3$, son of Nephi$_2$

Nephi$_3$ was the prophet who received the knowledge that the Savior would be born on the very night before the believers were to be put to death should the signs not be given (3 Ne. 1:9–14). He was one of the twelve disciples that the resurrected Christ chose when he appeared in Bountiful (3 Ne. 19:4). It is probable that it was Nephi$_3$'s short account of the Savior's visit that Mormon used as the basis for much of 3 Nephi (3 Ne. 5:9).

There is some confusion over the relationship between this Nephi$_3$ and the one for whom the book of 4 Nephi is named. Evidence suggests, however, that it was this very Nephi$_3$.

Section I:
The Nineteenth-Century Text

Chapter One

Joseph and Translation

An important foundation to any discussion of the nineteenth-century elements in the Book of Mormon is to understand the role Joseph Smith played in the production of the text. For those who do not believe in its ancient provenance, the answer is simple: Joseph did not translate anything, and the entirety of the text is from the nineteenth century.

On the other hand, belief in the declarations the text makes about its ancient historicity, as well as what later revelations say of Joseph's relation to the text, affirm that it is not merely a nineteenth-century production; instead, it is "an account written by the hand of Mormon upon plates. Taken from the plates of Nephi. Wherefore, it is an abridgment of the record of the people of Nephi, and also of the Lamanites—Written to the Lamanites, who are a remnant of the house of Israel; and also to Jew and Gentile" (Title Page).

That ancient text is declared to have been translated into English by some process that involved both Joseph and the "gift and power of God."[1] From this perspective, it is abundantly clear that Joseph is considered the text's translator:

- July 1828: "& when thou deliveredst up that Which that which God had given thee right to Translate."[2]
- Spring 1829: "It is wisdom in me that ye should translate this first part of the engravings of Nephi."[3]
- April 1830: "& gave unto him power by the means of which was before prepared that he should translate a Book which Book contained a record of a fallen People."[4]

Importantly, the same language was applied in March 1831 to the work Joseph did with the Bible: "I say unto you it shall not be given unto you to know any farther then this until the New Testament be translated."[5]

Joseph saw himself, and was therefore seen by his community, as a translator. The issue that remains difficult to understand is precisely what

---

1. Joseph Smith, "Preface," 1.
2. "Revelation Book 1," 2 [Doctrine and Covenants 3:12].
3. "Revelation Book 1," 11 [Doctrine and Covenants 10:45].
4. "Revelation Book 1," 53 [Doctrine and Covenants 20: 8–9].
5. "Revelation Book 1," 75 [Doctrine and Covenants 45:60].

is meant by the term "translate." On a macro level, Samuel M. Brown has produced an important examination of the way the word *translation* may explain the widest context of the Joseph's theology. He writes: "Translation was about more than words and sentences. Translation was also concerned with the transformation of human beings and the worlds they were capable of inhabiting."[6] That may be the best and most inclusive definition, but it is not helpful for understanding how the Book of Mormon's Nephite language was recreated in English. This is a topic that has long been discussed in Latter-day Saint scholarly literature.

One attempt to describe Joseph's own influence on the English text is Royal Skousen's triple delineation of iron-clad, tight, and loose control during Joseph's translation efforts.[7] However, Skousen's schema primarily relates to the controlled transmission of the text and not necessarily the process of translation itself.[8] Thus, Skousen would allow for a perhaps *loose* translation that was created prior to the time it was given to Joseph, who then *tightly* dictated what he saw through a seer stone.

To attempt to provide a different perspective to unravel the threads of the translation tangle, we may instead delineate the various stages of the movement of the ancient Nephite text into a modern English text. There are four that can be examined:

1. The ancient composition and its intended audience.
2. The agent of translation and the intended audience.
3. Joseph Smith's oral dictation.
4. The transcription of the dictated text.

Because it is only the fourth step—the translated dictation—that can be directly examined, it is there that this study will begin, working in reverse to induce what can be learned of each stage. They are further defined as follows:

Stage 4: The Transcription of the Dictated Text

An analysis of what was transcribed as Joseph spoke is thoroughly examined in Skousen's *Analysis of the Textual Variants of the Book of Mormon.*

---

6. Samuel Morris Brown, *Joseph Smith's Translation: The Words and Worlds of Early Mormonism*, 4.

7. Royal Skousen, "Translating the Book of Mormon: Evidence from the Original Manuscript," 64–65. A revised version is Royal Skousen, "How Joseph Smith Translated the Book of Mormon: Evidence from the Original Manuscript," 24.

8. Skousen, "Translating the Book of Mormon," 64–65.

That is unquestionably the work that should be consulted on this aspect of the creation of the modern text. This book has nothing to add.

Stage 3: Joseph Smith's Oral Dictation

When Joseph dictated to his scribes, he spoke English. This may seem too obvious to point out. However, an examination of the nature of the English text necessarily focuses on Joseph and the language of his time, environment, and culture. This stage explores if and how the early nineteenth century is reflected in the English text as dictated.

Stage 2: The Agent of Translation and the Intended Audience

The declaration that Joseph was the translator conflates stages 2 and 3. If Joseph is the agent of translation, then modern elements of the text may be attributed to him. If a divine being created the translation, and Joseph simply read it to his scribes, then modern elements must be assigned to that divine agent of translation. Thus, Section I spends time examining the arguments for Joseph being the agent.

Stage 1: The Ancient Composition and Its Intended Audience

The Book of Mormon declares that there are multiple compositional tasks behind this stage, with authors such as Nephi$_1$, Jacob, Mormon, and Moroni all writing of their own experiences and utilizing available records in the creation of their texts. The original, assumed audience for those writers would have driven some of their organization, literary structures, and selected events. Furthermore, these writers wrote in a different language, in a different culture, and from a much earlier time than the production of the English text. The examination of the creation of this stage is discussed in Sections II and III.

With that conceptual background of the process, we may examine Joseph's English dictation to identify elements that support him being the agent of translation and illustrate the way in which his nineteenth century cultural milieu appears in the dictated text.

Because the Book of Mormon is declared to have been translated by the gift and power of God, the invocation of the divine draws implicit assumptions about God into the discussion of its creation. There have been at least three basic assumptions about the nature of God's participation in the creation of the English text. The earliest was that God's involvement produced an infallible text. (Skousen calls this an "iron-clad" translation.)

A more recent development is that the divine influence occurred prior to Joseph consulting the translation instruments. Thus, there is a divine translation attributable to an entity from the heavenly realm rather than Joseph Smith. (This is Skousen's "tight control" position.)

Finally, the position this book recommends is that Joseph Smith was, indeed, the translator. When the English text is examined and elements are found that can be attributed to the nineteenth century, they are to be laid at his feet rather than at the feet of the ancient writers—or of God. (This is Skousen's "loose control" position.)

A Divinely Infallible Translation?

Because Joseph Smith gave little indication of his process of translation, we must turn to the many accounts given by those who were associated with him at the time. Joseph Knight's recollection is subtly more informative of the nature of the witnesses' recollection:

> Now, the way he translated was he put the urim and thummim into his hat and Darkned his Eyes then he would take a sentence and it would apper in Brite Roman Letters then he would tell the writer and he would write it[.] then <that would go away> the next sentence would Come and so on But if it was not Spelt rite it would not go away till it was rite[,] so we see it was marvelous.[9]

Royal Skousen lists four more people who supported the idea that the translation process was so accurate that even spelling errors were caught and corrected—Emma Smith, Martin Harris, David Whitmer, and Samuel W. Richards[10]—implying that God played a role in the very wording of the text, down to the spelling. However, other evidence suggests that their agreement is likely due to the communal refining of their understanding rather than an accurate description of what happened.[11]

The actual data from the Original Manuscript is more nuanced.[12] While there is support for statements that Joseph spelled names, there is no corresponding datum to support the correction of the spelling of basic English words.[13] According to Skousen,

> Frequently the first occurrence of a Book of Mormon name is first spelled phonetically, then that spelling is corrected; in some instances, the incorrect

---

9. Joseph Knight Sr., "Reminiscence, Circa 1835–1847," 4:17–18.
10. Skousen, "Translating the Book of Mormon," 65–66.
11. Brant A. Gardner, *The Gift and Power: Translating the Book of Mormon*, 119–34.
12. For an explanation of why the witness statements might agree on something that can be demonstrated to be incorrect, see Gardner, 109–18.
13. Skousen, "Translating the Book of Mormon," 76.

spelling is crossed out and followed on the same line by the correct spelling, thus indicating that the correction is an immediate one.[14]

Whatever process led to the spelling of names did not extend to the spelling of long words, which were often misspelled in the manuscript.[15] Furthermore, despite the control over (usually initial) spellings of names, there is no evidence demonstrating that this control continued for the spelling of those same names. Skousen notes: "[Joseph,] having learned to pronounce the difficult words, . . . would have simply relied on the scribe to correctly spell the words he dictated, except for unfamiliar names."[16] Thus, instead of the dictation being divinely spell-checked throughout, it seems more likely that these witnesses observed initial or occasional corrections and simply assumed consistent divine intervention. Given what the manuscripts show us, we should see these witness statements for their intention rather than their specific information. For example, Knight made his intention very clear when he declared that because of the spelling corrections, one could see that it was "marvelous." Knight was more interested in testifying of the miraculous process than defining the nature of it.

Perhaps the best indication that the words themselves were not seen as divinely perfect and therefore unchangeable was Joseph Smith's own willingness to alter some of the words, which he personally did for the 1837 edition of the Book of Mormon. Here, the only person who had actually experienced the process did not feel that the words themselves were divinely perfected and could not be improved.

A Divine, or Divine-adjacent, Translator?

There is no question that Joseph Smith was involved in the production of the modern text of the Book of Mormon. Numerous witnesses heard him dictating the text, and those who scribed for him confirm that they wrote what he said. In the model of the process of translation, stage 3 (the oral dictation of the text) is so well established that there is no need for examination of who transmitted the text to the scribes.

As for who translated the text, Joseph insisted: "Here then the subject is put to silence, for 'none other people knoweth our language' (Morm.

---

14. Skousen, 75.

15. Skousen, 76–77. That spelling errors would exist in the Original Manuscript is hardly surprising, as witnessed by the frequency with which modern spell checkers fail to do their job. Spelling was still in the process of stabilization in the early nineteenth century.

16. Skousen, 79.

9:34), therefore the Lord, and not man, had to interpret the Nephite record."[17] This statement leaves open the possibility that Joseph could have been the agent of transmission without being the agent of translation. That is, he could have simply been reading an existing text. If so, he would have had no input in the translation.

This is the position that some Latter-day Saint scholars have proposed. For example, Royal Skousen has long favored the idea of Joseph merely dictating an existing translation that he read from the interpreters or the seer stone.[18] More recently, that concept has been bolstered by research into the Book of Mormon's English. From such, Skousen concludes: "Based on the linguistic evidence, the [translator] . . . was not Joseph Smith."[19]

This conclusion is based on a comparison of vocabulary and grammatical forms found in the Book of Mormon (and other of Joseph's translation projects) that were supposedly archaic in 1830 and not part of Joseph's normal speech. Another scholar, Stanford Carmack, similarly declares:

> Smith himself—out of a presumed idiosyncratic, quasi-biblical style—would not have translated and could not have translated the text into the *form* of the earliest text. Had his own language often found its way into the wording of the earliest text, its form would be very different from what we encounter.[20]

This hypothesis is countered by the evidence of Joseph's mind in play during the translation process.

Joseph Smith as the Agent of Translation?

Born in 1805, Joseph Smith was unavoidably a man of the early nineteenth century, and the Book of Mormon, published in 1830, carries elements of the nineteenth century that have long been recognized in the text. Such modern elements should, however, be expected if Joseph had an involved role in the translation. One of the ways to understand how Joseph may be responsible for these more modern intrusions into the ancient content is to examine the ways that we can discern his mind in his other translation projects.

---

17. John W. Welch and Erick B. Carlson, eds., "Joseph Smith to the *Times and Seasons* (1843)," 127.

18. Skousen, "Translating the Book of Mormon," 64–65.

19. Royal Skousen, with Stanford Carmack, *The History of the Text of the Book of Mormon: The King James Quotations in the Book of Mormon*, 6.

20. Stanford Carmack, "Joseph Smith Read the Words," 41; emphasis in original.

Presence of Joseph in the Translation of the Bible

The Joseph Smith Translation contains changes to the King James Bible that range from revelatory expansion, to editorial changes, to a more mundane modernization of vocabulary. The process of translation was markedly different from that of the Book of Mormon. Unlike the translation of the Book of Mormon, Joseph rarely used a seer stone or similar instruments of translation.[21] Indeed, the "original" text that was *translated* was a King James Bible that he and Oliver Cowdery purchased from E. B. Grandin on October 8, 1829.[22] It was a Bible similar to the that used by most Latter-day Saints today, but some words had been modernized and some punctuation and italicized words were different.[23] Looking at his translation, we can observe two main ways in which changes were made to the Bible. The first involves Joseph interacting with the printed text and making relatively small changes; the second involves a revelatory process well exceeding the existing canon.

The physical Bible Joseph used in the translation process contains markings that clearly show him interacting with the text, but it rarely includes textual changes written into the margins or between the lines.[24] However, there are check marks, crosses, circles, dots, and other characters in ink or pencil.[25] The marks appear to be related to the two processes that Joseph used. In the shorter method directly involving the biblical text, the markings would indicate particular words or verses that were to be changed; he would then dictate the changes rather than provide an entire new text.[26] In the longer, revelatory method, Joseph would dictate an entire chapter or more. As he worked through his translation, Joseph eventually moved away from the long method of revealing completely new passages to the shorter method of marking up the text to indicate smaller changes to be made. From that point on, then, the first phase of

---

21. Kent P. Jackson, *Understanding Joseph Smith's Translation of the Bible*, 15.

22. Robert J. Matthews, *"A Plainer Translation": Joseph Smith's Translation of the Bible: A History and Commentary*, 26.

23. Scott H. Faulring, Kent P. Jackson, and Robert J. Matthews, eds., *Joseph Smith's New Translation of the Bible: Original Manuscripts*, 5.

24. Matthews, "Plainer Translation," 56.

25. Matthews comments that the marks may have been the result of more than one person's work (59). He suggests the possibility that some of the marks might have been entered after the Prophet's use of the Bible, perhaps by committees preparing the text for publication.

26. Matthews, 59–60.

translation involved reading the Bible text, deciding what type of changes needed to be made, and marking the text with the appropriate symbol.

One of the important similarities between the translation of the Bible and the Isaiah sections of the Book of Mormon is that both pay statistically significant attention to the King James Bible's italicized words. According to David P. Wright, "Many of the variants in the [Book of Mormon] Isaiah over against the King James Version occur precisely at these words."[27] Additionally, Wright found that the changes at those locations showed the same pattern as the later changes at italicized words in the translation of the Bible, though he did not explicitly make that comparison:

> The words omitted are those that translators would normally insert during translation for smooth conceptual and idiomatic flow in English. That these italicized words are missing is an indication that Smith was working from the KJV and at times made such modifications rather mechanically. This is more transparent in cases where the want of italicized words yields an ungrammatical and even incomprehensible reading. A recurring phrase in Isa. 5:25; 9:12, 17, 21; 10:4 is that God's "anger is not turned away, but his hand *is* stretched out still." In the [Book of Mormon] parallel passages, the verb "*is*" is absent, producing the syntactically incomplete phrase "his hand stretched out still" (2 Ne. 15:25; 2 Ne. 19:12, 17, 21; 20:4). The difficulty had to be remedied in later editions of the [Book of Mormon] by restoring the verb.[28]

In addition to simply excising italicized words, the Book of Mormon Isaiah passages also show the tendency to add or modify the text around them. Sometimes these changes removed the italicized word, yielding a complete sentence but supplying a slightly different reading. This pattern is simi-

---

27. David P. Wright, "Isaiah in the Book of Mormon: Or Joseph Smith in Isaiah," 159.

28. Wright, 164. Stan Spencer, "Missing Words: King James Bible Italics, the Translation of the Book of Mormon, and Joseph Smith as an Unlearned Reader and Editor of a Visioned Text," suggests: "In making these changes, Joseph Smith would not have been intending (or pretending) to restore ancient understanding, but rather to correct perceived errors of transmission of the English text. His focus during this process would not have been on italicized words per se, nor on intentionally revising the biblical text, but rather on supplying words where he thought they had been mistakenly (in his view) dropped" (64).

I agree that Joseph made changes in locations other than italicized words, but the only indication that he thought there was a "dropped" word is the removal of the italicized word that required a revision. He was not consistent, but the indication is that he was paying attention to the text in front of him and interacting. There is no good evidence that there were missing words that he had to supply.

larly found in the Joseph Smith Translation, where Joseph at times simply removed italicized words, but more often found new text to replace them.[29]

The similarity in process and the clear interaction with the physical Bible during the biblical revisions strongly suggest that the underlying relationship of Joseph to the Book of Mormon is similar. In both cases, Joseph was interacting with a text that included italicized words, which became an intermittent focus of his translation efforts. It is also very clear that Joseph was involved in that process as he *translated* the Bible.

The Joseph Smith Translation of the Bible makes clear that there was no divine pre-translated text from which Joseph read. In addition to the evidence of his interaction with the printed text, there are two instances where he translated the same text twice at different times during the translation of the Bible. Kent P. Jackson and Peter M. Jasinski provide the background for this interesting case:

> In light of what we know now about the creation of the New Translation, it is interesting to observe that, in two places in the Bible, Joseph Smith provided two original translations that vary from each other. The passages, one quite long (Matt. 26:1–71) and the other very short (2 Pet. 3:4–6), were translated twice, most likely because Joseph Smith had forgotten that he had produced the original translations and thus translated the material anew.[30]

As they conclude their comparison of the two translations, they note:

> The duplicate translation of [Joseph Smith Translation] material provides a unique opportunity to examine how Joseph Smith prepared his translation of the Bible. To a certain extent, we have in this situation the necessary components of a controlled test on how this kind of revelation worked—two independently produced prophetic revisions of the same texts.[31]

In addition to the interactive changes, there was also a significant revelatory process for parts of the text. Joseph created large sections of text that follow from the content of the Bible but are not directly dependent upon it. Kathleen Flake describes this extra-textual method of receiving the information to be written into the text:

> Smith is quoted as saying: "After I got through translating the Book of Mormon, I took up the Bible to read with the Urim and Thummim. I read the first chapter of Genesis, and I saw the things as they were done, I turned

---

29. Wright, "Isaiah in the Book of Mormon," 167–68.

30. Kent P. Jackson and Peter M. Jasinski, "The Process of Inspired Translation: Two Passages Translated Twice in the Joseph Smith Translation of the Bible," 36.

31. Jackson and Jasinski, 58.

over the next and the next, and the whole passed before me like a grand panorama; and so on chapter after chapter until I read the whole of it. I saw it all!" A more authoritative account is provided by Smith himself in February 1832. "Upon my return from Amherst [Massachusetts] conference, I resumed the translation of the Scriptures. . . . While translating St. John's Gospel, myself and Elder Rigdon saw the following vision" of the resurrection of the dead. Finally, in an 1843 funeral sermon, probably alluding to the account in Matt. 27:52 of graves opening at the death of Jesus, Smith spoke of "the visions that roll like an overflowing surge, before my mind." More specifically, he said, "I saw the graves open & the saints as they arose took each other by the hand . . . while setting up." Thus, although many emendations are editorial, the more radical of Smith's changes to the Bible were understood by him as a function of what he saw when reading it.

At least with respect to the [Joseph Smith Translation], it appears that when he read he saw events, not words. What he saw, he verbalized to a scribe.[32]

Flake concludes from this type of revelatory translation:

Arguably, then, 'translate' expressed Smith's experience of 'study[ing] it out in [his] mind' or his sense of agency in front of the text. Smith did not think of himself as God's stenographer. Rather, he was an interpreting reader, and God the confirming authority. He did not experience revelation "as dictated, as something whispered in someone's ear."[33]

Presence of Joseph in the Translation of the Book of Abraham

The Book of Abraham provides the most obvious evidence of Joseph's personal involvement in a translation project: the presence of Hebrew words that occur in the text after Joseph studied Hebrew with Joshua Seixas.[34] Matthew Grey explains:

This suggests once again that Smith felt free as a translator to incorporate words he learned from his academic studies into the translated content he derived from the papyri. In these instances, the Hebrew does not greatly alter the substance of the text; Smith easily could have conveyed the same ideas by simply translate the words as "star," "stars," or "eternal." Instead, his choice to articulate these concepts with Hebrew vocabulary seems to reflect his convictions that the

---

32. Kathleen Flake, "Translating Time: The Nature and Function of Joseph Smith's Narrative Canon," 505–6.

33. Flake, 507.

34. Matthew J. Grey, "Approaching Egyptian Papyri through Biblical Language: Joseph Smith's Use of Hebrew in His Translation of the Book of Abraham," 417–18.

Hebrew language was somehow represented on the papyri and that Hebrew vocabulary could be efficaciously used to illuminate the Egyptian text.[35]

It is important to note that Joseph used a vocabulary expanded by words he did not know and could not have known prior to learning Hebrew. However, once those words were part of his available vocabulary, he felt free to use them in the translation. This evidence strongly indicates that Joseph's available vocabulary was involved in the translation process, at least for the Book of Abraham. Grey further notes:

> This confluence of sources suggests that Smith's translation of the Book of Abraham was a dynamic and complex process involving a creative synthesis of his academic efforts and prophetic voice, which included his examination of characters and vignettes on the Egyptian papyri, attempts to create an Egyptian lexicon, interaction with the King James Version of the Bible, and claims to divine inspiration. In addition, the published text of the Book of Abraham shows that Joseph Smith incorporated into the translation process his knowledge of Biblical Hebrew—which he concurrently acquired through textbooks and formal study with a Hebrew Instructor—thus marking the first (and perhaps only) time Smith conscientiously used a conventional ancient language in his production of scripture.[36]

Like the Book of Mormon, the Book of Abraham also claims to be a *translation*, and in this case the resulting text shows an obvious interaction with Joseph's own vocabulary at the time of production.

Presence of Joseph in the Text of the Revelations

The Doctrine and Covenants, with the exception of Section 7, makes no claim to translation. Nevertheless, descriptions of how Joseph Smith received and dictated revelations bear a significant similarity to the description of the translation process. For example, Parley P. Pratt described Joseph giving a revelation in May 1831:

> After we had joined in prayer in his translating room, he dictated in our presence the following revelation:—Each sentence was uttered slowly and very distinctly, and with a pause between each, sufficiently long for it to be recorded, by an ordinary writer, in long hand. This was the manner in which all his written revelations were dictated and written. There was never any hesitation, reviewing, or reading back, in order to keep the run of the subject; neither did any of these communications undergo revisions, interlinings, or corrections. As he dictated them so they stood, so far as I have

---

35. Grey, 431.
36. Grey, 390.

witnessed; and I was present to witness the dictation of several communications of several pages each.[37]

As with his translating, Joseph pronounced revelation without hesitation and without the need to repeat or be reminded of what he had already said. The similarity suggests that there might be at least a conceptual similarity between some of what was translated in the Book of Mormon and Joseph's editorial process for many of his revelations. According to Grant Underwood,

> Scholars who have closely compared the wording of the revelation texts in the Doctrine and Covenants with that of earlier printings in the Star and the Book of Commandments have noticed that some passages read differently. It might be thought that this is because the Doctrine and Covenants corrected earlier errors and restored the pure, original text, but such is not the case. Actually the revised wording was designed to more fully and perfectly communicate the Word of God. Literally hundreds of these revisions, usually involving only a word or two but sometimes comprising an entire phrase or more, were made to the revelation texts between initial dictation and final publication in the Doctrine and Covenants.

He adds:

> Examination of the [Book of Commandments and Revelations] and the history of the D&C revelation texts from dictation to final form lead us to a richer, more nuanced view, one that sees Joseph as more than a mere human fax machine through whom God communicated finished revelation texts composed in heaven. Joseph had a role to play in the revelatory process.[38]

---

37. Parley P. Pratt, *Autobiography of Parley P. Pratt*, 62.

38. Grant Underwood, "Relishing the Revisions: Joseph Smith and the Revelatory Process." Karl F. Best, "Changes in the Revelations, 1833 to 1835," gives a similar explanation:

> Another possible explanation for changes in the revelations is that Joseph Smith had to interpret or transcribe the ideas that God placed in his mind; the words that he wrote or dictated were only his imperfect interpretation of what God intended. Joseph could then later rewrite or change the revelation to make it better fit what he remembered. . . This concept could be likened to transcribing a vision, a nonword event: any written account could be edited later to clarify the prophet's memory or interpretation of the experience, or to change the emphasis for a particular audience or purpose. (105–6)

Allowing for Joseph's Presence in the Translation of the Book of Mormon

Joseph Smith's revelations and other translations all involved his mind in some way without denying or diminishing any divine influence. The translation of the Book of Mormon need not be any different. In fact, the idea that Joseph's mind was also involved in the translation of the Book of Mormon was proposed in 1862 by Brigham Young, where he speculated: "Should the Lord Almighty send an angel to re-write the Bible, it would in many places be very different from what it now is. And I will even venture to say that if the Book of Mormon were now to be re-written, in many instances it would materially differ from the present translation."[39]

Many modern Latter-day Saint scholars have followed Brigham's idea and have suggested that the translation consisted of some conceptual connection to the plates that did not extend to precision in the selection of words or grammar. One of the most vocal and careful proponents of this view was B. H. Roberts:

> The view of the manner of translating the Book of Mormon here set forth furnishes the basis of justification for those verbal changes and grammatical corrections which have been made since the first edition issued from the press; and would furnish justification for making many more verbal and grammatical corrections in the book; for if, as here set forth, the meaning of the Nephite characters was given to Joseph Smith in such faulty English as he, an uneducated man, could command, while every detail and shade of thought should be strictly preserved, there can be no reasonable ground for objection to the correction of mere verbal errors and grammatical construction. There can be no reasonable doubt that had Joseph Smith been a finished English scholar and the facts and ideas represented by the Nephite characters upon the plates had been given him by the inspiration of God through the Urim and Thummim, those ideas would have been expressed in correct English; but as he was not a finished English scholar, he had to give expression to those facts and ideas in such language as he could command, and that was faulty English, which the Prophet himself and those who have succeeded him as custodians of the word of God have had, and now have, a perfect right to correct.[40]

---

39. Brigham Young, July 13, 1862, *Journal of Discourses*, 9:311.

40. Brigham H. Roberts, *New Witnesses for God, Volume 2: The Book of Mormon*, 145–46. Richard Lyman Bushman, *Joseph Smith: Rough Stone Rolling*, gives a similar explanation for the language used in the revelations contained in the Doctrine and Covenants: "The revelations were not God's diction, dialect, or native language. They were couched in language suitable to Joseph's time. The idioms, the grammar, even the tone had to be comprehensible to 1830s Americans" (174).

Roberts's explanation does not discount the Book of Mormon as a translation; instead, it posits that, just like any other translation, the vocabulary and syntax were artifacts of the translator. This perspective of Joseph being an active participant in the translation will inform the discussion of the next two chapters.

Chapter Two

Nineteenth-Century Influence on the Text

A translator's intended audience impacts the choices of words, images, and allusions they use. Commenting on efforts to translate the Bible, D. A. Carson declares: "The notion that one can translate responsibly *without* interpretation is, quite frankly, shockingly ignorant of the most basic challenges facing translators."[1] In Joseph Smith's case, the confluence of his own cultural and religious background with that of his reception audience impacted the literary style and interconnections with the King James Bible.

For both Joseph's original audience and subsequent readers, his role as a cultural translator was critical. Ana Rojo and Iraide Ibarretxe-Antuñano summarize the role that culture plays in translation:

> The emphasis of Cognitive Linguistics on cognitive aspects gives prominence to the role of the translator, who would no longer be considered just as a specialist in two languages, but rather an inter-cultural mediator between source and target texts. The translation as a product would be understood as a manipulation, a retextualization guided by a mediator who knows what is functionally appropriate in the target language, and not as a loyal and right transfer from a source into a target language. The translation as a process would be regarded as both a communicative and a cognitive process in which linguistic and conceptual aspects are perfectly integrated, and not as a mechanical equivalence transfer between two linguistic systems.[2]

Randall C. Davis elaborates on this type of translation:

> To illustrate this problem, we might examine what is generally considered the first English-language translation of a Native American literary text. Henry Timberlake's 1765 *Memoirs* offers what purports to be a translation of a Cherokee war song. It reads in part:
>
> > Where'er the earth's enlighten'd by the sun,
> > Moon shines by night, grass grows, or waters run,
> > Be't known that we are going, like men, afar,

---

1. D. A. Carson, "The Limits of Functional Equivalence in Bible Translation—and Other Limits, Too," 73; emphasis in original.
2. Ana Rojo and Iraide Ibarretxe-Antuñano, "Cognitive Linguistics and Translation Studies: Past, Present and Future," 13.

In hostile fields to wage destructive war;
Like men we go, to meet our country's foes,
Who, woman-like, shall fly our dreaded blows.

We might debate about how useful this text is as an ethnographic document, but it is obvious that Timberlake created this translation on the model of the dominant contemporary English verse form—the heroic couplet. Timberlake approached the original Cherokee text (or a translated version of it, since Timberlake himself apparently knew little of the Cherokee language) as raw material to be reworked before it may serve as "literature."[3]

In Timberlake's poem, the meaning of the actual original language (now lost) has been recast not only into another language, but into an expected literary form of the target language. It is unlikely that the heroic couplet was a Cherokee literary form. Timberlake's example makes it reasonable to examine the Book of Mormon for a similar attempt to translate language and form based upon the reception audience in preference over whatever the original might have been.

The Book of Mormon Reception Audience

The Book of Mormon intends to communicate; otherwise, it would have little purpose. However, because the translation's original 1830 audience had virtually nothing in common with the purported original language and culture recorded on the golden plates, what might have been effective communication when the Nephite text was finalized around AD 400 would be less effective with its primary audience fourteen centuries later. Effective communication—and thus, an effective translation—results from the interplay between communicator and audience, whether present or implied.[4]

---

3. Randall C. Davis, "Early Anglo-American Attitudes to Native American Languages," 230.

4. An interesting example of the interplay between a non-present audience and author is found in the Preface of Bob Bennett, *Leap of Faith: Confronting the Origins of the Book of Mormon*, x: "As I looked at the Book of Mormon from the vantage point of a neutral audience, I discovered aspects of it that I had never noticed before. As I probed the presentations of its critics, I discovered arguments that I had never understood before. As I recalled my own life experiences with forgeries, I saw applications that I had never thought of before." Bennett's vision of what he thought to write about occurred directly from assuming a particular type of audience. Where Bennett was explicit in describing the effect of the audience on what was written, that effect tends to appear more subtly, but just as forcefully, in Book of Mormon texts.

Candace Séguinot explains,

> Communication, above all, is between and about people, and not just about their need to sell refrigerators and make hotel reservations. It is the way we establish a sense of ourselves and our relationships to others and to the universe in which we live. That means that we bring certain needs and expectations to the act of understanding, and filter and interpret meaning from our individual perspectives.[5]

For the Book of Mormon, the task of communication across language, culture, and over fourteen hundred years required modifications of some sort for the translation to be comprehensible to its first readers. Without acceptance by that audience, later audiences would be much less likely to encounter the Book of Mormon.

Part of the Book of Mormon's early impact was due to its being a physical representation of a revelation from God. Janiece Johnson recalls the experience of Sarah DeArmon Pea:

> When Mormon elders shared the Book of Mormon with Sarah DeArmon Pea and her family in the Summer of 1835, Sarah "was anxious to see the Book" for herself. Rather than spending the evening with the Mormon visitors, Sarah asked to be excused so she could read. She spent "most of the night" reading the Book and was "greatly astonished at its contents." She detailed, "It left an impression upon my mind not to be forgotten:— For in fact the book appeared to be open before my eyes for weeks." At the outset, Sarah had no expectation of joining a new Church, but her connection to the Book blossomed. She became a Latter-day Saint as a result of that relationship. The Book unfolded the possibility of individual numinous experience not to be discarded once one accepted Smith as a prophet. A relationship with God was not just the prerogative of prophets: Smith's egalitarian impulse offered each Mormon convert the possibility of experiencing the divine.[6]

Johnson also notes that the early growth that would lead to the establishment of the Church of Christ (later, "of Latter-day Saints") was through the dissemination of the book as much as the missionary teaching about the book and the restoration:

> Charlotte Haven was visiting her brother in Nauvoo. . . . Not a Latter-day Saint herself, she offers a glimpse of Mormon practice as she experienced it. Writing to her family, she mentioned, "The saints take an interest in our

---

5. Candace Séguinot, "Translation Theory, Translating Theory and the Sentence," 86.

6. Janiece Johnson, "Becoming a People of the Books: Toward an Understanding of Early Mormon Converts and the New Word of the Lord," 2–3.

spiritual welfare, by sending us to read the Book of Mormon, The Voice of Warning, and the Book of Covenants, and invite us to attend prayer meetings." Sharing the books of the Restoration and encouraging reading was standard practice—it had not changed considerably in the intervening decade. If the content of the Book of Mormon and Restoration scripture played a significant role in one's own conversion, then Latter-day Saints worked to share that possibility with others.[7]

It is not surprising that the physical book would be an important part of the message beyond just preaching about its contents. The Book of Mormon entered both a literate culture and one that expected a book to be the basis of religious life. It is therefore unsurprising that the original binding of the Book of Mormon "echoed the Bible in many ways. . . . Its size and biding style strikingly resembled the most common Bible editions then being passionately produced and distributed by the ABS [American Bible Society]."[8] The first British editions "were also bound in a manner that corresponded to the portable Bibles printed by the Queen's official Bible publisher."[9]

It was not only the physicality of the Book of Mormon but also its language of translation that drew similarities between it and the Bible. Thus, for both detractors and believers, the two books were consciously compared. Eli Gilbert, an early convert, reported on the affinity he found between the two books of scripture: "[I] compared it with . . . The bible, (which book I verily thought I believed,) and found the two books mutually and reciprocally corroborate each other; and if I let go the book of Mormon, the bible might also do down by the same rule."[10] This is just one example of many that follows Philip L. Barlow's description of the Book of Mormon's reception:

> The new "gold bible" would have been incomprehensible apart from a biblical context. It was printed in biblical fashion as a collection of books, originally divided into chapters and later into verses. It contained two dozen chapters of material common to the Bible. The subjects of its narrative were originally biblical peoples, many of its episodes paralleled biblical stories, and it purported both to prophesy of the Bible as a book (from the vantage of 600 BCE) and to be itself a fulfillment of biblical prophecy. Indeed, the Book of Mormon explicitly identified itself as a companion to the Bible, written as a record of "a remnant of the House of Israel" "to the convincing of the Jew

---

7. Johnson, 20–21.
8. Paul C. Gutjahr, *The Book of Mormon: A Biography*, 5.
9. Johnson, "People of the Books," 22.
10. Quoted in Terryl Givens, with Brian Hauglid, *The Pearl of Greatest Price: Mormonism's Most Controversial Scripture*, 27.

and Gentile that Jesus is the Christ." Early Saints readily identified the angel Moroni with the angel from the "midst of Heaven" (Rev. 14:6) who was to have "the everlasting gospel to preach unto them that dwell on earth."[11]

Of course, not all who read the book had a favorable response. A famous comparison between the Bible and the Book of Mormon resulted in an unfavorable conclusion. Alexander Campbell said of his reading of the Book of Mormon:

> It admits the Old and New Testaments to contain the revelations, institutions, and commandments of God to Patriarchs, Jews, and Gentiles, down to the year 1830—and always, as such, speaks of them and quotes them. This admission at once blasts its pretentions to credibility. For no man with his eyes open can admit both books to have come from God. Admitting the Bible now received to have come from God, it is impossible that the book of Mormon came from the same Author.[12]

The King James Bible and Book of Mormon Language

Even though there were many who found the Book of Mormon lacking, it is interesting that their reasons were not based on the Book of Mormon's language, styled after the King James Bible. According to Eran Shalev,

> Remarkably, early opponents of the Book of Mormon who did note Smith's use of biblical language, as critical as they might otherwise be, did *not* criticize such use. One commentator, for example, alluding to the Book of Mormon as "full of strange narratives," remarked indifferently that it was written "in the style of the scriptures," and went on halfheartedly to applaud the Book for "bearing on its face the marks of some ingenuity, and familiar acquaintance it the Bible." Lack of concern about the use of the King James Bible's language seemed to have been the norm among its detractors.[13]

The obvious presence of "the style of the scriptures" can be seen at the beginning of the first chapter in the first book of Nephi. The book header reads, in part (taken from the Printer's Manuscript, with emphasis added):

> An account of Lehi and his wife Sariah, and his four sons—being called (beginning at the eldest) Laman, Lemuel, Sam, and Nephi. The Lord warns Lehi to depart out of the land of Jerusalem because he *prophesieth* unto the people concerning their iniquity, and they seek to destroy his life. He *taketh*

---

11. Philip L. Barlow, *Mormons and the Bible: The Place of the Latter-day Saints in American Religion*, 27.

12. Alexander Campbell, "Delusions," 91.

13. Eran Shalev, *American Zion: The Old Testament as a Political Text from the Revolution to the Civil War*, 115.

three days journey into the wilderness with his family. Nephi *taketh* his brethren and *returns* to the land of Jerusalem after the record of the Jews. The account of their sufferings.

The archaic *-eth* ending for the second person singular verbs is obvious. It was not part of quotidian speech in the nineteenth century but was quite familiar due to the prevalence of the King James Version of the Bible. Right at the beginning of the text, readers are introduced to verbs that imitate the King James Bible. We are also introduced to the fact that the translator must not have been completely comfortable with those forms. In the same sentence, with only three intervening words, we have "Nephi *taketh* his brethren and *returns* to the land of Jerusalem," where the archaic form is followed by the modern form. This strongly suggests that the *-eth* form is affected. While these and some other contradicting grammatical forms were reconciled for the 1920 and 1981 editions of the Book of Mormon,[14] this mixture of the modern and the archaic nevertheless appears throughout both the Original and Printer's Manuscripts.[15]

Why make the effort to mimic the language of the King James Bible? The answer is simple: it was expected. In Shalev's investigation of the American use of King James biblical language from 1770 to 1830, he writes:

> The language of the King James Bible was as strange and foreign to late eighteenth-century and nineteenth-century Anglophones as it is to twenty-first-century English-speakers. The staccato rhythms confined in short and numbered verses, the repetitive use of phrases such as 'and it came to pass,' and the use of verbs with suffixes such as '–eth,' had been long gone from the spoken language by the second half of the eighteenth century. Nevertheless, generations of Americans reverted to that language and its accompanying structures and forms to discuss their difficulties and represent their achievements, past and present. Surprisingly, this was not a predominantly religious idiom as Providence was notably absent from those texts as an active agent. Rather, American authors and commentators used this ontologically privileged language as a means to establish their claims for truth, as well as their authority and legitimacy in public discourse.[16]

The Book of Mormon veers from the more common use of the biblical language in that it is a religious text. Nevertheless, the desire to estab-

---

14. Royal Skousen, *Analysis of the Textual Variants of the Book of Mormon*, 1:47.
15. Gregory A. Bowen, "Sounding Sacred: The Adoption of biblical Archaisms in the Book of Mormon and Other 19th Century Texts," 2.
16. Eran Shalev, "An American Book of Chronicles, Pseudo-Biblicism and the Cultural Origins of the Book of Mormon," 137–38.

lish the text of the Book of Mormon "as a means to establish . . . claims for truth, as well . . . as authority and legitimacy" is obviously important to its publication. Nicholas J. Frederick and Joseph M. Spencer concur that the language and scriptural references lend "rhetorical authority to the Book of Mormon, allowing it to speak in the voice of authoritative scripture."[17]

The expectation that authoritative texts would be styled after the King James Bible wasn't taught. It was part of the atmosphere, and, as Shalev noted, "came naturally to generations of Americans writing and reading pseudobiblical texts, Joseph Smith and his audience included."[18] The cultural expectation both influenced the choices made in the language in which the Book of Mormon was dictated as well as fed the impressions of the text in its early readers. Shalev explains:

> Smith's timing was providential (no pun intended), however, for yet another reason: *The Book of Mormon* was published during the final efflorescence of a tradition of pseudo-biblical writing in the United States. Published later, *The Book of Mormon* might have not enjoyed Americans' fascination with pseudo-biblicism, the writing of American history in biblical language, which gradually lost its appeal in the years after 1830, as less and less of those distinct texts found their way to print. By the time the effects of the decline of pseudo-biblicism were felt, however, *The Book of Mormon* had already gained a momentum of its own, transcending the literary tradition that helped pave the way for that original American scripture.[19]

The presence of pseudo-biblical language in the Book of Mormon occurred at a time when the use of those forms was seen as lending an air of authenticity to the text. It was a choice made according to the expectations of the reception audience. Perhaps it was one of the things that might have changed had the translation occurred at a different time, as Brigham Young suggested.[20] The influence of that style of language was strong enough to influence the language of Joseph's later translation projects as well.

---

17. Eran Shalev, "An American Book of Chronicles, Pseudo-Biblicism and the Cultural Origins of the Book of Mormon," 137–38.

18. Eran Shalev, *American Zion*, 106.

19. Shalev, 114–15.

20. Brigham Young, July 13, 1862, *Journal of Discourses*, 9:311. Quoted previously but repeated here for convenience: "Should the Lord Almighty send an angel to re-write the Bible, it would in many places be very different from what it now is. And I will even venture to say that if the Book of Mormon were now to be re-written, in many instances it would materially differ from the present translation."

Quoting the King James Bible

As Daniel L. Belnap explains, "The presence of King James English and even KJV passages in the Book of Mormon functioned to establish the book's validity to the people already familiar with the words of God via King James English while making it easier to recognize the truths found therein because of the text's familiar cadence and sound."[21] Belnap's explanation is correct as a generalization, but there is more to the story. There are two major ways in which King James passages appear in the Book of Mormon. The first is in long quotations, and the second in shorter quotations or allusions.

Large direct quotations clearly point to a dependence upon the King James Bible rather than a re-translation of those chapters from a Nephite original text. Royal Skousen was able to determine that the edition of the King James Bible that served as the source for the included chapters must have been published after 1770.[22] Thus, the Book of Mormon is undeniably connected to the late eighteenth or early nineteenth centuries for the copied chapters.

The most obvious use of the King James Bible is seen in the inclusion of numerous chapters from Isaiah (at the end of 1 Nephi and extensively in 2 Nephi). Similarly, the representation of the Savior's teachings when he appeared to those gathered in Bountiful is indisputably based on Matthew 5–7 (3 Ne.12–14). These inclusions of whole chapters are the largest instances where the Book of Mormon leans upon the King James Bible. As Nicholas Frederick examined the numerous shorter allusions to biblical phrases, he found:

> It needs to be recognized that the Book of Mormon does not simply *adopt* the language of the Bible; it also *adapts* it, positioning the Book of Mormon as a careful redaction of the Bible. This adoption and adaptation can be seen in a variety of ways. Sometimes the Book of Mormon will integrate a single biblical phrase into its complex narrative. Sometimes the Book of Mormon will expand or condense the phrase, rendering a new phrase that may radically shift the context or meaning of the original biblical phrase. Sometimes the Book of Mormon will weave a single phrase from a specific biblical text or several phrases from a specific biblical text.[23]

---

21. Daniel L. Belnap, "The King James Bible and the Book of Mormon," 167.

22. Royal Skousen, with Stanford Carmack, *The History of the Text of the Book of Mormon: The King James Quotations in the Book of Mormon*, 5.

23. Nicholas J. Frederick, "The Book of Mormon and Its Redaction of the King James New Testament: A Further Evaluation of the Interaction between the New Testament and the Book of Mormon," 45–46; emphasis in original.

Frederick's analysis of the shorter quotations also applies to the way the chapter length quotations are integrated into the text. Both the Isaiah and Matthew chapters are integrated into the text in ways that are theologically important and adapted to the Nephite author's culture and concerns.

Both Nephi$_1$ and Jacob share a unique way of using scriptural texts. Nephi$_1$ quotes whole chapters of Isaiah before using information from those chapters for his intended purpose. Jacob similarly quotes extensively from Zenos's allegory of the olive tree before refocusing that text into the needs of his audience.

For Nephi$_1$, the inclusion of the Isaiah sections provided the textual grounding against which he reread his vision—the vision he had when he asked to see what his father had seen in the vision of the Tree of Life. This was the source of, and authority for, the discussion of the theological future Nephi$_1$ saw (1 Nephi 11–16). After entering the Isaiah chapters, Nephi$_1$ used allusions to Isaiah as the proof texts upon which he related that same vision of the future. Thus, Nephi$_1$ provided two "witnesses" to the veracity of that vision of the future: the first testimony was based on the authority of a vision, and the second was based on the authority of scripture. (Table 2A correlates the verses from Nephi$_1$'s prophecy based on Isaiah, with phrases or themes from his earlier vision in the Old World.)

Mormon's use of quoted scripture differed from that of Nephi$_1$ and Jacob. In the case of the Matthew passages in 3 Nephi, the King James Bible provides most of the text, but it is modified in places to recontextualize the sermon for a Nephite audience. A simple integration is the alteration from certain Old World words to Book of Mormon references. For example, one passage substitutes the Old World "farthing" for the Book of Mormon measurement "senine" (3 Ne. 12:26; Matt. 5:26).[24]

More subtle is the reframing of sections of Matthew to speak to two different audiences rather than the implied single audience of the original. Here, the resurrected Christ shifts the audience for his instructions from the whole multitude to his chosen twelve Nephite disciples, and then back to the multitude. First, at the end of 3 Nephi 11, Christ instructed the disciples (vv. 18–41). Then, at the beginning of 3 Nephi 12, "he stretched forth his hand unto the multitude, and cried unto them, saying: Blessed are

---

24. It should be noted that this process of recontextualizing words to the New World context is incomplete. There is no indication that Joseph, as a translator, was aware of the many cultural differences between the Old and New World contexts, and therefore many Old World specific references remain while only a few have been changed.

Table 2A

Isaiah-Based Theme	Tree of Life-Based Theme
2 Ne. 25:11–13	1 Ne. 11:33–34 (reference to "healing in his wings")
2 Ne. 25:16	1 Ne. 11:34–35
2 Ne. 25:17	1 Ne. 14:7
2 Ne. 25:18	1 Ne. 14:21–25, 39–41
2 Ne. 26:1	1 Ne. 12:6 (Christ appearing to Nephites)
2 Ne. 26:2	1 Ne. 12:3 (many generations pass away)
2 Ne. 26:6	1 Ne. 12:4 (thunderings and earthquakes)
2 Ne. 26:9	1 Ne. 12:12–13 (four-generation prophecy)
2 Ne. 26:10	1 Ne. 12:12–20 (destruction of Nephites)
2 Ne. 26:14	1 Ne. 14:20–29 (description of last days)
2 Ne. 26:15	1 Ne. 13:14–15 (gathering of the Gentiles against $Nephi_1$'s seed)
2 Ne. 26:17	1 Ne. 13:34–36 (coming of the Book of Mormon)
2 Ne. 26:21 "many churches" functions as the great and abominable, which is made explicit in 2 Ne. 28:18	2 Ne. 26:21 "great and abominable church"

ye if ye shall give heed unto the words of these twelve whom I have chosen from among you to minister unto you, and to be your servants" (v. 1). This is followed by a lengthy quotation of Matthew 5–6 of the Sermon on the Mount, which includes additional language wherein Jesus shifts from addressing the multitude to speaking directly to the Nephite twelve:

> No man can serve two masters; for either he will hate the one and love the other, or else he will hold to the one and despise the other. Ye cannot serve God and Mammon. *And now it came to pass that when Jesus had spoken these words he looked upon the twelve whom he had chosen, and said unto them: Remember the words which I have spoken. For behold, ye are they whom I have chosen to minister unto this people.* Therefore I say unto you, take no thought for your life, what ye shall eat, or what ye shall drink; nor yet for your body, what ye shall put on. Is not the life more than meat, and the body than raiment? (3 Ne. 13:24–25; cf. Matt. 6:24–25)

This shift in audience creates a rereading of the Sermon on the Mount to have the apparently more difficult instructions apply to the twelve rather than the entire gathered body.

Alluding to the King James Bible

An interesting artifact of the way that the Book of Mormon uses shorter quotations and allusions is that sometimes when the Nephite text could legitimately have been quoting from the brass plates, the dictated text instead uses the New Testament's retranslation of that passage. For instance, in 1 Nephi, written approximately 600 BC, we find a reference that is generally understood to point to John the Baptist:

> And he spake also concerning a prophet who should come before the Messiah, to prepare the way of the Lord—Yea, even he should go forth and cry in the wilderness: Prepare ye the way of the Lord, and *make his paths straight; for there standeth one among you whom ye know not; and he is mightier than I, whose shoe's latchet I am not worthy to unloose.* (1 Ne. 10:7–8)

The basic information legitimately alludes to Isaiah:

> The voice of him that crieth in the wilderness, Prepare ye the way of the Lord, make straight in the desert a highway for our God. Every valley shall be exalted, and every mountain and hill shall be made low: and the crooked shall be made straight, and the rough places plain. (Isa. 40:3–4)

However, the Book of Mormon phrasing instead seems to come from the Gospel of Mark:

> As it is written in the prophets, Behold, I send my messenger before thy face, which shall prepare thy way before thee. The voice of one crying in the wilderness, Prepare ye the way of the Lord, make his paths straight. . . . And preached, saying, *There cometh one mightier than I after me, the latchet of whose shoes I am not worthy to stoop down and unloose.* (Mark 1:2, 7. See also Luke 3:16 and John 1:27.)

Nicholas J. Frederick lays out the issue of biblical quotations such as this in the Book of Mormon:

> What can be at times jarring for readers of the Book of Mormon is the presence therein of the King James New Testament. While the incorporation of the King James Old Testament can be explained by Nephite access to the brass plates, it is more difficult to understand how the text of the New Testament, which was composed centuries after the Lehite migration to the Americas, could be found in the Book of Mormon. Yet there it appears. Passages mirroring the Gospel of Matthew, the Gospel of John, and the book of Revelation can easily be identified in the writings of Nephi, Alma, and Ether.[25]

For all the quotations that appear in the Book of Mormon, it is important to understand that they appear within the logical framework of

---

25. Nicholas J. Frederick, "The Language of Paul in the New Testament," 206.

the surrounding discussions.²⁶ They often serve as touchpoints for the development of doctrinal discussions in the text. As they are quoted or "likened to," they function similarly to Seth Perry's suggestion of intertextual biblical citations: "All moments of biblical citation create new texts; citation changes the text itself. Each moment of citation happens in a dialogic relationship with circumstance, and bringing the biblical text into such contingent relationships necessarily changes it."²⁷

The How and Why of the New Testament Quotations

Two important questions remain in the examination of the presence of New Testament quotations in the Book of Mormon: How did they get there, and how do they function in the text? The answer to the first lies in how translations work. The answer to the second lies in the way the text intends to attract its reception audience.

Eugene A. Nida expresses the process of translation this way:

> If a text has already been translated, whether into some other target language or into the same language that a translator is to employ, these existing translations constitute particularly important contexts because many receptors will undoubtedly be influenced by what they already know about the ST [source text] through the existing translations. This is a very important aspect in translating Classical texts of high literary quality because so often outstanding translators have already had a hand in establishing a model for rendering many key terms or well-known expressions. Such prior translations become especially important in translating religious texts, in which various ideas about divine inspiration can constitute real barriers to new and/or more correct renderings.²⁸

Walter W. Wessel confessed that even professional translators are profoundly affected by vocabulary and cadences of the King James Bible:

> In 1967 I joined a group of scholars who were invited to participate in a translation of the Bible that ultimately became known as the New International Version (NIV). We were not far into this project before most of us, especially the older members of the group, became keenly aware of how much we had

---

26. *The Plates of Mormon* provides footnotes marking the majority of these quotations and allusions.
27. Seth Perry, *Bible Culture and Authority in the Early United States*, 63.
28. Eugene A. Nida, "The Role of Contexts in Translating," 80.

been influenced by the wording of the King James Version. It took considerable effort and much vigilance to purge our minds of its antiquated language.[29]

Joseph Smith had no reason to attempt to purge his mind of the language and phrasing of the King James Bible. Indeed, the 1830 audience's cultural pressure was to retain as much of that language as possible. The strong influence of pseudo-biblical language on non-religious texts underscores the expectation that a religious text produced at the time should similarly use that style of language. The very same impetus to use the language of the King James Bible led to the use of the phrases found in the quotations and allusions. The extensive use of New Testament quotations and allusions underscores the probability that Joseph, like most Christians, was much more familiar with the New Testament than the Old, and therefore had easier access to those quotations.

Because the appearances of New Testament texts in the Book of Mormon constitutes a type of anachronism, they require more explanation than simply suggesting that they are the result of the impulse to use King James language. To understand why there might be obviously anachronistic quotations in the Book of Mormon, it is useful to make some observations. The following is a small selection of the list of approximately six hundred quotations or references to the New Testament in the Book of Mormon[30]:

- Mosiah 3:3 (Alma 13:22; Helaman 16:14)/**Luke** 2:10—Simple
- Mosiah 3:5/**Matthew** 11:5—Simple
- Mosiah 3:9 (3 Nephi 1:14)/**John** 1:11—Simple
- Mosiah 3:21 (Mosiah 5:15)/**Revelation** 19:6—Simple
- Mosiah 3:24/**Revelation** 20:13—Simple
- Mosiah 3:26/**Revelation** 14:10 (Revelation 16:19)—Simple
- Mosiah 3:27/**Revelation** 20:10 and 14:10–11—Compound
- Mosiah 4:11/**Acts** 22:16—Simple
- Mosiah 5:13 (Alma 12:7; 18:32; 21:6)/**Hebrews** 4:12—Simple
- Mosiah 5:15 (Alma 1:25)/**1 Corinthians** 15:58—Simple
- Mosiah 10:8/**Matthew** 3:4—Simple
- Mosiah 13:1/**Matthew** 8:29 (**Mark** 1:24)—Simple
- Mosiah 13:8 (Mosiah 25:7)/**Acts** 3:10—Simple
- Mosiah 13:34/**Philippians** 2:6–7—Simple
- Mosiah 15:2/**Luke** 1:35—Simple
- Mosiah 15:24/**Revelation** 20:6—Simple

---

29. Walter W. Wessel, "A Translator's Perspective on Alister McGrath's History of the King James Version," 199.

30. *The Plates of Mormon* has footnotes to most of the quotations and allusions.

- Mosiah 16:3 (Alma 42:10)/**James** 3:15—Simple
- Mosiah 16:7/**1 Corinthians** 15:14, 55—Paraphrase [Isaiah 25:8 and Hosea 13:14]
- Mosiah 16:8/**1 Corinthians** 15:54—Complex
- Mosiah 16:9/**John** 1:4–5—Simple—Expanded[31]

We know that the dictation of the published Book of Mormon text most likely began with Mosiah through Moroni, followed by the translation of the small plates in 1 Nephi through Words of Mormon. However, there does not seem to be any correlation between the dictation order of the Book of Mormon and the order of the New Testament; the above list presents verses containing quotations of the New Testament in the order of their dictation. Looking at the New Testament books, it is easy to see that there is no order to the selected quotations. Were Joseph using a Bible as his reference, he would have been required to jump back and forth from book to book. Even when we have three quotations in a row from Revelation, the references jump from chapter 20 to 14 and then back to 20. A reliance on a physical Bible for these quotations would have simply been too laborious and time consuming. Instead, the nature of the quotations themselves provides a better view of exactly how they are used. (Table 2B lists the biblical verse on the left side and the Book of Mormon quotation of that verse on the right.)

Although the quotations are obvious, it is also important to note that they are not precise. Rather, they often recreate new sentences using elements from separate passages in the New Testament. This both further argues against Joseph copying directly from an existing physical text and provides further evidence for the presence of Joseph's mind in the translation.

In addition, it is important to recognize that the quotations are not essential to the passages. That is, the shared language is not being presented as a quotation of another text and could have been phrased differently while retaining the same meaning. This suggests these quotations and allusions are at least subliminal, if not intentional connections to the New Testament. In a culture saturated with the King James Bible, where children often learned to read with their family Bible, these phrases would have been familiar both to the translator and the reception audience, placing them within a shared community of Christians.

---

31. Nicholas J. Frederick, "The Book of Mormon and Its Redaction of the King James New Testament: A Further Evaluation of the Interaction between the New Testament and the Book of Mormon," 79–80.

Table 2B

Biblical Verse	Book of Mormon Quotation
1 Corinthians 13:4–7 Charity suffereth long, and is kind; charity envieth not; charity vaunteth not itself, is not puffed up, Doth not behave itself unseemly, seeketh not her own, is not easily provoked, thinketh no evil; Rejoiceth not in iniquity, but rejoiceth in the truth; Beareth all things, believeth all things, hopeth all things, endureth all things.	Moroni 7:45 And charity suffereth long, and is kind, and envieth not, and is not puffed up, seeketh not her own, is not easily provoked, thinketh no evil, and rejoiceth not in iniquity but rejoiceth in the truth, beareth all things, believeth all things, hopeth all things, endureth all things.
Revelation 14:10–11 The same shall drink of the wine of the wrath of God, which is poured out without mixture into the cup of his indignation; and he shall be tormented with fire and brimstone in the presence of the holy angels, and in the presence of the Lamb: And the smoke of their torment ascendeth up for ever and ever:	Mosiah 3:27 And their torment is as a lake of fire and brimstone, whose flames are unquenchable, and whose smoke ascendeth up forever and ever.
Revelation 22:13 I am Alpha and Omega, the beginning and the end, the first and the last.	Alma 11:39 Yea, he is the very Eternal Father of heaven and of earth, and all things which in them are; he is the beginning and the end, the first and the last.
2 Peter 3:16 They that are unlearned and unstable wrest, as they do also the other scriptures, unto their own destruction.	Alma 13:20 Behold, the scriptures are before you; if ye will wrest them it shall be to your own destruction.
Hebrews 9:27 And as it is appointed unto men once to die, but after this the judgment:	Alma 12:27 But behold, it was not so; but it was appointed unto men that they must die; and after death, they must come to judgment, even that same judgment of which we have spoken, which is the end.

Table 2B continued

Biblical Verse	Book of Mormon Quotation
Hebrews 7:3 Without father, without mother, without descent, having neither beginning of days, nor end of life; but made like unto the Son of God; abideth a priest continually.	**Alma 13:9** Thus they become high priests forever, after the order of the Son, the Only Begotten of the Father, who is without beginning of days or end of years,
Matthew 13:6 And when the sun was up, they were scorched; and because they had no root, they withered away.	**Alma 32:38** But if ye neglect the tree, and take no thought for its nourishment, behold it will not get any root; and when the heat of the sun cometh and scorcheth it, because it hath no root it withers away, and ye pluck it up and cast it out.

This is similar to our own casual conversations with friends, or in presentations to groups, wherein we may quote a line from a movie assuming that the audience recognizes it. For example, if I say, "I don't think that word means what you think it means," I am not merely commenting on someone's naïve misuse of a term, but I am participating in a communal experience with the audience, who I assume recognize that I am quoting from the movie *The Princess Bride*. Younger speakers might do the same with quotations or references to *Harry Potter*. When those common quotations are used, they reinforce a recognition of, and sense of belonging in, a community.

The references to biblical quotations in Joseph's time were a common mode of expression even in contexts that did not require quotations. Lavina Fielding Anderson investigated the impact of the King James Bible on Joseph's biblicized home environment. From this she concludes:

> I argue that the Smith family's oral culture was so thoroughly imbued with biblical language, both the Old and New Testaments, that its use was fluent, easy, and familiar. When they reached for a colorful phrase, searched for a simile, or stressed a point, the vocabulary that their minds offered readily was an appropriate and often vivid phrase from the Bible. Seldom did the context of secondary use relate to the biblical context. It also seems likely that this easy familiarity with KJV language made it possible for them to quickly adopt and incorporate images and phrasing from specifically Mormon scriptures.[32]

---

32. Lavina Fielding Anderson, "Mother Tongue: KJV Language in Smith Family Discourse," 3–4.

Given the saturation of biblical language in Joseph's family, we can readily see how the presence of those New Testament quotations in the Book of Mormon stem from the common cultural familiarity and level of comfort with such quotations and references. They functioned to ease the reception audience into the scriptural familiarity of the Book of Mormon through reference to the Bible they knew and already accepted as authoritative. Internally, they function to further the development of the ideas encapsulated in the quoted verses or phrases.

Chapter Three

Translation Artifacts in the English Text

Beyond the use of King James language and quotations, there are additional ways in which the nineteenth century influenced elements of the Book of Mormon's English text. This chapter examines language-based anachronisms and the use of "Jesus Christ" as a name, both of which reflect cultural expectations. Furthermore, it will look at two other aspects of the text—the effect of fulfilled prophecy and the evidence for spontaneity in the dictation to show how Joseph Smith produced and influenced the English text.

Language-based Anachronisms

The Reverend M. T. Lamb published his criticism of the Book of Mormon in 1887. One of his arguments dealt with the problem of translation, wherein he used a hypothetical example to demonstrate what he saw as the problem of Book of Mormon language:

> Now, if upon examination, this book, purporting to be 200 years old, is found to be written in the current language of the present day, full of words and phrases and idiomatic expressions that were wholly unknown to the English language 200 years ago, this fact alone would furnish the most conclusive possible proof of the fraud.[1]

He followed that statement with what he felt was a powerful anachronistic example:

> But some of the above words will not allow of such an explanation. For instance, the word "faculties." "Arouse the *faculties* of your souls," [Jacob 3:11] "I myself have labored with all the power of *faculties* which I have possessed" [Mosiah 29:14].
>
> This use of the word is wholly *modern*. The ancients knew nothing of such a division of the mind or soul into faculties. And, hence there could have been no word found upon those ancient plates, that conveyed any such meaning.[2]

---

1. Martin Thomas Lamb, *The Golden Bible; Or, The Book of Mormon. Is It from God?*, 214.

2. Lamb, 219. His references to page numbers have been replaced with the modern verses to which he refers.

Lamb appears to have assumed that there would be a precise rendition of the words from the ancient language into the modern, and that finding a word that arguably postdated the beginnings of the Book of Mormon meant that the very vocabulary of the text witnessed to its anachrony.

All of Lamb's examples in this section of his book rely upon concepts of language and translation. First, if English were proposed as the original language of the text, then these anachronisms would be fatal to its truth claims. However, the Book of Mormon clearly declares that it is a translation of a document from another language. Suggesting that the concept of *faculties* would be a fatal anachronism simply assumes that an ancient culture could not have thoughts that modern English could have later developed its own words to describe.

Despite the problems with his logic, Lamb's analysis is still important because it highlights language and concepts that might be assigned to a modern textual layer rather than the purported ancient source. The Book of Mormon does contain words, phrases, and idioms that are more appropriate to the cultural context in which the dictation was produced rather than the ancient culture it declares to have been translated from.

In the context of a cross-cultural translation, the ability to adapt the source culture into something understandable to the target audience is the very task of a good translator. Our vocabulary is interwoven with the cultural contexts that give it function and meaning. As Michael Agar couches the issue, "Culture starts when you realize that you've got a problem with language, and the problem has to do with who you are. Culture happens *in* language, but the consciousness it inspires goes well beyond it."[3] When translation occurs in a cross-cultural environment, communication often requires a less than literal approach. Marcellus S. Snow provides an example of the problem of cross-cultural biblical translation:

> Christian missionaries of other faiths have encountered this challenge in its extreme form in translating the Bible for many of the primitive tribes of Africa and South America. How can one best translate "grace" into Mixtec? How can one be sure that an Indian tribe accustomed to planting seeds one at a time understands Christ's parable of the sower who scattered seeds by the handful? How can one convey to natives living on a small island with low hills an impression of the Judean mountains in their own language, which has a term for "hill" but none for "mountain"? What does one do if the

---

3. Michael Agar, *Language Shock: Understanding the Culture of Conversation*, 20–21; emphasis in original.

transliteration of "rabbi" into an African dialect is dangerously close to an obscene word?[4]

Numerous examples demonstrate how Joseph used imagery and vocabulary from a familiar historical and agricultural background for his translation. For example, Mormon uses a particular metaphor to describe his people: "The Spirit of the Lord hath already ceased to strive with their fathers; and *they are without Christ and God in the world; and they are driven about as chaff before the wind*" (Morm. 5:16). A modern English-speaking audience might easily understand this verse because we descend from cultures heavily dependent upon wheat. That grain was so crucial to the formation of sedentary communities—so fundamental to the ability to establish society—that we have inherited metaphors that require an intimate understanding of how the raw grain becomes food. We understand the idiom even when many modern readers are far removed from any agricultural experience with wheat. For this metaphor to have any sense to the audience, they must have a basic knowledge of wheat, chaff, and the production method by which chaff is blown in the wind. None of these requirements existed anywhere in the New World, and thus an authentic ancient document written there could not have originally contained a sentence where chaff was used metaphorically.

Elsewhere, there is familiarity with Western agriculture, but rather with biblical animal husbandry. For example, in 3 Nephi 15:17 we read of "other sheep." This passage alludes to John 10:16 and reflects a biblical culture familiar with herding sheep. Jesus is the good shepherd and brings his flock together. While clearly familiar to the reception audience, it was a practice that was unknown to Book of Mormon writers.[5]

Conversely, the translated Book of Mormon does not provide any specific animals and agricultural products that would exclusively reflect cultures of the pre-Columbian Western hemisphere. This would coincide with it being unlikely that Joseph knew anything at all about the animals and agricultural practices that we now know from history or archaeology. Nevertheless, the Book of Mormon is a text in translation, and the prob-

---

4. Marcellus S. Snow, "Translating Mormon Thought," 49–50.

5. The only place where herd animals were domesticated, of which I am aware, was in South America. Llamas are herd animals and could be adapted to the shepherd/flock imagery. I favor a Mesoamerican location where there was no available herd animal. Note, however, that there is a difference between domesticated and tamed. Mesoamerica did have tamed animals, an important issue in the story of Ammon at the waters of Sebus.

lem of finding words for animals or plants that are unfamiliar is a known problem in the clash between cultures and languages.

Following the colonization of the Western continents, indigenous cultures had to find ways to adapt to the imposition of artifacts, animals, and plants that accompanied European immigrants. Cecil H. Brown explains:

> In 1493, as head of an armada of 17 ships, Columbus made his second voyage to America. In addition to 1,200 men, on board these vessels were animals and plants never before seen by native Americans: horses, pigs, cattle, chickens, sheep, and goats; and barley, wheat, chick-peas, melons, radishes, salad greens, sugarcane, and fruit trees in the forms of seeds, stones, and cuttings. . . .
>
> Both Native Americans and Europeans adjusted in various ways to novel items encountered in the great exchange. This adjustment often initially entailed the linguistic problem of deciding what names to give new things.[6]

Elements of the ways in which humankind has resolved the need for lexical acculturation with other human languages shed light on prophetic acculturation to the divine. Brown found that Native American languages tended to borrow European words for animals more often than for artifacts.[7] This distinction may provide clarification for certain choices Joseph made while translating that required him to process meaning into language. When that meaning could be correlated to available categories, it would have triggered a lexical acculturation that could adapt current language to the new information. The presence of modern relabeling does not mean that there was no authentic Nephite animal or plant that was named in their own language; rather, it simply declares that the selected English word is the result of translation.

We see something similar in the King James Bible: "Neither do men light a candle, and put it under a bushel, but on a candlestick" (Matt. 5:15). Candles and candlesticks are technically anachronisms, as they were not in use in Palestine during Jesus's day. They are, however, reasonable representations of the meaning of the source text behind the English translation (which most modern Bibles accurately translate as "lamp" and "stand"). Translation anachronisms in the Book of Mormon simply suggest that Joseph expressed meaning using his available vocabulary.

This explanation also provides the reason for the mixture of familiar and unfamiliar animals in Ether 9:19: "And they also had horses, and asses, and there were elephants and cureloms and cumoms; all of which were useful unto man, and more especially the elephants and cureloms

---

6. Cecil H. Brown, *Lexical Acculturation in Native American Languages*, 3.
7. Brown, 158.

and cumoms." The presence of translated and untranslated animals is unusual. We only see it in Ether. The translation methodology that converted Nephite meaning into English suggests that the translated animals in the sentence were animals with which Moroni was familiar, and that familiarity suggests relabeling as Joseph translated. However, it may be the case that Moroni did not know what curelons and cumoms were and therefore left those terms untranslated in his Nephite writing. As unknowns, Joseph also left them untranslated.[8]

The Use of "Christ" as a Name

The Book of Mormon intentionally focuses on Jesus Christ, and understanding Jesus as the Messiah is a central theme throughout the Nephite text. However, what belongs to the nineteenth-century translation is the way in which the title of the "anointed one" becomes altered from a title to a surname.

This obvious modernity is best represented in 2 Nephi 25:19: "For according to the words of the prophets, the Messiah cometh in six hundred years from the time that my father left Jerusalem; and according to the words of the prophets, and also the word of the angel of God, *his name shall be Jesus Christ*, the Son of God." The first problem with this verse is that we have both "Messiah" and "Christ" in the same sentence—as they are both translations of the exact same concept of the "anointed one." "Messiah" comes to English by transliteration from Hebrew (*mashiach*); Christ comes to English by transliteration of the Greek (*khristós*) translation of *mashiach*.

---

8. It should be noted that there have been other explanations of why we find anachronisms in the text. Some have argued that many of the animals and plants assumed to have been anachronistic have been found. (See, for example, Wade E. Miller, "Animals in the Book of Mormon: Challenges and Perspectives.") Recent research has found horse bones that date to pre-Columbian times, with at least one during Book of Mormon times. (See "When Lehi's Party Arrived in the Land, Did they Find Horses There?," Book of Mormon Central.) Others have used the argument about loan-shifting (which is the term for what Brown examined in his study of cross-cultural linguistic labeling). That has been suggested to have occurred with the Nephites rather than Joseph as suggested here. (See John L. Sorenson, *An Ancient American Setting for the Book of Mormon*, 289–90.) The identification of the Nephites as the source of the language shift is implicit in his arguments. Although each of those positions have their arguments, they fail to adequately explain the range of these cultural anachronisms as fully as understanding them within the context of translation.

The second problem is also introduced in the verse, but it is characteristic of how the paired words "Jesus Christ" appear throughout the Book of Mormon, where they are together seemingly used as a compound name rather than a name and title. Edward J. Brandt examined the combination of Jesus and Christ in the Book of Mormon and notes: "The continued use of the name Jesus Christ in the Book of Mormon, in view of all of the other names and titles used in the scriptures, shows it had an important influence on the Nephites throughout their history."[9] Brandt argues that "Christ" (the title) is used frequently in association with the concept of "name." As an example, he cites Mosiah 15:21,[10] which reads: "And there cometh a resurrection, . . . even a resurrection of those that have been, and who are, and who shall be, even until the resurrection of Christ—for so shall he be called."

Brandt emphasizes "for so shall he be called" as justification for using "Christ" as a name, concluding that the Nephites "knew as Peter knew that there was no 'other name given under heaven save it be this Jesus Christ, . . . whereby man can be saved.'"[11] Acts 4:12, to which Brandt compared the quoted scripture from 2 Nephi 25:20, reads: "Neither is there salvation in any other: for there is none other name under heaven given among men, whereby we must be saved." The sentiment is clearly the same, but it is only in the Book of Mormon that "Jesus Christ" is used as a name rather than as a name and title.

One of the subtle issues behind the problem of the way a "name" is assumed in the Book of Mormon translation is that it leans upon modern perceptions of what a name is rather than the ancient context of it that we see in both the Old and New Testament. Walther Eichrodt explains:

> In order to understand this it is necessary to realize the vital reciprocal relationship which according to ancient ideas subsisted between the name and its owner. When it is believed that the nature of a thing is comprehended in its name, then on the one hand emphasis is laid on the idea that knowledge of the name mediates a *direct relationship with the nature*, and on the other the name is regarded to such an extent as *expression of the individual character* of its owner that it can, in fact, stand for him, become a concept interchangeable with him.[12]

---

9. Edward J. Brandt, "The Name *Jesus Christ* Revealed to the Nephites," 203.
10. Brandt, 204.
11. Brandt, 205. See 2 Nephi 25:20; compare Acts 4:12; see also 2 Nephi 31:20–21; Mosiah 3:17, 5:8; D&C 18:23; Moses 6:52, 57.
12. Walther Eichrodt, *Theology of the Old Testament*, 2:40; emphasis in original.

When we read Acts 4:12, the *name* is the essence of the Messiah as Savior, not the more mundane designation of an individual. Although the Book of Mormon contains the word *name*, it modernizes the meaning. That small shift to a modern understanding diminishes the title *Christ* to the point where Jesus Christ functions almost as name and surname.

Returning to the presence of both Messiah and Christ in 2 Nephi 25:19, we can understand that Joseph, as translator, was unaware of the language contexts that led to two different English words for the same meaning. He was similarly unaware of the ancient contexts surrounding the importance of a *name*. Perhaps had the King James translators only given us "Jesus the Christ" rather than "Jesus Christ," the confusion might have been avoided. It is the nineteenth-century concept of name that is represented in the way "Jesus Christ" is used in the Book of Mormon rather than the more ancient understanding.

Fulfilled Prophecy and Translation

Scriptural prophecy is typically generalized and thus often only understood as fulfilled after specific historical events seem to line up with the less-specific prophecy. While it is not a case of fulfilled prophecy, there is a possible instance in the Book of Mormon where Joseph Smith's later experiences influenced the way we understand one aspect of the Nephite text.

In 1829, Joseph made a statement about the title page of the Book of Mormon:

> I wish to mention here that the title-page of the Book of Mormon is a literal translation, taken from the very last leaf on the left hand side of the collection or book of plates, which contained the record which has been translated, the language of the whole running the same as all Hebrew writing in general; and that said title page is not by any means a modern composition, either of mine or of any other man who has lived or does live in this generation.[13]

Normally, there would be no reason to doubt Joseph's statements about the Book of Mormon plates, as he was the only person who could speak with any authority about them. Nevertheless, part of this statement may not refer to an understanding from the time of translation but rather reflects Joseph's later understanding of Hebrew. By 1839, when he made the statement about the title page, Joseph had studied Hebrew as part of his education in the School of the Prophets in Kirtland. The specific refer-

---

13. "History, circa June–October 1839 [Draft 1]," The Joseph Smith Papers, 9.

ence to "the whole running the same as all Hebrew writing in general" highlights how his Hebrew studies were informing his description.

The reason for questioning this statement is the set of characters commonly known as the Anthon Transcript. The pen strokes and movement of the characters indicate the left-to-right writing movement that is conventional in English, not the right-to-left writing in Hebrew. If the characters are reasonable representations of what was on the plates, the characters, and therefore sentences, were written left to right. In short, the physical evidence of the transcript contradicts Joseph's own description of the writing on the plates.[14]

That Joseph made this description so late suggests that after he learned of the writing and reading pattern of Hebrew, he retrojected that information onto the translation process. Because that process does not seem to have included the physical examination of the plates,[15] it is quite possible that he translated the entire set of plates without even being aware of the reading direction of the characters on them.

Those same characters appear in another more extensive retrojection of the modern onto the ancient. Martin Harris's visit to Charles Anthon was a seminal event for the publication of the Book of Mormon, as it convinced Harris that he should support the translation and publication process. Important to this study, the visit was also behind the way in which Joseph translated 2 Nephi 27. That chapter is $Nephi_1$'s reworking of the themes of Isaiah 29 into a prediction of the future redemption of Zion. Nephi begins the process as early as 2 Nephi 27:3:

> And all the nations that fight against Zion, and that distress her, shall be as a dream of a night vision; yea, it shall be unto them, even as unto a hungry man which dreameth, and behold he eateth but he awaketh and his soul is empty; or like unto a thirsty man which dreameth, and behold he drinketh but he awaketh and behold he is faint, and his soul hath appetite; yea, even so shall the multitude of all the nations be that fight against Mount Zion.

---

14. Of course, it is also possible that the physical act of writing them on paper created some of the strokes that show the left-to-right formation. Nevertheless, the flow of the shapes suggests a left-to-right motion in the same way that our Latin alphabet shows a left-to-right design. Hebrew characters show a right-to-left flow.

15. John W. Welch with Erick B. Carlson, eds., "Emma Smith Bidamon, as interviewed by Joseph Smith III (1879)," 130, explains that she wrote as Joseph had his face in his hat and the plates lay covered on the table. The number of testimonies about the face-in-the-hat method indicate that, even if the plates were nearby, Joseph was not consulting them during the translation.

This is a reworking of Isaiah 29:7–8:

> And the multitude of all the nations that fight against Ariel, even all that fight against her and her munition, and that distress her, shall be as a dream of a night vision.
>
> It shall even be as when an hungry man dreameth, and, behold, he eateth; but he awaketh, and his soul is empty: or as when a thirsty man dreameth, and, behold, he drinketh; but he awaketh, and, behold, he is faint, and his soul hath appetite: so shall the multitude of all the nations be, that fight against mount Zion.

Nephi$_1$ restructures the introduction to apply specifically to Zion rather than to Ariel (another name for Jerusalem),[16] but he retains the "dream of a night vision" because it fits his restructuring of the "voice from the dust" into a message from those who "slumber" in death. This passage is not simply altering, adding, or omitting a few words as has been the case up to this point. Rather it is a complex thematic reworking of Isaiah's original. It is well crafted, taking literary themes and weaving them together into a new fabric.

This reworking fits with the way Nephi$_1$ used Isaiah as he develops his vision of the future of Zion. Regarding the examination of how Joseph's information environment affected the translation, it is interesting that the predicted future becomes very precise when Nephi$_1$ was interacting with Isaiah 29:

> And the vision of all is become unto you as the words of a book that is sealed, which men deliver to one that is learned, saying, Read this, I pray thee: and he saith, I cannot; for it is sealed:
>
> And the book is delivered to him that is not learned, saying, Read this, I pray thee: and he saith, I am not learned.
>
> Wherefore the Lord said, Forasmuch as this people draw near me with their mouth, and with their lips do honour me, but have removed their heart far from me, and their fear toward me is taught by the precept of men:
>
> Therefore, behold, I will proceed to do a marvellous work among this people, even a marvellous work and a wonder: for the wisdom of their wise men shall perish, and the understanding of their prudent men shall be hid. (vv. 11–14)

The Isaiah prophecy is generic. As Joseph translated this section, Harris's experience colored the way the Nephite text was recreated in English. Isaiah's (and Nephi$_1$'s) prophecy had been fulfilled, and that ful-

---

16. Victor L. Ludlow, *Unlocking Isaiah in the Book of Mormon*, 206.

filled prophecy allowed the retranslation of Isaiah/Nephi$_1$ to reveal that fulfillment:

> But behold, it shall come to pass that the Lord God shall say unto him to whom he shall deliver the book: Take these words which are not sealed and deliver them to another, that he may show them unto the learned, saying: Read this, I pray thee. And the learned shall say: Bring hither the book, and I will read them.
>
> And now, because of the glory of the world and to get gain will they say this, and not for the glory of God.
>
> And the man shall say: I cannot bring the book, for it is sealed.
>
> Then shall the learned say: I cannot read it.
>
> Wherefore it shall come to pass, that the Lord God will deliver again the book and the words thereof to him that is not learned; and the man that is not learned shall say: I am not learned.
>
> Then shall the Lord God say unto him: The learned shall not read them, for they have rejected them, and I am able to do mine own work; wherefore thou shalt read the words which I shall give unto thee. (2 Ne. 27:15–20)

The translation stops short of naming names, but the description clearly knows of Harris's experience with Anthon.[17]

The influence of fulfilled prophecy can similarly be seen in the way that the Gospel of Matthew transforms a different passage from Isaiah: "Therefore the Lord himself shall give you a sign; Behold, a virgin shall conceive, and bear a son, and shall call his name Immanuel" (Isa. 7:14). The author of Matthew sees the birth of Christ as the fulfillment of Isaiah's prophecy and renders it in the context of Jesus of Nazareth:

> But while he thought on these things, behold, the angel of the Lord appeared unto him in a dream, saying, Joseph, thou son of David, fear not to take unto thee Mary thy wife: for that which is conceived in her is of the Holy Ghost.
>
> And she shall bring forth a son, and thou shalt call his name JESUS: for he shall save his people from their sins.
>
> Now all this was done, that it might be fulfilled which was spoken of the Lord by the prophet, saying,

---

17. David E. Sloan, "The Anthon Transcripts and the Translation of the Book of Mormon: Studying It Out in the Mind of Joseph Smith," 62. According to the 1832 history, Joseph could not translate the very same characters that he had previously copied off the plates; furthermore, it was not until the characters were returned to him that he "commenced" translating them (Sloan, 62). This corresponds closely to the sequence of events identified in 2 Ne. 27 and Isa. 29, and it is significant that the Prophet specifically saw in these events the fulfillment of Isa. 29.

Behold, a virgin shall be with child, and shall bring forth a son, and they shall call his name Emmanuel, which being interpreted is, God with us. (Matt. 1:20–23)

Most interesting about this reworking of Isaiah is that Matthew eventually influenced the translators of Isaiah. According to Robert Alter, a better translation of that passage in Isaiah would be: "Therefore the Master Himself shall give you a sign: *a young woman* is about to conceive and bear a son, and she shall call his name Immanuel."[18] The Hebrew *'almâ* (young woman) became the Greek *parthenos* in Matthew (following the Septuagint's Greek translation of Isaiah). The King James translators then accepted the fulfilled prophecy and made the connection tighter by translating the Hebrew term in Isaiah as "virgin."

For a translator living after a perceived fulfillment to phrase a passage in terms of it is understandable. This is particularly true if we are not dealing with an academic translation attempting to retain more of the sense of the original. Thus, it may be expected that Joseph would clarify and expand on previously generic prophecies in his translation, as the Book of Mormon was not intended to be a resource on New World native architecture or agriculture but rather to bolster the reader's testimony of Christ.

A similar process may explain another unusual and fulfilled prophecy in 2 Nephi that was said to be contained on the brass plates:

And thus prophesied Joseph [of Egypt], saying: Behold, that seer will the Lord bless; and they that seek to destroy him shall be confounded; for this promise, which I have obtained of the Lord, of the fruit of my loins, shall be fulfilled. Behold, I am sure of the fulfilling of this promise;

And his name shall be called after me; and it shall be after the name of his father. And he shall be like unto me; for the thing, which the Lord shall bring forth by his hand, by the power of the Lord shall bring my people unto salvation. (2 Ne. 3:14–15)

That there was a prophecy on the brass plates can be accepted. It is the prophecy of a seer named Joseph—who would bring forth the Book of Mormon and whose father was also named Joseph (an obvious reference to Joseph Smith Jr.)—that may be best understood as a translation being more specific as the result of a fulfilled prophecy.

---

18. Alter's translation of Isaiah 7:14. Robert Alter, *The Hebrew Bible: A Translation with Commentary: Prophets*, vol. 2, 645; emphasis added.

Spontaneity in the Dictated Text

The dictated text contains several types of sentences that are best understood as the result of spontaneous creation rather than simply reading a pre-written text. Before examining these sentences, we need background on some essential differences between orality and literacy. Both use words in the same language, and both can be parsed into sentences and perhaps paragraphs. Nevertheless, there are significant differences among the similarities. Walter Ong explains:

> Writing establishes in the text a "line" of continuity outside the mind. If distraction confuses or obliterates from the mind the context of which emerges the material I am now reading, the context can be retrieved by glancing back over the text selectively. Backlooping can be entirely occasional, purely ad hoc. The mind concentrates its own energies on moving ahead because what it backloops into lies quiescent outside itself, always available piecemeal on the inscribed page. In oral discourse, the situation is different. There is nothing to backloop into outside the mind, for the oral utterance has vanished as soon as it is uttered. Hence the mind must move ahead more slowly, keeping close to the focus of attention much of what it has already dealt with. Redundancy, repetition of the just-said, keeps both speaker and hearer surely on the track.[19]

Thus, a significant marker of orality is the need for error correction but without an easy way to accomplish it. In any written text, context can easily be retrieved, and errors can be quickly edited. Oral presentations, on the other hand, have no such means of correction. Once the utterance is pronounced, it cannot be taken back. Instead, it can only be corrected in the next utterance. Ong continues: "With writing, words once 'uttered', outered, put down on the surface, can be eliminated, erased, changed. There is no equivalent for this in an oral performance, no way to erase a spoken word: corrections do not remove an infelicity or an error, they merely supplant it with denial and patchwork."[20]

Sentences Correcting Their Own Errors

The problem of correcting an oral text is perhaps clearest in sentences with an error that is corrected with a statement beginning with "or" (or "or rather"). Ruth Scodel underscores the oral underpinnings of self-correction:

---

19. Walter J. Ong, *Orality and Literacy*, 39–40.
20. Ong, 103.

> In genuinely spontaneous speech, self-correction and shifts of direction happen all the time. (Avoiding too much self-correction is an important measure of competence in such everyday oral narration as telling jokes.)[21]

She also notes:

> Self-correction presents very different issues, depending on whether it occurs within a single text or between texts. For a speaker to change his mind, stop himself, or announce that he has spoken inappropriately, generally implies an extemporaneous situation, since with preparation the speaker could presumably have gotten it right the first time.[22]

Applying this concept to the text of the Book of Mormon at least suggests that corrections might represent a spontaneous creation.[23]

Perhaps the most obvious use of the corrective "or" is found in Alma 24:19:

> And thus we see that, when these Lamanites were brought to believe and to know the truth, they were firm, and would suffer even unto death rather than commit sin; and thus we see that *they buried their weapons of peace, or they buried the weapons of war, for peace.*

The phrase "weapons of peace" makes no sense and was immediately corrected to "weapons of war." However, the correction doesn't treat it as a complete error, only an unfortunate compression of the idea. Thus, the extended, and presumably correct, phrase was to bury "the weapons of war, for peace."

Mary Lee Treat examined this type of correction, including this very example. She concludes: "It is clear that this consistent use of a phrase for a correcting purpose would not appear if the writer were using pen, ink and paper. Only in a situation where corrections were impossible would this configuration emerge."[24] Treat recognized the problem of such a correction when a complete rewrite could not be made. However, she suggested the difficulty was due to the medium of writing on metal plates and not an essential difference between speaking and writing.

The problem with her explanation is that the very solution she suggested for pen and paper is also available on metal. The writer can simply cross out a mistake. The assumption is that the more permanent medium

---

21. Ruth Scodel, "Self-Correction, Spontaneity, and Orality in Archaic Poetry," 64.
22. Scodel, 62.
23. I offered a different analysis in Brant A. Gardner, "Literacy and Orality in the Book of Mormon," 72–73. I have since changed my mind.
24. Mary Lee Treat, "No Erasers," 1:54.

would make that more difficult, but that is demonstrably untrue. It takes less effort to cross out a word than to use several new words to avoid the cross-out. In the case of "weapons of peace," the correction would only require crossing out a single word. The word "peace" could have been crossed out and followed immediately by "war." The "or" correction required much more work. Parsimony suggests that writing on the more difficult medium would select the shorter, therefore easier, solution.

Examining other instances of the corrective "or" allows for more insight into the process that created those sentences. For example, a similar change in a single word would have repaired 1 Nephi 19:4:

> Wherefore, I, Nephi, did make a record upon the other plates, which gives an account, or which gives a greater account of the wars and contentions and destructions of my people. And this have I done, and commanded my people what they should do after I was gone; and that these plates should be handed down from *one generation to another, or from one prophet to another,* until further commandments of the Lord.

If this "or" is read as a corrective rather than an expansion, the correction only had to cross out the word "generation" and then write "prophet." Another passage that is more clearly correcting an error is found in Jacob 5:21:

> And it came to pass that the servant said unto his master: How comest thou hither to *plant this tree, or this branch of the tree?* For behold, it was the poorest spot in all the land of thy vineyard.

Once again, the error of "plant this tree" could have been repaired by crossing out the word *tree* and then continuing with *branch of the tree.*

A different type of corrective "or" functions to correct an incorrect impression rather than an outright mistake. In Jarom 1:14 we have:

> And I, Jarom, do not write more, for the plates are small. But behold, my brethren, ye can go to the other plates of Nephi; for behold, upon them the records of our wars are engraven, according to *the writings of the kings, or those which they caused to be written.*

The phrase "writings of the kings" is not incorrect, but it could leave the impression that it was the kings themselves who wrote. Therefore, the phrase is corrected to note that the kings had caused the plates to be written.

The motivation for the correction in Alma 35:15 clarifies the use of the wrong word in the initial clause:

> Now Alma, being grieved for the iniquity of his people, yea for the wars, and the bloodsheds, and the contentions which were among them; and *having been to declare the word, or sent to declare the word,* among all the people in

every city; and seeing that the hearts of the people began to wax hard, and that they began to be offended because of the strictness of the word, his heart was exceedingly sorrowful.

The first clause is only somewhat awkward, but the clear intent would have been to create the phrase "having been sent to declare." The word *sent* was left out, and then added as a correction in the next phrase.

There are also problem-solving corrections that do not use the corrective "or."

> For the things which some men esteem to be of great worth, both to the body and soul, others set at naught and trample under their feet. Yea, even the very God of Israel do men trample under their feet; *I say, trample under their feet but I would speak in other words*—they set him at naught, and hearken not to the voice of his counsels. (1 Ne. 19:7)

> And in the fifty and first year of the reign of the judges there was peace also, save it were the pride which began to enter into the church—*not into the church of God, but into the hearts of the people who professed to belong to the church of God*. (Hel. 3:33)

In an important paper that examined improvisation and extemporaneous change in the text of the Book of Mormon, Gerald E. Smith writes:

> It is sometimes difficult to know precisely who inserted the corrective conjunction phrase into a passage; whether Smith did while translating in the nineteenth century; whether the engravers of the actual plate text did, such as Mormon, Nephi, or Moroni; or whether even earlier authors or orators did, those whose words are quoted or embedded by the engravers, such as Alma, Abinadi, Limhi, or Benjamin.[25]

Smith correctly notes that there are different possibilities for the person who generated these obviously extemporaneous changes; however, he consistently assumes antiquity of the corrections without any examination of why the different types of corrective conjunctions must have occurred in antiquity.

Some uses of "or" are obviously ancient, such as those found in Isaiah:

> For shall the prey be taken from the mighty, *or* the lawful captives delivered? (1 Ne. 21:24/Isa. 49:24)

> Yea, for thus saith the Lord: Have I put thee away, or have I cast thee off forever? For thus saith the Lord: Where is the bill of your mother's divorcement? To

---

25. Gerald E. Smith, "Improvisation and Extemporaneous Change in the Book of Mormon, Part 1: Evidence of an Imperfect, Authentic, Ancient Work of Scripture," 5.

whom have I put thee away, *or* to which of my creditors have I sold you? Yea, to whom have I sold you? Behold, for your iniquities have ye sold yourselves, and for your transgressions is your mother put away. (2 Ne. 7:1/Isa. 50:1)

These are examples of what Smith calls his "Type 2: Amplifying, clarifying, or augmenting the meaning of an original expression."[26] This type is literary rather than corrective and is part of the Hebrew scripture as augmentations.

Smith's argument that the corrective conjunctions must have been original to the text is based solely on the assumption that if Joseph Smith had made them, he would have corrected them in later editions.[27] That explanation, however, assumes that the Prophet fully understood the entire translation process—an assumption that does not seem supported by the evidence. As Michael Hubbard Mackay puts it, "[Joseph Smith] experienced the process but he did not know through personal experience that it was correct or whether its modern translation represented a historical ontology or a nineteenth-century ontology. He simply could not know."[28]

There are two cases (at least) of the corrective "or" where the nature of the correction points more clearly to Joseph Smith than to any other possible author of the sentence. The first is in Alma 17:18:

> Now Ammon being *the chief among them, or rather he did administer unto them*, and he departed from them, after having blessed them according to their several stations, *having imparted the word of God unto them, or administered* unto them before his departure; and thus they took their several journeys throughout the land.

Although this is clearly a correction, it is perhaps not immediately clear what the correction would be. Alma$_1$ *was* chief among all his people. He was at one time the chief judge, though by the time of this sentence he had relinquished that position. Nevertheless, he had retained the position of the High Priest, and that would qualify him as chief among those of the same religion. Nevertheless, this was changed to "or rather he did administer unto them," as though being chief and an administer were to be considered somehow equivalent.

The most logical explanation for this conflation of "chief" and "administer" would be that this sentence intentionally echoed Matthew 29:27:

---

26. Smith, 11.

27. Gerald E. Smith, "Improvisation and Extemporaneous Change in the Book of Mormon, Part 2: Structural Evidences of Earlier Ancient versus Later Modern Constructions," 71.

28. Michael Hubbard MacKay, "The Secular Binary of Joseph Smith's Translations," 7.

"And whosoever will be chief among you, let him be your servant."[29] The logical oral process would be the production of the sentence with the word "chief," which could trigger the memory of the passage in Matthew. That triggered remembrance explains the correction that serves more as a theological amplification. It is an amplification that only occurs in Matthew, or the similar phrase in Mark 10:44. Because the textual model is from the New Testament, it is unlikely that anything similar would have been in the original text to suggest the need for this correction.

Perhaps more interesting is the correction in Mosiah 8:17:

> But a seer can know of things which are past, and also of things which are to come, and by them *shall all things be revealed, or, rather, shall secret things be made manifest, and hidden things shall come to light*, and things which are not known shall be made known by them, and also things shall be made known by them which otherwise could not be known.

This correction depends upon the context of the seer and Joseph's contemporaneous context that understood the particular talent of the seer as making secret (or hidden) things manifest. The correction comes in the middle of a description of a seer in the Book of Mormon, and the context of the verse is clearly comfortable with the concept that "all things be revealed." It is the addition of the "or rather" phrase that deviates from the Book of Mormon context and inserts information from Joseph's cultural perceptions. While finding secret or hidden things is demonstrably a definition applicable to the cultural understanding in Joseph's time as a local seer, it is not a demonstrable explanation for the use of a seer stone in the Book of Mormon that is used to translate.[30] The concepts could be tied together, but the need to explain how the Book of Mormon's position of the revelation of all things fit into Joseph's contemporaneous seeric culture is external to the text.

Incomplete Sentences

Oral texts have a greater tendency to create incomplete or run-on sentences than written ones do.[31] The underlying cause is the differing access to memory. For a written text, having the written portion available

---

29. See also Mark 10:44: "And whosoever of you will be the chiefest, shall be servant of all."
30. See Omni 1:20 and Mosiah 8:13.
31. For example, see Oregon Department of Transportation Research Section, "Guide to Transcribing and Summarizing Oral Histories," 2. The Guide notes that often an editing pass is required to fix run-on sentences.

takes over the function of memory; what has been written is available for consultation. In contrast, oral utterances rely both upon the memory of the speaker and the hearer to create understanding. For both, there is no external memory, only the availability of internal memory. Short-term memory is the key to understanding the differing types of incomplete sentences in the dictated text.

There are two interrelated aspects of the study of short-term memory: the formation of memory and the production of language. Most studies have concentrated on the processing of items to be remembered. That is an intake function. Language production reverses the direction of memory. Nevertheless, both the intake and production functions use short-term memory in similar ways.

The most important aspects of short-term memory to the investigation of possible spontaneous creation in the dictation of the Book of Mormon are the capacity of short-term memory and its temporal duration. Short-term memory has inherent limitations. George Miller proposes that the magic number for the number of discrete items to be held in short-term memory was seven, plus or minus two.[32] Daniel Bor notes that more recent studies show that "a conscious limit of 4 objects turns up faithfully in almost any kind of experiment one tries."[33]

In addition to a limited capacity to hold many items in short-term memory, it also appears to have a time limitation. We can hold that number of discrete elements for only about thirty seconds.[34] While Miller and others were studying the ability to remember, or the intake, the same limitations exist on the externalization of short-term memory through language. Steven Pinker notes:

> Phonological short-term memory lasts between one and five seconds and can hold from four to seven "chunks." (Short-term memory is measured in chunks rather than sounds because each item can be a label that points to a much bigger information structure in long-term memory, such as the content of a phrase or sentence.)[35]

The reason for discussing memory in chunks rather than items is that a chunk is stored in memory much as a single word might, even though it

---

32. George Mandler, "Organization and Memory," 314.

33. Daniel Bor, *The Ravenous Brain: How the New Science of Consciousness Explains our Insatiable Search for Meaning*, 137.

34. Julia Shaw, *The Memory Illusion: Remembering, Forgetting and the Science of False Memory*, 7.

35. Steven Pinker, *How the Mind Works*, 89–90; parentheses in original.

consists of more than one word. Pinker elaborates: "*Kicking the bucket* is not a kind of kicking, and buckets have nothing to do with it. The meanings of these phrase-sized units have to be memorized as listemes, just as if they were simple word-sized units, and so they are really 'words' in this sense."[36] It is not the number of words that weighs heavily on short-term memory, but the phrases that may be produced as "chunks." This becomes relevant to the Book of Mormon translation in that most problems with incomplete sentences revolve around multiple phrases that come between the introduction of the sentence and its intended conclusion. Many of those phrases were likely present as listemes and count as one unit rather than the number of words in the phrase.

This crucial aspect of memory formation and language production becomes an issue only in spontaneous utterances. Written texts substitute the functionally permanent record for the mental effort required to produce language. Reading does not tax the memory in the same way as the production of spontaneous utterances does.[37] In the case of the incomplete sentences, it is precisely the tax on memory that creates the conditions under which the sentences drift in meaning, and either never find their way to a grammatical conclusion or essentially start over to correct the deviations.

In addition to the inherent difficulties of creating spontaneous speech, the very process described for the oral dictation of the Book of Mormon increases the memory load. According to David Whitmer,

> He [Joseph] put the stone in his hat and putting his face in his hat so as to exclude the light and before his eyes would appear what seemed to be parchment, on which would appear the charters of the plates in a line at the top and immediately below would appear the translation, in English, which Smith would read to his scribe, who wrote it down exactly as it fell from his lips. The scribe would then read the sentence written, and if any mistake had been made the characters would remain visible to Smith until corrected, when they faded from sight to be replaced by another line.[38]

---

36. Steven Pinker, *The Language Instinct: How the Mind Creates Language*, 148.
37. Paul M. Postal, "Transformational Grammar: An Introduction," 151: "It is well known that *written* performances may use longer sentences on the average than spoken performances. The reason is that with the written medium, the use of language makes fewer demands on memory, and more of the total number of sentences can be used."
38. Larry E. Morris, ed., *A Documentary History of the Book of Mormon*, 346.

Although this is a late description giving details that Whitmer could not see, it still provides the important observation that the dictation was an interrupted process. Rather than a smooth flow of words, Skousen suggests that the dictation blocks contained between twenty to thirty words at a time.[39] The time between the dictation of one block and the next was determined by the speed at which the scribe could complete writing that block and read it back. Thus, the problem of memory is compounded with the time lag for the scribe.

John and Jeannie Welch experimented with reproducing the physical translation experience:

> In order to test the feasibility of these calculations of how fast Joseph and Oliver actually could have worked, my wife, Jeannie, and I decided to try it out ourselves. We picked two pages in Royal Skousen's Yale edition of the Book of Mormon, since that version breaks the text lines into thought clauses that would have been about the length of each translational unit. At first, I played the role of Joseph and read the first line slowly and distinctly, while she, playing the role of Oliver, began immediately writing those words down. When she reached the end of that line, she read it back to me, and I confirmed that it was correct or pointed out mistakes. Then I paused, gazed again at the page, uncovered the next line, and read it aloud, which Jeannie likewise recorded and read back. And so we proceeded to the end of the page. . . .
>
> Altogether, our results showed empirically that a translation rate of right around 20 words per minute was quite possible. But we couldn't imagine sustaining that rate hour after hour, day after day. Our hands got tired, and the one playing Joseph needed to catch his or her breath and clear his or her voice. We used ballpoint pens. We imagined Oliver dipping and using his quill pen.[40]

They personally experienced how dramatically the translation process complicated the problem of production. In this case, however, they were only testing the reading of the text and were not looking at the problem of short-term memory. As already noted, reading does not tax memory in the same way that spontaneous utterances do.[41] If the process was physically taxing when only reading and scribing, it can be understood how the memory tax was even greater in the spontaneous dictation of the text.

There are two types of incomplete sentences in the dictated Book of Mormon. They can best be seen in either the Original or Printer's

---

39. Royal Skousen, "Translating the Book of Mormon: Evidence from the Original Manuscript," 71–72.

40. John W. Welch, "Timing the Translation of the Book of Mormon: 'Days [and Hours] Never to Be Forgotten,'" 38–39.

41. Postal, "Transformational Grammar," 151.

Manuscripts, as some (but not all) were corrected in later editions.[42] The problems of incomplete sentences recur throughout the text and across authors, books, and, importantly, across both the small plates and the large plates. This suggests that the problem lies with the consistent mind that crosses all those elements: Joseph Smith, the self-identified translator.

Incomplete Sentences Corrected by Repetitive Resumption

The first type of incomplete sentence is one in which the sentence is corrected by starting over.[43] Royal Skousen calls this process repetitive resumption. He notes:

> In the Book of Mormon text, a sentence may begin with a long clause or phrase that is never completed. In most cases the passage will recover from its uncomplete state by starting over, more or less. This resumption is generally accomplished by repeating some aspect of the initial part of the uncompleted sentence, thus tying the text back to what was first stated.[44]

Before proceeding to examples, Skousen's statement that such sentences "begin with a long clause or phrase" should be highlighted. That is the key to taxing short-term memory that requires the restart rather than the completion of the sentence.

The following examples are formatted according to the thought lines that Skousen uses to reproduce the text:

1 Nephi 1:4:

For it came to pass *in the commencement of the first year*
Of the reign of Zedekiah king of Judah
—my father Lehi having dwelt at Jerusalem in all his days—
And *in that same year* there came many prophets prophesying unto the people
That they must repent or the great city Jerusalem must be destroyed.[45]

There is a hanging phrase at the beginning: "For it came to pass in the commencement of the first year . . ." The phrase ends with "my father Lehi having dwelt at Jerusalem in all his days," which is an interruptive phrase. At that point the perhaps intended way to resolve the sentence was lost, and Joseph started over.

---

42. These examples are taken from *The Plates of Mormon*.
43. Larry G. Childs, "Epanalepsis in the Book of Mormon." Childs uses the term *epanalepsis* to describe repetitive resumption on the sentence level.
44. Royal Skousen, with Stanford Carmack, *The History of the Text of the Book of Mormon: The Nature of the Original Language*, 4:808.
45. Skousen, with Carmack, 819.

Mosiah 2:36–37:

And now I say unto you my brethren *that*
After ye have known and have been taught all these things
If ye should transgress and go contrary to that which hath been spoken
That ye do withdraw yourselves from the Spirit of the Lord
That it may have no place in you to guide you in wisdom's paths
That he may be blessed prospered and preserved—
I say unto you that the man that doeth *this*
The same cometh out in open rebellion against God.[46]

The sentence has five intervening phrases and then pauses. Rather than attempt any completion, the text repeats "I say unto you" to restart the flow of the idea.

Mosiah 7:27–28:

And because he saith unto them that Christ was the God the Father of all things
And saith that he should take upon him the image of man
And that it should be the image after which man was created in the beginning
—or in other words he said that man was created after the image of God
And that God should come down among the children of men
And take upon him flesh and blood and go forth upon the face of the earth—
And now because he said this they did put him to death.[47]

This example is interesting in that the sentence could have been completed without the repetition. However, the length of the sentence up to that point likely made Joseph unsure of the most economical method of completion. There are five clauses, and one of those is a dependent clause, which increases the complexity of holding the sentence in memory.

Perhaps the most interesting sentence is found in 1 Nephi 13:29, where the various internal clauses require that repetitive resumption be used twice to complete the sentence; it has been reformatted to highlight the resumptions.

And after these plain and precious things were taken away
    it goeth forth unto all the nations of the Gentiles;
    and after it goeth forth unto all the nations of the Gentiles,
    yea, even across the many waters which thou hast seen
    with the Gentiles which have gone forth out of captivity, thou seest—
because of the many plain and precious things which have been taken out of the book,
    which were plain unto the understanding of the children of men,
    according to the plainness which is in the Lamb of God—

---

46. Skousen, with Carmack, 816.
47. Skousen, with Carmack, 817.

> *because of these things which are taken away out of the gospel of the Lamb,* an exceedingly great many do stumble, yea, insomuch that Satan hath great power over them.

The intended sense of the sentence could be simply stated by taking the first and last lines: "And after these plain and precious things were taken away . . . an exceedingly great many do stumble, yea, insomuch that Satan hath great power over them." The inserted clauses add important information, but they are interruptive of the original intent, requiring the use of repetitive resumption to start over. The first attempt is similarly delayed with two more explanatory phrases before the final repetitive resumption finishes the sentence.

Incomplete Sentences Left Without Resolution

Skousen says of the second type of incomplete sentence: "It should be noted at the start that sometimes the uncompleted initial portion is never followed by any kind of resumption. Instead, the writer simply moves on to another topic without finishing what he started to write."[48] These are best explained by the heavy toll on memory created by a particular type of sentence.

Pinker explained that there are certain types of sentences which complicate the problem of both the number of chunks in short-term memory but also the time they are required to be held in memory:

> People . . . must dedicate some of their short-term memory to dangling phrases. But short-term memory is the primary bottleneck in human information processing. Only a few items—the usual estimate is seven, plus or minus two—can be held in mind at once, and the items are immediately subject to fading or being overwritten.[49]

He notes that these types of sentences are called "top-heavy," which means that they heavily load the memory requirement at the beginning of a long sentence. These are not only difficult to complete but are often more difficult to understand.[50] When there are sentences that begin with a dangling phrase, and particularly when there are three or more intervening clauses before the conclusion, they are frequently left incomplete.

---

48. Skousen, with Carmack, 808.
49. Pinker, *Language Instinct*, 201.
50. Pinker, 202.

The following examples come from the Printer's Manuscript of 1 Nephi 13:29:[51]

> And after it goeth forth unto all the nations of the Gentiles—yea, even across the many waters (which thou hast seen with the Gentiles, which have gone forth out of captivity)—and thou seest—because of the many plain and precious things which have been taken out of the book (which were plain unto the understanding of the children of men, according to the plainness which is in the Lamb of God).

The beginning "after" suggests a conclusion that will indicate that something happened. There are seven following clauses but no conclusion as to what should have come "after." The following verse then simply changes the subject, with no conclusion to what comes "after it goeth forth unto all the nations of the Gentiles."

The next examples comes from 1 Nephi 18:20–21:

> For had not the Lord been merciful, to show unto me concerning them—even as he had prophets of old. For he surely did show unto prophets of old, all things concerning them.

The beginning of the sentence begins with "had not," which suggests some conclusion of what happened. What happens is that the definition of his mercy, to show them all things, is repeated as a statement. The initial "had not" is never completed.

Mosiah 10:17 likewise detours with a clause without concluding its initial thought:

> But I, having sent my spies out round about the land of Shemlon—that I might discover their preparations—that I might guard against them—that they might not come upon my people and destroy them.

This verse is an example of several verses starting with "having."[52] Many of these have no resolution. This incomplete sentence is unresolved after three following clauses.

The nature of these sentences is that there is a condition set up at the beginning of the sentence, and then there are multiple inserted clauses

---

51. Formatted as in *The Plates of Mormon*.
52. Other examples include 2 Nephi 6:2, Jacob 4:1, Mosiah 7:21–22, Mosiah 10:7 (*having* has been changed to *had* in the current edition), Alma 9:1 (repetitive resumption at the end of the verse attempts to resolve the first part of the sentence), Alma 13:4 (*having* has been changed to *have* in the current edition), and Alma 15:21 (the first *having* has been changed to *had*, but the sentence remains unresolved in the current edition).

(remembering that the clause can be considered as a listeme). Those intervening clauses created both the mental and conceptual separation from the beginning of the sentence that so overtaxed Joseph's memory that the sentences were not resolved. In these cases, there does not appear to have been any understanding of the incompleteness of the sentence, and therefore it did not even have repetitive resumption used to create a type of resolution.

The difference between the typical completed sentences and the various examples of incomplete sentences lies in the combination of a dangling verb and a quantity of intervening clauses. When at least three clauses followed the initial hanging verb, Joseph typically lost track of the hanging verbal clause and did not resolve it. That is consistent with the capacity of short-term memory list items. The interrupted nature of the translation added time to the dictation and thus increased the memory load. In these cases, the memory tax was so high that the sentences were left without resolution.

The nature of these incomplete sentences indicates orality. The memory taxation that caused them simply does not exist in most written texts, as the very act of writing removes the problem of memory. According to Werner Kelber,

> As words are transposed into visible signs, they are lined up in rectilinear rows. The line now becomes a dominant factor in the formation of language. The effects of linearization upon cognitive processes, largely taken for granted by the modern, literate mentality, are not to be underrated. The most obvious result is the introduction of an ordering agent into language. . . . Fundamentally this is because the mind is relieved of the burden or retaining knowledge by remembering. Writing enables one to produce language over a prolonged period of time, at one's own pace, with self-chosen interruptions and without a direct commitment to audiences.[53]

Ong concurs: "With writing, the mind is forced into a slowed-down pattern that affords it the opportunity to interfere with and reorganize its more normal, redundant processes."[54] The very fact of writing eliminates the problem of holding dangling sentences in memory. When a writer begins such a phrase, the dangling verb is held on paper and available for consultation. None of the problems of short-term memory come into play.

---

53. Werner H. Kelber, *The Oral and the Written Gospel: The Hermeneutics of Speaking and Writing in the Synoptic Tradition, Mark, Paul, and Q*, 106–7, 109.

54. Ong, *Orality and Literacy*, 40.

The contrast between writing and oral production argues against these incomplete sentences as having originated from the written Nephite text. An original writer would have different solutions available to fix these before they were transmitted. It is the ephemerality of the oral utterance that creates the conditions for the types of incomplete sentences that are seen in the Book of Mormon.

Chapter Four

Translating Meaning

This section began with a discussion of Joseph Smith as the agent of translation, and it ends by returning to that issue of translation. After discussing what elements can be assigned to the translation layer, the next question is how those elements might coexist in a text that Joseph declared was translated by the gift and power of God.

Stanford Carmack recently suggested that examining the English text of the Book of Moses might help discern "whether words were revealed to Joseph Smith in 1830, or whether ideas were revealed to him."[1] He previously proposed that the Book of Mormon resulted from Joseph reading the words of a pre-existing translation.[2] Carmack only offered two options, and there are problems with both. On the one hand, if Joseph only received ideas, then the relationship of the English text to the Nephite text is tenuous and potentially so distant as to be unreliable. On the other hand, the idea that someone else created the text that Joseph read simply relocates every question about the translation from Joseph to some other translator. Whether the language came from Joseph or someone else, the English text displays elements best assigned to the nineteenth-century translation layer.

There is another option beyond the two Carmack suggested. In *The Gift and Power: Translating the Book of Mormon*, I proposed that the linguistic concept mentalese provides the explanation for the nature of the English language of the Book of Mormon. Unfortunately, my explanation has proven insufficient to adequately communicate the concept. Mentalese has too often been assumed to be a different name for *ideas* and was thus subject to the same problems noted for Carmack's first option above. Accepting that the previous explanation was insufficient means that this chapter will have both a small review and an expanded explanation of what mentalese is and how it helps explain the nature of the dictated English translation.[3]

---

1. Stanford Carmack, "The Importance of Book of Moses English for Determining Authorship." YouTube video, minutes 1:03 to 1:06.

2. Stanford Carmack, "Joseph Smith Read the Words," 41–64.

3. See Michael R. Ash, *Rethinking Revelation and the Human Element in Scripture: The Prophet's Role as Creative Co-Author,* for an interesting example of

Steven Pinker, who coined the term "mentalese," describes the way the brain elevates meaning into words and sentences:

> Mentalese [is] the language of thought in which our conceptual knowledge is couched. When you put down a book, you forget almost everything about the wording and typeface of the sentences and where they sat on the page. What you take away is their content or gist. (In memory tests, people confidently "recognize" sentences they never saw if they are paraphrases of the sentences they did see.) Mentalese is the medium in which content or gist is captured. . . . Mentalese is also the mind's lingua franca, the traffic of information among mental modules that allows us to describe what we see, imagine what is described to us, carry out instructions, and so on.[4]

Mentalese deals in meaning rather than ideas. That is an important and significant difference. Mentalese can certainly represent the meaning contained in ideas. However, it also lies underneath precise information such as reciting the alphabet or giving someone a phone number. Mentalese is not a question of precision or imprecision; rather, it is simply the way that the brain encodes meaning into language. Sentences are produced that may convey ideas. Sentences are also produced that provide specific information.

Because mentalese describes the way all language is generated from meaning, that meaning can yield very specific translations. For instance, there is textual evidence from the manuscripts that there were corrections to the spelling of names during the translation of the Book of Mormon. Thus, there is evidence that there was a precise mode of production for those names. Such precision does not preclude mentalese. Information

---

how inadequate my previous explanation was, evidenced in Ash's discussion of how his concept of translation differs from mine:

> Like Brant Gardner, I believe that God implanted the Book of Mormon narrative into Joseph's native prelanguage (or mentalese). While Gardner believes that his mentalese came from the Book of Mormon plate text, I believe this prelanguage reflected memories of the mental architecture created while forming the pre-written oral composition. The mentalese in Joseph's brain would have formed the intended English words to "translate" the gist of the narrative in most instances but could have recalled more details (such as names and narrative structure) as necessary. (p. 594)

Ash appears to distinguish his understanding from mine with his reference to the ability of mentalese to recall specific details. It is unfortunate that my original discussion led to the assumption that details were not transmitted. I am attempting to rectify that misunderstanding in this chapter.

4. Steven Pinker, *How the Mind Works*, 90.

stored as meaning and specific meanings are elevated to speech just as concepts might be.

One difficulty encountered with comprehending mentalese comes from our common-sense assumptions about language. It is difficult to think without thinking in words. Ossie Davis writes: "*Thinking* itself is sub-vocal speech—in other words, one must use *words* in order to think at all."[5] For all that this statement *feels* right, it isn't the whole picture. It is true that we often conduct internal dialogues, but there is an important division between our awareness of thinking and the subconscious activities that precede the ability to even sub-vocalize.

We are so aware of ourselves that we assume that our consciousness is who we are.[6] Without attempting a philosophical or scientific definition of either consciousness or the self, there is an important biological division between brain activity and awareness that plays into the discussion of mentalese and translation.

An example of that division can be seen in the discovery of a phenomenon called blindsight. There are individuals who have properly functioning eyes, but are blind because of damage to parts of the brain that process vision. However, it was discovered that while some of these people knew that they were blind, they were yet able to "see" the orientation of objects without being able to consciously see them. For example, they might be given an envelope and told to put it in a slot that would alternatively be horizontal or vertical. They could do so with a high degree of accuracy, even though they could not "see" the slot. As Ian Glynn explains: "Blindsight seems very strange because it is impossible to imagine getting visual information and at the same time being unable to see."[7] Yet those with blindsight could see without awareness of seeing. The type of vision they use is a separate visual circuit in the brain from the one of which we

---

5. Ossie Davis, "The English Language is My Enemy!," 242; emphasis in the original.

6. Daniel Bor, *The Ravenous Brain: How the New Science of Consciousness Explains Our Insatiable Search For Meaning*, 4–7, discusses Descartes' famous concept "I think, therefore I am." He notes: "It is worth pointing out that Descartes, like everyone else who thought about such things until a century or so ago, assumed that the mental realm simply meant everything he was conscious of. Descartes would probably have believed the concept of unconscious thoughts as an oxymoron, and certainly would never have accepted that our unconscious minds could influence our consciousness, as we all now largely assume" (p. 7).

7. Ian Glynn, *An Anatomy of Thought: The Origin and Machinery of the Mind*, 219.

are aware. Both systems exist, and we use both while only being aware of our conscious visualizing.

Other research suggests that there is a difference between an action and our awareness of that action, even for those we believe we consciously initiate. An experiment was conducted that examined what happens when a person is asked to move a finger: "Brain activity relating to the preparation to move a finger began to ramp up a good third of a second, on average, before the subjects consciously believed they had decided to move—and sometimes this brain marker was deterred a whole second beforehand."[8] The ability of our unconscious to act apart from and prior to our awareness is so pervasive that Christopher C. French and Krissy Wilson conclude: "Research has shown that most human information processing occurs outside of awareness."[9]

It is in that realm of the unconscious that speech is generated prior to our awareness. Pinker explains: "We have all had the experience of uttering or writing a sentence, then stopping and realizing that it wasn't exactly what we meant to say. To have that feeling, there has to be a 'what we meant to say' that is different from what we said."[10] There can be a disconnect between our awareness of intent and the production of whatever speech form we produce.

Mentalese is not a type of translation. Rather, it is a description of the way any language is generated from the underlying meaning. As Pinker further explains,

> Knowing a language, then, is knowing how to translate mentalese into strings of words and vice versa. *People without a language would still have mentalese, and babies and many nonhuman animals presumably have simpler dialects.* Indeed, if babies did not have a mentalese to translate to and from English, it is not clear how learning English could take place, or even what learning English would mean.[11]

---

8. Bor, *Ravenous Brain*, 103. This phenomenon has led some people to suggest that we somehow anticipate the future. The more accurate explanation is that it is our awareness that lags behind. We do not decide to move a finger before we decide to move a finger. What happens is that our awareness of our intent lags behind the unconscious physical process involved in producing the movement.

9. Christopher C. French and Krissy Wilson, "Cognitive Factors Underlying Paranormal Beliefs and Experiences," 17.

10. Steven Pinker, *The Language Instinct: How the Mind Creates Language*, 57.

11. Pinker, *The Language Instinct*, 82; emphasis added.

The subconscious assembles information and processes its meaning outside of the stream of our awareness, rising to the level of our conscious understanding in our "eureka" moments.[12] This concept becomes important in the discussion of the translation of the Book of Mormon (and Joseph's other translated or revelatory texts) because it speaks to the way he generated the English text. The transference of unconscious mentalese to a spoken language occurred naturally as Joseph spoke.

The translation issue for the Book of Mormon is not really the English language that Joseph dictated. It is a question of where the underlying mentalese meaning came from. If we believe that it was a translation, there can be no other source than God. Thus, Joseph understood what the Nephite text said at a level below language. That meaning was elevated to language through the normal processes by which we generate our spoken language, which was translated into words that Joseph knew and into the King James language style he intentionally used. Were God to have chosen a different translator, the resulting text may have differed in the words and sentences but would have preserved the same essential meaning. That preserved meaning might have been a theological concept, or it might have been a particular name. Mentalese produces both.

Perhaps some understanding of the role of mentalese can be seen by considering two translations of the same text by the same person. Allen J. Christenson is fluent in Quiché, the language of the Maya classic text, the Popol Vuh. He is also conversant in their culture, making him an excellent translator. He has provided two different types of translation of the Popol Vuh. The first was created for an English reading audience, and the second represents a more literal translation:

> This is the beginning of the ancient traditions of this place called Quiché.
> Here we shall write. We shall begin to tell the ancient stories of the beginning, the origin of all that was done in the citadel of Quiché, among the people of the Quiché nation.[13]

> This its root ancient word,
> Here Quiché its name.
> Here we shall write,
> We shall plant ancient word,
> Its planting,

---

12. Kate Douglas, "How Powerful is the Subconscious?," 32; Kate Douglas, "The Subconscious Mind: Your Unsung Hero."

13. Allen J. Christenson, *Popol Vuh, the Sacred Book of the Maya: The Great Classic of Central American Spirituality, Translated from the Original Maya Text*, 59.

> Its root-beginning as well,
> Everything done in
> Citadel Quiché,
> Its nation Quiché people.[14]

One can see how the more flowing version comes from the more literal version, but there are interesting cultural concepts related to planting that were lost when the translation was made for the modern audience. It can be assumed that Christenson was fully aware of the complexities and differences. At the level of mentalese, Christenson understood the Quiché original well enough that he could express it in both the literal and the more fluid translations, according to his purpose in generating an English text. Both versions represent the meaning of the original. Importantly, some literary aspects of the original might be lost in the more fluid translation. In contrast, when presented in a literal translation, what was elegant in Quiché is stilted in English.

Douglas R. Hofstadter published a masterful example of the variability of translation. He began with a simple poem from Clément Marot, written in French in the 1500s. He provided the original poem and then numerous translations, each taking a slightly different method of presenting the meaning of the poem, from a quite literal translation to attempting to preserve the ideas of rhyme or whimsy of the original.[15] Every version was a translation. Every version was created by the same person from the same original. Every version attempted to preserve something from the original. Preservation of the words that were closest to the original did not always capture its intent. For example, he saw whimsy in the original, but that aspect was not preserved in the literal translation. It is an excellent example of how mentalese can generate the same poem in multiple versions, depending upon the reason for generating the different poems.

How does the understanding of mentalese fit into the question of the translation of the Book of Mormon? It gives us a mechanism by which Joseph's culture and language could generate the inconsistent archaisms of the translation layer along with the more remarkable ancient cultural content (discussed in the next two sections). It is proposed, therefore, that the divine source of the information contained in the Nephite plates transmitted mentalese, not ideas. It was more precise than ideas. The delivery of a

---

14. Allen J. Christenson, *Popol Vuh: Literal Poetic Version, Transcription and Translation*, 13.

15. Douglas R. Hofstadter, *Le Ton Beau de Marot: In Praise of the Music of Language*.

mentalese "text" functioned in the way that any translator might take his or her understanding of one language to represent it in another. Just as Christenson could generate two different types of translation from meaning of an original text, the translation of the Book of Mormon is the representation of meaning in sets of words Joseph selected. Thus, the resulting translation transmits the Nephite meaning, but it was filtered through Joseph's culture, vocabulary, and experiences.

Section II:
The Nephite Book of Mormon

Chapter Five

A Written Original Behind the Translation

In his book, *Visions in a Seer Stone*, William L. Davis suggests that Joseph Smith used techniques of extemporaneous speech preparation that were common in his time to create the Book of Mormon text as he dictated. The evidence for spontaneous creation in the dictation of the text presented in Chapter 3 might provide evidence for his general thesis of extemporaneous production. Ironically, however, the very concept of the heavy memory tax that supported the types of sentences exhibiting spontaneous creation argues against Davis's hypothesis that extemporaneous production might explain the entire text of the Book of Mormon.

Davis understands that a completely spontaneous textual dictation cannot account for a text as long and complex as the Book of Mormon. He explains:

> The evidence reveals that behind the project lay a systematic approach of careful planning and preparation, which, in turn, suggests that Smith spent a significant amount of time in the creation of the work. In addition, the content of the stories also suggests a process of elaborate preparatory construction. Grant Hardy, for example, records a litany of textual features that reveal such a process, including, among many others, the presence of flashbacks, parallel narratives, a hundred-year chronicle of Nephite leaders and judges, as well as several genealogies and successions of rulers.
>
> When combined together, all of these factors suggests that Smith began his work on the Book of Mormon long before he actually started to dictate the text. Taking into consideration the textual evidence and the array of historical accounts surrounding the production of the work, the best explanation of Smith's process involves a scenario in which he announced the existence of the gold plates containing the narrative of the Book of Mormon in September 1823, after which he spent several years constructing and revising preliminary outlines (*not* fully written manuscripts) that framed the work before dictating the current texts.[1]

---

1. William L. Davis, *Visions in a Seer Stone: Joseph Smith and the Making of the Book of Mormon*, 163.

Davis sees extensive preparation of outlines and intricate textual interrelationships that must have been written down, revised, and revisited to produce the extemporaneous text. Important to his hypothesis is that while the outlines may have been written down, the entire text was not.

Nevertheless, just as a careful analysis of the sentences shows evidence of spontaneity due to the problems of short-term memory, there are aspects of the text that would stretch even long-term memory and point to the likelihood of there being a written original behind the dictation. Of course, such an underlying text may still be of a purely nineteenth-century origin if it were first written and then memorized. It is certainly not beyond human capabilities to memorize that much text, although there is no evidence that Joseph was capable of doing so.[2] For this discussion, however, it isn't the memorization of a text that is important; rather, it is the required existence of a written text.

The book of Ether provides an important example of the high memory tax that would be required to extemporaneously create the dictated text, even from a previously written outline. The first chapter of that book presents a genealogy list of at least thirty generations (1:6–32) that is recreated in reverse order as the story of the Jaredites unfolds. However, the recreation is not a simple reversed list. The names and ordering of the genealogy are integrated into the events relevant to those individuals (see Table 5). For an even greater level of complexity, the genealogy has two men named Com who had different parents and sons and who are listed generations apart, and yet the text is able to keep the two men with the same name in their correct reversed order in the narrative of Jaredite history. The commonality of names did not create any issues in remembering how the two fit into the larger genealogical pattern.

The challenge of keeping all this information in memory is compounded by the fact that the men listed in the genealogy are not always protagonists in the narrative. Often, persons outside of that genealogy are the driving characters. Thus, even as a mnemonic list, this list cannot be

---

2. Perhaps even for Davis's comprehensive outlines, but certainly for a fully written text, the quantity of paper required surely would have been noticed. In a family of limited economic means, the diversion of money from the family to the purchase of paper would have been noticed. In such a small community, the purchase of quantities of paper that had no apparent reason would certainly have been noticed. One would have expected that someone noticed that Joseph spent a lot of time alone with pen and paper. None of these things were ever reported, or even suggested.

Table 5

Genealogy as It Appears in Ether 1:6–32	Later Appearance in Ether
He that wrote this record was Ether,	11:23: Ether
and he was a descendant of Coriantor.	11:18: Coriantor
Coriantor was the son of Moron.	11:14: Moron
And Moron was the son of Ethem.	11:11: Ethem
And Ethem was the son of Ahah.	11:10: Ahah
And Ahah was the son of Seth	11:9: Seth
And Seth was the son of Shiblon.	11:4: Shiblom
And Shiblon was the son of Com.	10:31: Com
And Com was the son of Coriantum.	10:31: Coriantum
And Coriantum was the son of Amnigaddah.	10:31: Amnigaddah
And Amnigaddah was the son of Aaron.	10:31: Aaron
And Aaron was a descendant of Heth	10:31: Heth
who was the son of Hearthom.	10:29: Hearthom
And Hearthom was the son of Lib.	10:18: Lib
And Lib was the son of Kish.	10:17: Kish
And Kish was the son of Corom.	10:16: Corom
And Corom was the son of Levi.	10:14: Levi
And Levi was the son of Kim.	10:13: Kim
And Kim was the son of Morianton.	10:9: Morianton
And Morianton was a descendant of Riplakish.	10:4: Riplakish
And Riplakish was the son of Shez.	10:1: Shez
And Shez was the son of Heth.	9:25: Heth
And Heth was the son of Com.	9:25: Com
And Com was the son of Coriantum.	9:21: Coriantum
And Coriantum was the son of Emer.	9:14: Emer
And Emer was the son of Omer.	8:1: Omer
And Omer was the son of Shule.	7:7: Shule
And Shule was the son of Kib.	7:3: Kib
And Kib was the son of Orihah,	6:27: Orihah
who was the son of Jared;	1:33: Jared

the basis for the prolonged narrative. The memory tax to keep this list of thirty individuals in their correct relation while telling stories that often feature other named characters creates a sufficient strain that would likely require consulting a written original.

A second type of evidence for a written original comes in an examination of Mormon's textual insertions. Ironically, the technique of repetitive resumption that was highlighted in Chapter 3 to demonstrate spontaneity in sentences also provides evidence of a written original when applied to longer texts. David E. Bokovoy and John A. Tvedtnes describe this type of repetitive resumption:

> When working with a document, biblical editors often framed their textual insertions between two parallel statements. "The repetition in question need not be verbatim," observes biblical scholar Bernard Levinson, "more often it is approximate and may abridge the earlier unit.". . .
>
> A biblical editor would often mark his insertion by restating several key elements that occurred prior to the editorial interruption. Following this resumption, the original account would then continue by supplying the primary literary elements.[3]

This technique is not exclusive to biblical editors. Tzvi Abusch not only noticed the technique in Mesopotamian incantations; he used it to discern when newer sections had been interpolated into an earlier text. His critical analysis of the text itself was born out by the discoveries of other copies of those incantations without the inserted text.[4]

For Abusch, there are two requirements to qualify as a repetitive resumption. The first is that there must be a repetition of a phrase (the repetition itself). The second is that the material in between the repetitions must not be directly related to the preceding text—meaning that it must be an intrusion into the flow of the primary text.

What sets this use of repetitive resumption apart from the sentence-level spontaneous corrections is the quantity of intervening text. Although some of the examples are short, many of them are quite long. Each of these exceeds the ability of a person to hold the phrases to be repeated in memory across so much inserted material. Indeed, the discovery of the technique and explanations for it are based on the analysis of written texts.

---

3. David E. Bokovoy and John A. Tvedtnes, *Testament: Links Between the Book of Mormon and the Hebrew Bible*, 117–18.

4. I. Tzvi Abusch, "Maqlû III 1–30: Internal Analysis and Manuscript Evidence for the Revision of an Incantation," 307.

A Written Original Behind the Translation

This type of repetitive resumption occurs multiple times in the separate books written or edited by Mormon. A short example comes at the end of Alma 30:

> And it came to pass that the curse was not taken off of Korihor; but he was cast out, *and went about from house to house begging for his food.*
>
> Now the knowledge of what had happened unto Korihor was immediately published throughout all the land; yea, the proclamation was sent forth by the chief judge to all the people in the land, declaring unto those who had believed in the words of Korihor that they must speedily repent, lest the same judgments would come unto them.
>
> And it came to pass that they were all convinced of the wickedness of Korihor; therefore they were all converted again unto the Lord; and this put an end to the iniquity after the manner of Korihor.
>
> *And Korihor did go about from house to house, begging food for his support.* (Alma 30:56–58)

The material in between the italicized departure and repetition temporarily moves away from focusing on what happened to Korihor to the way his story had been passed around. That information was perhaps needed to explain why he was killed in Antionum, but it interrupts the storyline.

A much longer example occurs earlier in the same chapter:

> But it came to pass in the latter end of the seventeenth year, there came a man into the land of Zarahemla, *and he was Anti-Christ, for he began to preach unto the people against the prophecies which had been spoken by the prophets, concerning the coming of Christ.*
>
> Now there was no law against a man's belief; for it was strictly contrary to the commands of God that there should be a law which should bring men on to unequal grounds.
>
> For thus saith the scripture: Choose ye this day, whom ye will serve.
>
> Now if a man desired to serve God, it was his privilege; or rather, if he believed in God it was his privilege to serve him; but if he did not believe in him there was no law to punish him.
>
> But if he murdered he was punished unto death; and if he robbed he was also punished; and if he stole he was also punished; and if he committed adultery he was also punished; yea, for all this wickedness they were punished.
>
> For there was a law that men should be judged according to their crimes. Nevertheless, there was no law against a man's belief; therefore, a man was punished only for the crimes which he had done; therefore all men were on equal grounds.
>
> *And this Anti-Christ, whose name was Korihor,* (and the law could have no hold upon him) *began to preach unto the people that there should be no Christ.* And after this manner did he preach. (Alma 30:6–12)

Again, the departure and resumptive repetition are italicized. The interruptive insertion deals with the nature of Mosiah$_2$'s law, not Korihor.

An even longer insertion found in the book of Helaman comes with intrusive information about geography:

> *And it came to pass in the forty and sixth, yea, there was much contention and many dissensions*; in the which there were an exceedingly great many who departed out of the land of Zarahemla, and went forth unto the land northward to inherit the land.
>
> And they did travel to an exceedingly great distance, insomuch that they came to large bodies of water and many rivers.
>
> Yea, and even they did spread forth into all parts of the land, into whatever parts it had not been rendered desolate and without timber, because of the many inhabitants who had before inherited the land.
>
> And now no part of the land was desolate, save it were for timber; but because of the greatness of the destruction of the people who had before inhabited the land it was called desolate.
>
> And there being but little timber upon the face of the land, nevertheless the people who went forth became exceedingly expert in the working of cement; therefore they did build houses of cement, in the which they did dwell.
>
> And it came to pass that they did multiply and spread, and did go forth from the land southward to the land northward, and did spread insomuch that they began to cover the face of the whole earth, from the sea south to the sea north, from the sea west to the sea east.
>
> And the people who were in the land northward did dwell in tents, and in houses of cement, and they did suffer whatsoever tree should spring up upon the face of the land that it should grow up, that in time they might have timber to build their houses, yea, their cities, and their temples, and their synagogues, and their sanctuaries, and all manner of their buildings.
>
> And it came to pass as timber was exceedingly scarce in the land northward, they did send forth much by the way of shipping.
>
> And thus they did enable the people in the land northward that they might build many cities, both of wood and of cement.
>
> And it came to pass that there were many of the people of Ammon, who were Lamanites by birth, did also go forth into this land.
>
> And now there are many records kept of the proceedings of this people, by many of this people, which are particular and very large, concerning them.
>
> But behold, a hundredth part of the proceedings of this people, yea, the account of the Lamanites and of the Nephites, and their wars, and contentions, and dissensions, and their preaching, and their prophecies, and their shipping and their building of ships, and their building of temples, and of synagogues and their sanctuaries, and their righteousness, and their wicked-

ness, and their murders, and their robbings, and their plundering, and all manner of abominations and whoredoms, cannot be contained in this work.

But behold, there are many books and many records of every kind, and they have been kept chiefly by the Nephites.

And they have been handed down from one generation to another by the Nephites, even until they have fallen into transgression and have been murdered, plundered, and hunted, and driven forth, and slain, and scattered upon the face of the earth, and mixed with the Lamanites until they are no more called the Nephites, becoming wicked, and wild, and ferocious, yea, even becoming Lamanites.

And now I return again to mine account; therefore, what I have spoken had passed after there had been great contentions, and disturbances, and wars, and dissensions, among the people of Nephi.

The forty and sixth year of the reign of the judges ended;

And it came to pass that there was still great contention in the land, yea, even in the forty and seventh year, and also in the forty and eighth year. (3:3–19)

The narrative is moving toward a description of contention when Mormon inserts information about some people moving to a land northward, giving a long description of that region. It has no direct, or at least immediate, relevance to the "great contentions, and disturbances, and wars, and dissensions, among the people of Nephi" (v. 17).

In a final example from Alma VIII (10–11), an obvious interruption has its departure and repetitive phrase obscured by the modern division of what was, in 1830, a single chapter:

Now the object of these lawyers was to get gain; and they got gain according to their employ.

[Chapter 11, not an original chapter break]

Now it was in the law of Mosiah that every man who was a judge of the law, or those who were appointed to be judges, should receive wages according to the time which they labored to judge those who were brought before them to be judged.

Now if a man owed another, and he would not pay that which he did owe, he was complained of to the judge; and the judge executed authority, and sent forth officers that the man should be brought before him; and he judged the man according to the law and the evidences which were brought against him, and thus the man was compelled to pay that which he owed, or be stripped, or be cast out from among the people as a thief and a robber.

And the judge received for his wages according to his time—a senine of gold for a day, or a senum of silver, which is equal to a senine of gold; and this is according to the law which was given. . . .

[Continues through verse 19]

> Now, *it was for the sole purpose to get gain, because they received their wages according to their employ*, therefore, they did stir up the people to riotings, and all manner of disturbances and wickedness, that they might have more employ, that they might get money according to the suits which were brought before them; therefore they did stir up the people against Alma and Amulek. (10:32–11:20)

This insertion is long and intrusive enough that Orson Pratt parsed it into its own chapter in 1879.

The fact of deviation from intent does not necessarily suggest a written text. What suggests the written text is the repetitive resumption of the departure phrase following the intrusive passage. Memorization might allow for this, but it would nevertheless first require a written original to be first memorized.

These long examples of repetitive resumption do not fit the qualities of oral texts. Werner Kelber describes an essential difference between an oral and a written text that can be witnessed in these examples:

> From textuality's retrospective cast it is but a small step toward its potential for self-reflection and self-criticism. The mnemonics of oral culture require repetition and foster redundancy. Knowledge that has to rely on memory is uneasy about innovative departures from orally stored and transmitted tradition. Thinking, for this reason, proceeds less by deviation from, and more in imitation of, oral forms and authorities. . . .
>
> Fundamentally this is because the mind is relieved of the burden or retaining knowledge by remembering. Writing enables one to produce language over a prolonged period of time, at one's own pace, with self-chosen interruptions and without a direct commitment to audiences.[5]

There is no evidence that mnemonic prompts could have produced the complicated use of the genealogy list in the book of Ether or the repetitive resumption in Mormon's writing. Instead, the text conforms more to the characteristics of a written narrative than an extemporaneous one, pointing to an original text that underlies the dictated translation.

---

5. Werner H. Kelber, *The Oral and the Written Gospel: The Hermeneutics of Speaking and Writing in the Synoptic Tradition, Mark, Paul, and Q*, 108–9.

CHAPTER SIX

STRUCTURING THE TEXT[1]

When the Book of Mormon's first readers encountered the book, the physical binding and the similarity to the language of the King James Bible encouraged them to see it in the context of previously accepted scripture. That impression was enhanced by the division of the Book of Mormon into separate books bearing a man's name. Nephi$_1$, Jacob, Enos, and Jarom were not familiar names, but the parallel to Isaiah, Jeremiah, Ezekiel, and Daniel was clear. Nevertheless, where the physical binding and the style of the language can be assigned to aspects of its nineteenth-century production, the named books and the original chapters were part of the Nephite text.

Latter-day Saints encounter the Book of Mormon in a way that is fundamentally different from what Mormon intended. The absence of the so-called lost 116 pages means that we no longer have Mormon's introduction and everything preceding the current first chapter of the book of Mosiah.[2] Instead, modern readers are introduced to the Book of Mormon through the inclusion of the small plates that narratively take the place of those missing pages. While Words of Mormon allows readers to see a change in ancient authorship occurring with the book of Mosiah, in many ways the subtle construction of assumptions already began with Nephi$_1$'s personal book, which colored their understanding of Mormon's abridged history.

This is demonstrated in how each of the individual books are named. The connection between author and book name is explicit in the small

---

1. Much of the material in this chapter appeared in Brant A. Gardner, *Labor Diligently to Write: The Ancient Making of a Modern Book*. Some text has been edited, some expanded. I have included it in this book because it is important evidence that the minds behind the ancient text used a different logic than would be expected of a modern book.

2. The identification of the lost original translation as 116 pages is an accepted label, but perhaps does not correctly identify the number of the lost pages. According to research done by Don Bradley, the number of pages dictated to and lost by Martin Harris may have actually been as high as 300 pages, with the number 116 being instead the page count of the small plates translation contained in the Printer's Manuscript. See Don Bradley, *The Lost 116 Pages: Reconstructing the Book of Mormon's Missing Stories*, 92–103.

plates (save for the book of Omni). For example, Nephi₁ designated his book after his own name. He named his second book after his own name as well (similar to the way he named both his small plates and large plates the "plates of Nephi"³). Nephi₁ did provide a way to separate the two books, but not by calling them "1 Nephi" and "2 Nephi". Instead, he called our 1 Nephi "The Book of Nephi: His Reign and Ministry"; and the second, simply "The Book of Nephi." (The distinguishing "First" and "Second" were added to the Printer's Manuscript at some point after the text had been copied from the Original Manuscript.)

Jacob followed with a book titled after his own name and with the clarification that he was "the brother of Nephi." Enos and Jarom follow this model by naming their books after themselves. The exception comes with the book of Omni, which is named after its first writer; however, the brevity of the entries apparently allowed three generations of subsequent writers, including a pair of brothers, to simply add their short accounts to Omni's set of plates.

While this relationship between author and book is correct for those on the small plates, they were never intended by Mormon to be a part of the Book of Mormon (see Chapter 15), and this method of naming books is not what we find in Mormon's history. Instead, a close examination suggests that the named books in that history replicate book names on the large plates that Mormon relied on as his primary source. The logic for that suggestion is explored in Chapter 12.

Book of Mormon Chapters

In addition to named books, the original division of the text into chapters was based on features contained on the Nephite plates. Royal Skousen explains:

> Evidence from both the original and printer's manuscripts shows that Joseph Smith apparently saw some visual indication at the end of a section that the section was ending. Although this may have been a symbol of some kind, a more likely possibility is that the last words of the section were followed by blankness. Recognizing that the section was ending, Joseph then told the

---

3. "And now, as I have spoken concerning these plates, behold they are not the plates upon which I make a full account of the history of my people; for the plates upon which I make a full account of my people I have given the name of Nephi; wherefore, they are called the plates of Nephi, after mine own name; and these plates also are called the plates of Nephi" (1 Ne. 9:2).

scribe to write the word *chapter*, with the understanding that the appropriate number would be added later.[4]

Further indications that the original chapters belong to the golden plates rather than the modern translation come from the unexpected ways in which the Book of Mormon formed these chapters.

One place where the Book of Mormon's often unusual chapter breaks can be easily seen is in the Isaiah chapters included in 2 Nephi. When Orson Pratt created new chapter and verse designations for the 1879 edition, one of his considerations was to format and reversify passages in the text that were clearly quoting the Bible in order to have them closely parallel the biblical chapters. To do this, Pratt recut the Isaiah passages to mirror the standard biblical chapters. For example, the original chapter VIII of 2 Nephi was broken up into five separate chapters: Nephi$_1$'s introduction to the Isaiah material (2 Ne. 11) and our distinct Isaiah chapters (2 Ne. 12–15). According to Skousen, "What is especially striking is that the original Book of Mormon chapters for the biblical quotations are based on thematic and narrative cohesiveness and they do not generally correspond with the King James chapter breaks."[5]

John Gee explains this usage in further detail:

> When quoting lengthy passages, Book of Mormon prophets intentionally start and stop in certain specific places, reflecting natural breaks in Isaiah's text. Nephite writers normally marked breaks in passages through a syntactic or phrasal marker at the beginning of a new section. One of these is a statement of acknowledging the presence of a quotation; such statements are common in ancient authors and we will refer to them as "inquit" statements after the most common Latin phrase *inquit*, "he said. . . . "
>
> Jacob chose with care the long Isaiah passage that he quotes in 2 Nephi 6:6–8; 25 (see 2 Ne. 6:4); he is not simply rambling on until he gets tired. Inquit statements mark the boundaries of the passage he quotes. The selection Jacob quotes from Isaiah contains four sections, each of which begins with the phrase "Thus saith the Lord" (Isa. 49:22, 25; 50:1; 51:22; parallel to 2 Ne. 6:6, 17; 17:1; 8:22), and the final sections ends just before a fifth "Thus saith the Lord" (Isa. 52:3).
>
> Nephi also quotes part of this passage (1 Ne. 21:22–26; parallel to Isaiah 49:22–26), but he stops earlier. The words immediately after his stopping point are "Thus saith the Lord" (Isa. 50:1; parallel to 2 Ne. 7:1), and he

---

4. Royal Skousen, "How Joseph Smith Translated the Book of Mormon," 27–28.

5. Royal Skousen, with the collaboration of Stanford Carmack, *The History of the Text of the Book of Mormon: Part Five, The King James Quotations in the Book of Mormon*, 11.

began with a phrase just as distinctive: "Hear ye this, O house of Jacob" (Isa. 48:1; parallel to 1 Ne. 20:1).[6]

The chapter endings for the quoted Isaiah material correspond to the *inquit* beginnings rather than those in the King James Bible. Interestingly, Gee points out that these chapters were triggered by a beginning statement rather than by an ending. This is probably due to the presence of those divisions on the brass plates that were copied and not created. Thus, this mode of separating chapters represented an Old World concept but does not represent Nephi$_1$'s or Mormon's editorial styles.

Mormon's chapters have a much more complex set of triggers that determine when a chapter ends than those in Nephi$_1$'s writings. In 1 Nephi, the original chapters are generally separated by the ending of a story or scene—although Nephi$_1$ often includes multiple stories in a chapter.[7] In Mormon's writings, however, we find a very different set of chapter-ending types. Whereas Nephi$_1$'s writings (particularly in 1 Nephi) are nicely structured and appear to have chapters that were conceived prior to writing, Mormon's chapters give the impression that he was writing extemporaneously until there was some trigger that caused him to stop.

Sermon Endings May End Chapters

A significant feature of Mormon's writing style is the inclusion of large sections of material copied directly from his secondary sources. For example, there is significant text copied from Zeniff's record, Alma$_2$'s personal record, and Nephi$_3$'s personal record. Mormon also quoted letters, which may or may not have been included on the large plates.[8] However, the most often quoted material are sermons, which Mormon preferred to copy rather than restate.

Selected for their theological instruction, these sermons are presented by Mormon within their historical context. Whereas Mormon's abridged narration was at least a step removed from his sources—as it would require him to read the large plates or other sources and then create his own sum-

---

6. John Gee, "'Choose the Things That Please Me': On the Selection of the Isaiah Sections in the Book of Mormon," 68–69; internal subheadings silently removed.

7. An interesting technique Nephi$_1$ used to demarcate stories inside chapters is discussed at the end of this chapter.

8. Mormon quotes letters written by Ammoron (Alma 54:16–24), Captain Moroni (Alma 54:5–14, 60:1–36), Helaman (Alma 56:2–58:41), Pahoran (Alma 61:2–21), and Giddianhi (3 Ne. 3:2–10). Moroni quotes letters from Mormon (Moro. 8:2–30, 9:1–26).

mary narrative of the events—the act of directly copying these sermons would have involved a more intensive and interactive relationship with the source material. Perhaps for that reason, Mormon frequently introduces a chapter break when a sermon ends and before resuming his narration in the next chapter. Thus, the end of the sermon not only signals a chapter break, but it may also reflect his own mental switch from the process of directly copying material to reading and summarizing recorded history.

For example, Mosiah II (4) closes at a break in King Benjamin's discourse.[9] The following chapter (III, 5) then opens with Benjamin's people testifying to what he had told them. In a thematically conceived chapter, this material might have been kept together, but it seems that Mormon instead inserted a break where he did because he was physically and mentally transitioning from directly copying from the large plates to summarizing the narrative in his own words.

There are instances, however, when Mormon includes entire sermons in the body of a chapter without any break between the sermon and his own narration. For example, Alma$_2$'s sermon to the poor of the Zoramites ends in Alma 32. Then Amulek preaches, with his sermon ending in chapter 34. The original Alma XVI, however, contained the current chapters 30–35. Chapter 35 gives some of the aftermath of the sermon, but it was not separated by a chapter break in the 1830 edition. The reason for the difference in the way Mormon handled internal versus chapter-ending sermons is not clear.

Testificatory Amen Endings

Most of Mormon's chapters continue through multiple events until something in the text triggers a chapter break. A sermon ending was one of those, but the most important one was the presence of a testificatory "amen."[10] The first occurrence closes Mosiah I (1–3) and also marks the end

---

9. In the following discussion, Roman numerals indicate the chapter numbers and structuring from the Printer's Manuscript; the Arabic numerals represent the post-1879 chapters.

10. According to Daniel B. McKinlay, "The Hebrew word, meaning 'truly,' is transliterated into Greek in the New Testament, and thence to the English Bible. It is found many times in the Book of Mormon. The Hebrew infinitive conveys the notions 'to confirm, support, uphold, be faithful, firm.' In antiquity the expression carried the weight of an oath. By saying 'amen' the people solemnly pledged faithfulness and assented to curses upon themselves if found guilty (Deut. 27:14–26). And by saying 'amen' the people also sealed their praises of

of a sermon. Importantly, it is not just the word "amen" that triggers a chapter ending; rather, it is only when it functions as a testimony to the preceding sermon or commentary. Thus, the two instances of "amen" in 3 Nephi 11:25 and 13:13 are not immediately followed with chapter breaks, as they were instead parts of prayer that were within the instructions and sermons of Jesus. Elsewhere, however, when "amen" serves to testify of the preceding content, it triggers a chapter break even if narrative itself has not yet ended. Similar to the way a chapter ending on a copied sermon relocated the story's closing narration to the beginning of the next chapter, testificatory *amens* required that the closing narration be moved to after the break.

For example, Alma V–VI (7–8) illustrates the way that a testificatory "amen" creates a chapter break even though the shorter narrative arc has not yet come to a conclusion. Chapter V (7) contains a sermon by Alma to the people of Gideon and ends with verse 27:

> And now, may the peace of God rest upon you, and upon your houses and lands, and upon your flocks and herds, and all that you possess, your women and your children, according to your faith and good works, from this time forth and forever. And thus I have spoken. Amen.

This is followed by a chapter break that initiates Chapter VI (8) but concludes the narrative of Alma's preaching in Gideon:

> And now it came to pass that Alma returned from the land of Gideon, after having taught the people of Gideon many things which cannot be written, having established the order of the church, according as he had before done in the land of Zarahemla, yea, he returned to his own house at Zarahemla to rest himself from the labors which he had performed.
>
> And thus ended the ninth year of the reign of the judges over the people of Nephi.
>
> And it came to pass in the commencement of the tenth year of the reign of the judges over the people of Nephi, that Alma departed from thence and took his journey over into the land of Melek, on the west of the river Sidon, on the west by the borders of the wilderness. (8:1–3)

The division between chapters V (7) and VI (8) occurred because there was a sermon that ended with "amen" at the end of V (7). When Mormon began chapter VI (8), he started with the aftermath of the sermon, with Alma returning from Gideon.

Although we do not have access to the large plates that Mormon largely relied on as his source material, we think he learned the testificatory

---

God (1 Chr. 16:36; Ps. 106:48; Rom. 11:36; 1 Pet. 4:11)." Daniel B. McKinlay, "Amen," 1:38.

"amen" from them—given Nephi₁'s own consistent inclusion of chapter breaks after his use of it in his small plates, which we can surmise was also present in his large plates. See 1 Nephi II (6–9), which ends with "amen." Similarly, "amen" ends 1 Nephi III (10–14) and 1 Nephi VII (22), which also closes the First Book of Nephi. In 2 Nephi, it closes chapters III (3), IV (4), VI (9), VII (10), XIII (31), and XV (33), which also marks the end of 2 Nephi.[11]

As noted, the first extant "amen" ending in Mormon's own writing occurs at the close of Mosiah I (1–3), which was a part of Benjamin's discourse that Mormon copied. A similar "amen" closes a sermon at the end of Mosiah III (5). Mosiah VI (9–10) is a direct quotation of the record of Zeniff, which Zeniff ends with: "And now I, being old, did confer the kingdom upon one of my sons; therefore, I say no more. And may the Lord bless my people. Amen" (Mosiah 10:22). A final "amen" in Mosiah concludes chapter VIII (13:25–16:15) at the close of Abinadi's sermon before Noah and his priests.

In the book of Alma we find multiple chapters ending immediately after a closing "amen" in speeches and sermons copied by Mormon: Alma IV (6), V (7), XIV (23–26), XV (27–29), and XIX (42–43). In Helaman, Mormon concludes his own inserted testimony with it at the end of chapter IV (11–12). Similarly, 3 Nephi II (3–5) ends with Mormon's testimony, again punctuated by an "amen."

At the close of his own writings on the golden plates, Mormon signs off with an "amen" at the end of Mormon III (6–7). His son Moroni continued the trend, using it to end the book of Mormon IV (8–9). Interestingly, in his editing of the book of Ether, Moroni only uses an "amen" when inserting his own testimony into the abridged record. This occurs at the end of Ether I (1–4), II (5), V (12), and at the end of VI (13–15), which closes the book of Ether.

Anomalous and Missing Chapter Breaks

Although a testificatory "amen" was the strongest trigger to end a chapter, there are some important exceptions. For example, our Alma 33 ends with a quoted sermon and the copied "amen" (v. 23). However, this chapter break was added by Orson Pratt for the 1879 edition. The original chapter XVI spanned the modern chapters 30–35, placing this "amen" in the middle of the chapter.

---

11. In Jacob, "amen" ends chapter IV (6). The book of Enos also ends with an "amen." There are no more such endings on the small plates.

A plausible explanation for the lack of a break is that Mormon here is copying material from the large plates (or elsewhere) and perhaps merely replicating the existing structure of the source text. In this case the original chapter XVI is heavily copied from Alma$_2$'s personal record, with Mormon transcribing two sermons that appear one after the other—the first by Alma$_2$, and the second by Amulek. Between them there is only one sentence: "And now it came to pass that after Alma had spoken these words unto them he sat down upon the ground, and Amulek arose and began to teach them" (Alma 34:1). It is also possible that Mormon simply missed an existing chapter break while his focus was on copying from his source material. As noted above, the nature of the required physical interaction with the source text was much higher when he was directly copying rather than summarizing with his own words. Thus, the mode of copying perhaps allowed "amen" to be used without Mormon creating his own chapter.

A second example occurs when the original chapters VII (11:1–13:24) and VII (13:25–6) of Mosiah split in the middle of Abinadi's sermon. The division makes so little sense to a modern reader that Orson Pratt combined the two sections of Abinadi's speech so that it was all within the same chapter.[12] What caused Mormon to create a chapter ending at a place that seems unnecessary? The original chapter ending for Mosiah VII comes at a pause in Abinadi's speech (13:24), and when chapter VIII begins, we have Abinadi speaking again, with only a brief segue: "And it came to pass that after Abinadi had made an end of these sayings that he said unto them" (v. 25).

Here, the part of Abinadi's sermon that ends in Mosiah 13:24 (and thus concludes the original Mosiah VII) was the completion of Abinadi's own quotation of the Decalogue. It was thus a quotation within a quotation, and the end of that quoted material from the brass plates appears to have been the cause. In this case, we don't have enough information to know if Mormon copied the break from his source or if he added the break himself because he felt that one was required after the quoted material.

---

12. A similar modification of the chapter breaks often occurs in Lynn A. Rosenvall and David L. Rosenvall, eds., *A New Approach to Studying the Book of Mormon*. The Rosenvalls provide a text "organized by events, emphasizing narrators, speakers, locations, dates and quoted passages" (title page). The structuring of the text by events often crosses chapter boundaries, implicitly underscoring my suggestion that the concept of finishing a story was not part of Mormon's criteria for ending one chapter and beginning another.

Another similar chapter break, however, suggests that in these instances Mormon was copying existing breaks rather than creating them. This break occurs at the end of 3 Nephi VI (13:25–14:27) and follows the Savior "quoting" from the Sermon on the Mount (Matt. 7:23–27).[13] As with the previous example, the break occurs at the end of a quotation of a biblical passage within a larger sermon (with 3 Nephi VII (15) continuing Jesus's sermon to those at the temple in Bountiful). It differs, however, in that this quotation is of a text that would have been previously unknown to the Nephites. Either way, including a break here seems to be a variation of ending a quotation of a larger sermon. Perhaps there was something in the sermon that allowed the original recorder, Nephi$_3$, to understand that there was a break, and in turn Mormon copied that into his plates.

A similar implied ending that Nephi$_3$ created, and which Mormon copied, is seen in the division between 3 Nephi IX (19–21:21) and X (21:22–23:13):

> And I will execute vengeance and fury upon them, even as upon the heathen, such as they have not heard.
> [Original chapter break]
> But if they will repent and hearken unto my words, and harden not their hearts, I will establish my church among them, and they shall come in unto the covenant and be numbered among this the remnant of Jacob, unto whom I have given this land for their inheritance. (3 Ne. 21:21–22)

The "But" in verse 22 clearly links that statement to the concluding text of the previous chapter, and Pratt likely removed the break to provide a continuous sermon. However, what is not as obvious is that (similar to the two previous examples) verse 21 marks the end of a quotation of scripture, this time Micah 5:8–15. (It is not a simple copy, though, as verses 19–20 are inserted between verses 14 and 15 of Micah 5.) Again, the quotation of a biblical passage is immediately followed with a chapter break.

Another chapter break later in 3 Nephi, this time between chapters XII (26:6–27:22) and XIII (27:23–29:9), does not follow the previous pattern and is even more difficult to understand:

> Therefore, if ye do these things blessed are ye, for ye shall be lifted up at the last day.
> [Original Chapter Break]
> Write the things which ye have seen and heard, save it be those which are forbidden. (3 Nephi 27:22–23)

---

13. See the discussion of the presence of New Testament quotations in the Book of Mormon in Chapter 2.

This break involves neither an "amen" nor any change from quotation to discourse. Instead, there is simply a change in topic, where the previous chapter deals with appropriate gospel actions and the subsequent chapter begins with the command to write what had been taught. Nevertheless, for Mormon this would have been all a quotation from his original source, and there is nothing in the way he typically copied material that suggests that he created this chapter break himself. This may just be the case that for whatever reason the break already existed on the large plates.

The Original Book and Chapter Headers

Latter-day Saints today are accustomed to short introductory statements at the beginnings of books, including every chapter of the Book of Mormon. Most of these chapter headings are modern additions, and their presence obscures those that were in the original text. In the case of the original chapter headings, modern editions place them above the chapter number rather than below, where they were originally, and the modern chapter summary now follows the number. Thus, the new chapter heading is more prominent, and the original chapter heading can easily be lost. (For example, the record of Zeniff in Mosiah VI–IX (9–21) begins with an original heading for the record that comes after the break, which begins VI; in modern editions, that heading precedes both the chapter break and modern chapter headings.)

Book headers appear as synopses or introductory material right after the title of the book. The original text has them included at the beginning of each book that Mormon compiled and edited from the large plates, but not with his or his son Moroni's personal writings (Words of Mormon and the books of Mormon, Ether, and Moroni).[14] Among the books of the small plates, headers were only included at the beginnings of 1 Nephi, 2 Nephi, and Jacob; they are not present for Enos, Jarom, and Omni.

In the extant pages of the Original Manuscript, the only remaining synoptic book header comes at the beginning of the book of Helaman. There, a long line is drawn to separate the header from the beginning of the first chapter.[15] When Oliver Cowdery and other scribes copied the text of the Original Manuscript to create the Printer's Manuscript, a similar

---

14. The beginning of the book of Mosiah was part of the initial manuscript lost by Martin Harris. There surely was a synoptic header at the beginning that book, but its first chapters were never retranslated.

15. Royal Skousen and Robin Scott Jensen, eds., *Revelations and Translations, Volume 5: Original Manuscript of the Book of Mormon*, 437.

line was drawn at the same place to separate the header from the text, suggesting that the line was considered a part of the original.[16] Elsewhere in the Printer's Manuscript, another line clearly separates 3 Nephi's header from the beginning of its first chapter, but there the book title itself is not clearly separated from the header.[17] That the scribes tried to exactly copy the Original Manuscript by even duplicating such lines suggests that the absence of a line dividing the text in the Printer's Manuscript accurately represents what was on the Original. Thus, when typesetting the manuscript to begin printing, there were times when John Gilbert, the compositor for the first printing, was able to use a textual marker to determine the separation of the headers from the main text, but in other cases there was nothing but the text itself to aid in his decision making.[18]

The problem of separating the header from the text becomes evident in the very first pages of the Book of Mormon, where the header for 1 Nephi is set apart from the text of its initial chapter. The latter part of the header reads:

> The account of their sufferings. They take the daughters of Ishmael to wife. They take their families and depart into the wilderness. Their sufferings and afflictions in the wilderness. The course of their travels. They come to the large waters. Nephi's brethren rebel against him. He confoundeth them, and buildeth a ship. They call the name of the place Bountiful. They cross the large waters into the promised land, and so forth. This is according to the account of Nephi; or in other words, I, Nephi, wrote this record.

The fascinating issue here is the very last sentence. While the entirety of the header is in the third person, the final sentence switches to the first person (which $Nephi_1$ uses throughout his own writing). The Printer's Manuscript lacks an initial chapter indicator and therefore yields no assistance in how or where the header should be divided from the text, and thus Gilbert opted to have the entire block of text act as the book header.

Alternatively, this text could be divided into both a book header and a chapter header. Taking this approach, the book header would be:

> *The account of their sufferings. They take the daughters of Ishmael to wife. They take their families and depart into the wilderness. Their sufferings and afflictions in the wilderness. The course of their travels. They come to the large waters. Nephi's brethren rebel against him. He confoundeth them, and buildeth a ship.*

---

16. Skousen and Jensen, *Printer's Manuscript of the Book of Mormon*, 1:356–57.
17. Skousen and Jensen, 1:356–57, 2:206–7.
18. Skousen and Jensen, 1:20–21, 110–11, 208–9.

> *They call the name of the place Bountiful. They cross the large waters into the promised land, and so forth.*

The final sentence would then be a chapter header, indicating the authorship of the chapter:

> *This is according to the account of Nephi; or in other words, I, Nephi, wrote this record.*

This smaller chapter header would then naturally run into the first chapter and act similarly to other chapter headers that provide the source of the history—this one being Nephi$_1$'s firsthand account.

Textual Markers In Lieu of Punctuation

Apart from the larger structural elements of books and chapters, the Original and Printer's Manuscripts provide no punctuation or formatting to specify the finer structural elements of sentences or paragraphs. Instead, these were both determined by John Gilbert. In general, he did an excellent job of creating the sentences, and his paragraphing was in line with the way other books of the time would use them. While official editions of the Book of Mormon by The Church of Jesus Christ of Latter-day Saints have long ago done away with paragraphs in the text in lieu of distinct verses, there are several editions today that have alternate paragraphing based on modern sensibilities.[19] Similarly, there are other ways to delineate sentences, although the official Church practice has been to maintain Gilbert's sentences in the first edition besides Joseph Smith's own edits to later editions, as well as some others based on reviews of the manuscript pages. Despite the lack of punctuation, Gilbert did not randomly decide how to separate sentences and paragraphs; there are internal textual markers that can assist in both the creation of sentences and paragraphs. For example, most of the sentences follow regular English patterns and structures that would make adding punctuation not very difficult in most cases.[20]

---

19. Some editions that have edited the Book of Mormon to recreate paragraphs are Grant Hardy, ed., *The Book of Mormon: Another Testament of Jesus Christ*; Jack M Lyon, ed., *The Readable Scriptures: The Book of Mormon: The Standard Works Reformatted for Clarity and Structure*; and Rosenvall and Rosenvall, eds., *A New Approach to Studying the Book of Mormon*.

20. The experience of recreating sentences in *The Plates of Mormon* produced sentences that most often followed the original compositor's choices. In many cases, the modern preference for shorter sentences influenced the punctuation, but the vast majority of sentences retain the 1830 punctuation.

Punctuation as a visual symbol is unique to written texts, but it has not always been used. According to Ernst R. Wendland, writing in Ancient Near Eastern times

> was an extremely difficult, time-consuming, and hence also expensive procedure. Therefore, everything was done to conserve space on the scarce writing material available; a typical scroll, for example, or later book-like codex or tablet reveals no word or sentence breaks and few, if any punctuation marks.[21]

There were, however, ways in which readers could make sense of the text. Thus, as Werner H. Kelber writes, "In the absence of punctuation signs, texts were likely to be composed in conformity with a phenomenology of sound more than sight."[22] Oral presentations use a number of conventions for listeners to understand the orator. These include repeated forms and verbal markers that would signal the listener as to how to follow the course of the presentation.

There is no way to know exactly how language was represented on the plates; all we have is the way that Joseph Smith's translation dictation represented it. Thus, we have the interesting recontextualization of a written document into an oral form that used artificial oral pauses surrounding the approximately twenty-word segments to create meaning.

Paratextual Function of "And Now" and "And It Came To Pass"

Both "and now" and "and it came to pass" are textual markers that move the reader through a narrative, with the difference between the two being the location of the story on a conceptual temporal timeline. "And now" marks new information that is associated within the same timeframe as the previous information.[23] "And it came to pass" moves the narrative

---

21. Ernst R. Wendland, "Orality and its Implications for the Analysis, Translation, and Transmission of Scripture," 17.

22. Werner H. Kelber, *The Oral and the Written Gospel: The Hermeneutics of Speaking and Writing in the Synoptic Tradition, Mark, Paul, and Q*, xxiv.

23. According to John Gee, "An analysis of the original Book of Mormon chapter division shows that the phrase 'and now' serves as verbal punctuation marking a major break in the text both between and within chapters. The Book of Mormon phrase is a literal translation of the Hebrew expression *w't(h)*, which is used both in the Hebrew Bible and in Epigraphic Hebrew to mark a transition between major sections of text." John Gee, "Verbal Punctuation in the Book of Mormon I: (And) Now," 48. While I agree that "and now" marks divisions, my reading of the function in the Book of Mormon text comes from the text itself rather than comparison to any ancient language.

through time.[24] In Skousen's terminology, they are a narrative connector.[25] The latter still bridges the subsequent narrative to the previous, but it shifts the timeframe to a later event. In modern English the two might be alternatively rendered as "at the same time" and "later."

In the following examples, it can be easily seen how "and now" segues between different foci within the same event or sermon. The first is from Lehi₁ speaking to his sons and others prior to his death in the promised land:

> And it must needs be that the power of God must be with him [Nephi], even unto his commanding you that ye must obey. But behold, it was not he, but it was the Spirit of the Lord which was in him, which opened his mouth to utterance that he could not shut it.
>
> *And now* my son, Laman, and also Lemuel and Sam, and also my sons who are the sons of Ishmael, behold, if ye will hearken unto the voice of Nephi ye shall not perish. And if ye will hearken unto him I leave unto you a blessing, yea, even my first blessing.
>
> But if ye will not hearken unto him I take away my first blessing, yea, even my blessing, and it shall rest upon him.
>
> *And now*, Zoram, I speak unto you: Behold, thou art the servant of Laban; nevertheless, thou hast been brought out of the land of Jerusalem, and I know that thou art a true friend unto my son, Nephi, forever. (2 Ne. 1:27–30)

Verses 28 and 30 in this example begin with "and now" and mark a shift of the person being addressed within the same event rather than later in time.

A more interesting series of this phrase comes from Jacob's discourse to the Nephites after they had fled from the Lamanites:

---

24. Donald W. Parry, "Why is the Phrase 'and it came to pass' so Prevalent in the Book of Mormon?":

> But why does the phrase "and it came to pass" appear in the Book of Mormon so much more often, page for page, than it does in the Old Testament? The answer is twofold. First, the Book of Mormon contains much more narrative, chapter for chapter, than the Bible. Second, but equally important, the translators of the King James Version did not always render *wayehi* as "and it came to pass." Instead, they were at liberty to draw from a multitude of similar expressions like "and it happened," "and . . . became," or "and . . . was."
>
> Wayehi is found about 1,204 times in the Hebrew Bible, but it was translated only 727 times as "and it came to pass" in the King James Version. Joseph Smith did not introduce such variety into the translation of the Book of Mormon. He retained the precision of "and it came to pass," which better performs the transitional function of the Hebrew word.

25. Skousen, *The History of the Text of the Book of Mormon*, 166.

> Nevertheless, I speak unto you again; for I am desirous for the welfare of your souls. Yea, mine anxiety is great for you; and ye yourselves know that it ever has been. For I have exhorted you with all diligence; and I have taught you the words of my father; and I have spoken unto you concerning all things which are written, from the creation of the world.
>
> *And now*, behold, I would speak unto you concerning things which are, and which are to come; wherefore, I will read you the words of Isaiah. And they are the words which my brother has desired that I should speak unto you. And I speak unto you for your sakes, that ye may learn and glorify the name of your God.
>
> *And now*, the words which I shall read are they which Isaiah spake concerning all the house of Israel; wherefore, they may be likened unto you, for ye are of the house of Israel. And there are many things which have been spoken by Isaiah which may be likened unto you, because ye are of the house of Israel.
>
> *And now*, these are the words: Thus saith the Lord God: Behold, I will lift up mine hand to the Gentiles, and set up my standard to the people; and they shall bring thy sons in their arms, and thy daughters shall be carried upon their shoulders.
>
> And kings shall be thy nursing fathers, and their queens thy nursing mothers; they shall bow down to thee with their faces towards the earth, and lick up the dust of thy feet; and thou shalt know that I am the Lord; for they shall not be ashamed that wait for me.
>
> *And now* I, Jacob, would speak somewhat concerning these words. For behold, the Lord has shown me that those who were at Jerusalem, from whence we came, have been slain and carried away captive. (2 Ne. 6:3–8)

The first "and now" marks the transition from the introduction to the topic of the discourse. The second declares that Jacob will read from Isaiah, whereupon the quotation is also introduced with a subject changing "and now." The final introduces the commentary on that verse.

With the phrase "and it came to pass," note how the temporal state changes chronologically from one event to the next. For instance, the following are all from a timeline of events repeated by $Nephi_1$ in 2 Nephi 5:

> *And it came to pass* that the Lord did warn me, that I, Nephi, should depart from them and flee into the wilderness, and all those who would go with me.
>
> Wherefore, *it came to pass* that I, Nephi, did take my family, and also Zoram and his family, and Sam, mine elder brother and his family, and Jacob and Joseph, my younger brethren, and also my sisters, and all those who would go with me.... (vv. 5–6)
>
> *And it came to pass* that we began to prosper exceedingly, and to multiply in the land. (v. 13)

> *And it came to pass* that I, Nephi, did cause my people to be industrious, and to labor with their hands. *And it came to pass* that they would that I should be their king. But I, Nephi, was desirous that they should have no king; nevertheless, I did for them according to that which was in my power. (vv. 17–18)
>
> *And it came to pass* that I, Nephi, did consecrate Jacob and Joseph, that they should be priests and teachers over the land of my people. *And it came to pass* that we lived after the manner of happiness. And thirty years had passed away from the time we left Jerusalem. And I, Nephi, had kept the records upon my plates, which I had made, of my people thus far. *And it came to pass* that the Lord God said unto me: Make other plates; and thou shalt engraven many things upon them which are good in my sight, for the profit of thy people. (vv. 26–30)

Each time, "and it came to pass" moves the narrative forward by marking a new event that follows the previous. Thus, while this phrase is used so often throughout the Book of Mormon, due to 2 Nephi's emphasis on sermons and likening scripture over providing narrative history, it appears only a total of thirteen times in that book—all of them in chapters 4 and 5.[26] In contrast to its relatively sparse use in 2 Nephi, 1 Nephi (which is more historical in focus) uses the phrase 109 times.

The narrative function of these two textual markers provides a key to how the uninterrupted flow of Joseph Smith's translation dictation might be best separated into paragraphs.[27] Thus, the reformatted text found in *The Plates of Mormon* most often uses these markers to create paragraphs, even when so many are found in sequence. Although that results in some very short paragraphs, it preserves the immediacy of the narrative movement through time.

---

26. It also occurs where Isaiah uses the phrase in a context that similarly marks time: "And it came to pass in the days of Ahaz the son of Jotham . . ." (2 Ne. 17:1).

27. With no known connection to Hebrew, Maya texts also have verbal markers that indicate similar meanings of "and now" and "and it came to pass." The similarity results from a similar solution to the problem of visually representing speech without a system of punctuation rather than a connection to any Book of Mormon language. Michael D. Coe and Mark Van Stone, *Reading the Maya Glyphs*, 33, has entries for glyphs that have the same functions as "and now" and "and it came to pass." When the Maya glyph was originally translated, it was translated as "and it came to pass." When Latter-day Saint authors were too quick to see that glyph as a proof for the Book of Mormon, the standard translation has now shifted to "it happened."

Paratextual Function of "And" and "Now"

Additional paratextual keys that assist in deciphering the paragraph and sentence structures are the words "and" and "now."[28] According to John Gee, such usage can be seen in other ancient languages:

> Sentences in Anatolian languages like Hittite and Luwian, usually start with a particle to which various enclitic particles are attached. The particle functions as verbal punctuation because it signals where a new sentence starts. Consider, for example, the simple Hittite sentence:
> Nu-wa-ra-aš TI-an-za
> Now he will live.
> The Hittite particle *nu* "now" (the Hittite and English words are, in fact, cognates) functions as verbal punctuation to let the sentence start.[29]

Gee notes that Hebrew sentences also often start with common particles.[30]

In the Book of Mormon, the overwhelming function of "and" to begin sentences can be easily seen in Nephi$_1$'s account of his own vision of the Tree of Life. The following, taken from 1 Nephi 12:1–4, is a reconstruction of sentences and paragraphing based on the more archaic function of these markers:

> And it came to pass that the angel said unto me: "Look, and behold thy seed—and also the seed of thy brethren."
>
> *And* I looked, and beheld the land of promise. *And* I beheld multitudes of people—yea, even as it were in number as many as the sand of the sea.
>
> And it came to pass that I beheld multitudes gathered together to battle one against the other. *And* I beheld wars and rumors of wars, and great slaughters with the sword among my people.
>
> And it came to pass that I beheld many generations pass away after the manner of wars and contentions in the land. *And* I beheld many cities—yea, even that I did not number them.
>
> And it came to pass that I saw a mist of darkness on the face of the land of promise.
>
> *And* I saw lightnings.
>
> *And* I heard thunderings, and earthquakes—and all manner of tumultuous noises.
>
> *And* I saw the earth, and the rocks—that they rent.
>
> *And* I saw mountains tumbling into pieces.
>
> *And* I saw the plains of the earth—that they were broken up.
>
> *And* I saw many cities—that they were sunk.

---

28. Gee, "Verbal Punctuation," 36.
29. Gee, 33–34.
30. Gee, 35.

And I saw many—that they were burned with fire. And I saw many—that they did tumble to the earth, because of the quaking thereof.

The use of "now" in the Book of Mormon differs from "and now." Where "and now" is a temporal marker, "now" can signal additional information or an explanatory expansion on what had just been noted:

> And it came to pass that I, Nephi, said many things unto my brethren, insomuch that they were confounded and could not contend against me; neither durst they lay their hands upon me nor touch me with their fingers, even for the space of many days. *Now* they durst not do this lest they should wither before me, so powerful was the Spirit of God; and thus it had wrought upon them. (1 Ne. 17:52)

> Wherefore, we would to God that we could persuade all men not to rebel against God, to provoke him to anger, but that all men would believe in Christ, and view his death, and suffer his cross and bear the shame of the world; wherefore, I, Jacob, take it upon me to fulfil the commandment of my brother Nephi.
>
> *Now* Nephi began to be old, and he saw that he must soon die; wherefore, he anointed a man to be a king and a ruler over his people now, according to the reigns of the kings. (Jacob 1:8–9)

> And he said unto the servant: Behold, the branches of the wild tree have taken hold of the moisture of the root thereof, that the root thereof hath brought forth much strength; and because of the much strength of the root thereof the wild branches have brought forth tame fruit. *Now*, if we had not grafted in these branches, the tree thereof would have perished. *And now*, behold, I shall lay up much fruit, which the tree thereof hath brought forth; and the fruit thereof I shall lay up against the season, unto mine own self. (Jacob 5:18)

The example from Jacob 5:18 demonstrates the difference of "now" fulfilling the role of explanation verses "and now" introducing new information that occurs at the same time.

Nephi$_1$'s Internal Story Demarcation

Nephi$_1$'s spiritual biography in 1 Nephi had an interesting problem and a more interesting solution. While telling stories from his life, he did not use chapters or visual markers to differentiate between each story. (The first chapter of the original dictation spanned chapters 1 through 5 of the modern editions, detailing multiple narratives including Lehi$_1$'s early preaching and initial revelation, the family leaving Jerusalem, and the quest for the brass plates.) Instead, and in line with the rest of the orally influenced elements of the text, Nephi₁ distinguished narrative arcs with a verbal division. However, his method was unique in the Book of Mormon to his personal writing, and its nature limited its effectiveness. His method was to mention his father's tent.

The first instance of this occurs in 1 Nephi 2 following Lehi₁'s admonition to his murmuring sons Laman and Lemuel:

> Neither did they believe that Jerusalem, that great city, could be destroyed according to the words of the prophets. And they were like unto the Jews who were at Jerusalem, who sought to take away the life of my father.
>
> And it came to pass that my father did speak unto them in the valley of Lemuel, with power, being filled with the Spirit, until their frames did shake before him. And he did confound them, that they durst not utter against him; wherefore, they did as he commanded them.
>
> *And my father dwelt in a tent.*
>
> And it came to pass that I, Nephi, being exceedingly young, nevertheless being large in stature, and also having great desires to know of the mysteries of God . . . (vv. 13–16)

While Nephi₁'s note about his father dwelling in his tent fits into the context of the narrative, it also occurs at a shift in that narration. At this point in his overall story, Nephi₁'s family has departed from Jerusalem and temporarily settled in a valley. From there the story shifts away from the family as a whole and begins to focus more and more on Nephi₁ himself, beginning with his own prayerful confirmation of his father's words.

Following a pair of communications from the Lord, Nephi₁ writes, "And it came to pass that I, Nephi, returned from speaking with the Lord, *to the tent of my father*" (1 Ne. 3:1). In response to his prayers, Nephi₁ receives a revelation that calls him to be the prophet to the people of the New World. The revelation spoke of the choice land promised to Nephi₁. It spoke of Nephi₁ as the ruler and teacher over his brothers. It spoke of how, when the Lamanites would not accept him, they would be a scourge to Nephi₁'s people. Nephi₁ ends that story with a verse that simply notes that he returned to the tent of his father.

Such a mention seems rather uninteresting, given that Nephi₁ has just finished speaking with the Lord. However, throughout 1 Nephi, he repeatedly uses the return to his father's tent as a literary phrase marking the boundary of a story. Returning to the tent ends the story of Nephi₁'s first revelations. It is also a transition because it places Nephi₁ before his father. With Nephi₁ at his father's tent, he is in a place to begin the story of the retrieval of the brass plates, which, again, ends with Nephi mentioning his father's tent: "And it came to pass that we took the plates of brass and the servant of Laban, and departed into the wilderness, and journeyed unto *the tent of our father*" (1 Ne. 4:38). This, however, does not signal the complete end to the narrative arc, as Nephi₁ briefly takes a tangent to acknowledge how difficult their excursion had been for his parents, and particularly his mother (5:1–6). Instead, the narrative wraps up several verses later to include the impact of their return on his parents: "And when we had returned *to the tent of my father*, behold their joy was full, and my mother was comforted" (v. 7). Thus ends the story of the return for the plates of brass. Nephi₁ resolves the tension between his mother and father and signals that he has finished that story by repeating their return to his father's tent.

Nephi₁'s next mention of going to his father's tent again signals the end of one narrative (returning to Jerusalem for Ishmael's family) and the beginning of a new one (the rebellion in the wilderness):

> And it came to pass that we went up unto the house of Ishmael, and we did gain favor in the sight of Ishmael, insomuch that we did speak unto him the words of the Lord.
>
> And it came to pass that the Lord did soften the heart of Ishmael, and also his household, insomuch that they took their journey with us down into the wilderness *to the tent of our father*.
>
> And it came to pass that as we journeyed in the wilderness, behold Laman and Lemuel, and two of the daughters of Ishmael, and the two sons of Ishmael and their families, did rebel against us; yea, against me, Nephi, and Sam, and their father, Ishmael, and his wife, and his three other daughters. (1 Ne. 7:4–6)

Then, again, Nephi₁ uses his father's tent to signal the end of that rebellion and their repentance and the beginning of their renewed travelling through the wilderness:

> And it came to pass that they were sorrowful, because of their wickedness, insomuch that they did bow down before me, and did plead with me that I would forgive them of the thing that they had done against me.
>
> And it came to pass that I did frankly forgive them all that they had done, and I did exhort them that they would pray unto the Lord their God for forgiveness. And it came to pass that they did so. And after they had done praying unto the Lord we did again travel on our journey *towards the tent of our father*.
>
> And it came to pass that we did come down unto *the tent of our father*. And after I and my brethren and all the house of Ishmael had come down

unto *the tent of my father*, they did give thanks unto the Lord their God; and they did offer sacrifice and burnt offerings unto him.

And it came to pass that we had gathered together all manner of seeds of every kind, both of grain of every kind, and also of the seeds of fruit of every kind. (1 Ne. 7:20–8:1)

These verses come at a major shift in the story of Nephi$_1$ and his family. They have been sedentary for a while, and this appearance of the "tent of our father" begins the new journey to Bountiful. Perhaps the significance of this shift explains the triple repetition of the "tent of our/my father." However, as they are setting forth again toward the promised land, Lehi$_1$ receives and shares with his family the vision he had of the Tree of Life—an account that Nephi$_1$ again ends with a mention of his father's tent:

> And after he had preached unto them, and also prophesied unto them of many things, he bade them to keep the commandments of the Lord; and he did cease speaking unto them.
>
> And all these things did my father see, and hear, and speak, *as he dwelt in a tent*, in the valley of Lemuel, and also a great many more things, which cannot be written upon these plates.
>
> And now, as I have spoken concerning these plates, behold they are not the plates upon which I make a full account of the history of my people; for the plates upon which I make a full account of my people I have given the name of Nephi; wherefore, they are called the plates of Nephi, after mine own name; and these plates also are called the plates of Nephi. (1 Ne. 8:38–9:2)

The first verse is Nephi$_1$'s ending of the story of the dream. We get his segment-ending phrase "dwelt in a tent." As with other times when Nephi$_1$ speaks of his father's tent, the function is to separate sections of the story being told in the larger chapter. What is most important in this case is that Nephi$_1$ mentions that many other things happened "which cannot be written upon these plates" (1 Ne. 9:1). This begins a brief tangent where Nephi$_1$ discusses his plates and the visions and revelations recorded on them, ending again with mention his father's tent:

> And after this manner of language did my father prophesy and speak unto my brethren, and also many more things which I do not write in this book; for I have written as many of them as were expedient for me in mine other book.
>
> And all these things, of which I have spoken, were done *as my father dwelt in a tent*, in the valley of Lemuel.
>
> And it came to pass after I, Nephi, having heard all the words of my father, concerning the things which he saw in a vision, and also the things

which he spake by the power of the Holy Ghost, which power he received by faith on the Son of God—and the Son of God was the Messiah who should come—I, Nephi, was desirous also that I might see, and hear, and know of these things, by the power of the Holy Ghost, which is the gift of God unto all those who diligently seek him, as well in times of old as in the time that he should manifest himself unto the children of men. (1 Ne. 10:15–17)

This occurrence of "my father dwelt in a tent" comes as Nephi$_1$ separates his father's vision of the tree of life and his own, which he again ends with his trademark phrase before moving on to the next story about his brothers once again murmuring about their father:

And now I make an end of speaking concerning the things which I saw while I was carried away in the Spirit; and if all the things which I saw are not written, the things which I have written are true. And thus it is. Amen.[31]

And it came to pass that after I, Nephi, had been carried away in the Spirit, and seen all these things, I returned *to the tent of my father.*

And it came to pass that I beheld my brethren, and they were disputing one with another concerning the things which my father had spoken unto them. (1 Ne. 14:30–15:2)

Finally, Nephi$_1$ signals the end of this interaction with his brothers with the same mention, then uses it to mark the next major stage of their travels into the wilderness with Lehi$_1$'s discovery of the Liahona at his tent door:

And it came to pass that I, Nephi, did exhort my brethren, with all diligence, to keep the commandments of the Lord.

And it came to pass that they did humble themselves before the Lord; insomuch that I had joy and great hopes of them, that they would walk in the paths of righteousness.

Now, all these things were said and done *as my father dwelt in a tent* in the valley which he called Lemuel.

And it came to pass that I, Nephi, took one of the daughters of Ishmael to wife; and also, my brethren took of the daughters of Ishmael to wife; and also Zoram took the eldest daughter of Ishmael to wife.

And thus my father had fulfilled all the commandments of the Lord which had been given unto him. And also, I, Nephi, had been blessed of the Lord exceedingly.

---

31. Chapter III (10–14) ends with a testificatory "amen" that, as noted above, forces a chapter break in the writing. Thus, although the "tent of my father" occurs at the beginning of a chapter rather than as an internal division, it still functions as a story boundary. Were it not for the testificatory amen, it is plausible that Nephi would not have ended the chapter at this point.

And it came to pass that the voice of the Lord spake unto my father by night, and commanded him that on the morrow he should take his journey into the wilderness.

And it came to pass that *as my father arose in the morning, and went forth to the tent door*, to his great astonishment he beheld upon the ground a round ball of curious workmanship; and it was of fine brass. And within the ball were two spindles; and the one pointed the way whither we should go into the wilderness. (1 Ne. 16:4–10)

Chapter Seven

Influence of the Assumed Audience

While the Book of Mormon itself had an audience to which it spoke when it was published in 1830, the audience of the individual ancient authors varied. Furthermore, for those authors who intended to speak to a future audience, it cannot be known how accurately they envisioned those who would read their translated writings.

In *The Oral and the Written Gospel*, Werner Kelber examines the possible influence of orality on the New Testament, and his findings are instructive to what Book of Mormon writers experienced:

> In the broadest terms, oral and written compositions come into existence under different circumstances. A speaker addresses an audience in front of him, and its presence in turn affects the delivery of his speech. There is a sense in which performer and audience share in the making of the message. An author, by contrast, writes for readers who are normally absent at the time and from the place of writing. This relative detachment from social context allows the author to exercise controls over his composition in a manner unknown to the performer of live speech.[1]

Although the Book of Mormon is obviously a written text, we can still see some of the effect of a present audience when an author quotes a sermon or dialogue. Of course, there is the proviso that because the speeches were written down they were necessarily created after the event they describe. It is likely that they were improved in the writing by eliminating verbal hesitations or misspeaking. Nevertheless, the essential interaction with the original present audience is preserved.

An obvious influence of the present audience can be seen in Alma$_2$'s discourse outside of Antionum. There, we have an interesting description of a change in his audience:

> Now, as Alma was teaching and speaking unto the people upon the hill Onidah, there came a great multitude unto him, who were those of whom we have been speaking, of whom were poor in heart, because of their poverty as to the things of the world.

---

1. Werner H. Kelber, *The Oral and the Written Gospel: The Hermeneutics of Speaking and Writing in the Synoptic Tradition, Mark, Paul, and Q*, 14–15.

> And they came unto Alma; and the one who was the foremost among them said unto him: Behold, what shall these my brethren do, for they are despised of all men because of their poverty, yea, and more especially by our priests; for they have cast us out of our synagogues which we have labored abundantly to build with our own hands; and they have cast us out because of our exceeding poverty; and we have no place to worship our God; and behold, what shall we do?
>
> And now when Alma heard this, he turned him about, his face immediately towards him, and he beheld with great joy; for he beheld that their afflictions had truly humbled them, and that they were in a preparation to hear the word.
>
> *Therefore he did say no more to the other multitude*; but he stretched forth his hand, and cried unto those whom he beheld, who were truly penitent, and said unto them . . . (Alma 32:4–7)

Alma$_2$ had started preaching to one audience, but a new audience then arrived. Alma$_2$ then not only redirected his attention, he tailored his sermon to this newly arrived group.

Nevertheless, it is still important to remember that no Book of Mormon writer had an immediate audience. As Walter Ong puts it, "The writer's audience is always a fiction."[2] The audience is a fiction because they are not actually present as the text is written; they are rather imagined. Yet the fictive audience provides the context for at least some of the way the text is presented. For example, a book about dolphins could be written for children or for marine biologists. The resulting texts may have the subject in common, but they will be written very differently. While we modern readers of the Book of Mormon are generally presumed to be its intended audience—and that might ultimately be God's intention—the envisioned audience for Nephi$_1$ and Mormon was likely one much closer to their culture and time.

Nephi$_1$ began the tradition of record keeping with explicitly defined purposes, and he managed to reiterate those in writing four different times. The first time comes right after Nephi$_1$ mentions that he cannot write everything his father saw and heard (1 Ne. 9:1). That perhaps triggered Nephi$_1$'s realization that he hadn't told his readers anything about the plates. He makes up for that lack by inserting an explanation that takes his narrative slightly off track for a few verses, but it functions to explain the plates to his audience:

---

2. Walter J. Ong, *Orality and Literacy*, 100.

> And now, as I have spoken concerning *these plates, behold they are not the plates upon which I make a full account of the history of my people*; for the plates upon which I make a full account of my people I have given the name of Nephi; wherefore, they are called the plates of Nephi, after mine own name; and these plates also are called the plates of Nephi.
>
> Nevertheless, I have received a commandment of the Lord that I should make these plates, for the special purpose that there should be an account engraven of the ministry of my people.
>
> Upon the other plates should be engraven an account of the reign of the kings, and the wars and contentions of my people; wherefore these plates are for the more part of the ministry; and the other plates are for the more part of the reign of the kings and the wars and contentions of my people.
>
> Wherefore, the Lord hath commanded me to make these plates for a wise purpose in him, which purpose I know not. (1 Ne. 9:2–5)

The essential information is that Nephi$_1$ wrote two different sets of plates. One was to be a dynastic record (an account of the reign of the kings). Nephi$_1$ points out that what his reading audience has before them is not related to that dynastic record but to another set of plates that has a different purpose (the ministry of his people). He then returns to his narrative in the next verse (10:1). What is important is that this is an aside that appears to have been triggered by a realization that his future audience may not have the information his contemporaries would have known. Rather than continuing with his planned text, Nephi$_1$ inserted intrusive material.

The second discussion similarly interrupts the planned flow of the text. In this case, the trigger was arriving in the New World and discussing the finding of certain metals (gold, silver, and copper) that likely made up the alloy used for the golden plates (see 1 Ne. 18:25).[3] It appears that mentioning the metals used to create the plates caused Nephi$_1$ to provide another explanation for the plates:

> And it came to pass that the Lord commanded me, wherefore *I did make plates of ore* that I might engraven upon them the record of my people. And upon the plates which I made I did engraven the record of my father, and also our journeyings in the wilderness, and the prophecies of my father; and also many of mine own prophecies have I engraven upon them.
>
> And I knew not at the time when I made them that I should be commanded of the Lord to make these plates; wherefore, the record of my father, and the genealogy of his fathers, and the more part of all our proceedings in

---

3. Jerry Grover, *Ziff, Magic Goggles, and Golden Plates: Etymology of Zyf and a Metallurgical Analysis of the Book of Mormon Plates*, 74–81.

the wilderness are engraven upon those first plates of which I have spoken; wherefore, the things which transpired before I made these plates are, of a truth, more particularly made mention upon the first plates.

And after I had made these plates by way of commandment, I, Nephi, received a commandment that the ministry and the prophecies, the more plain and precious parts of them, should be written upon these plates; and that the things which were written should be kept for the instruction of my people, who should possess the land, and also for other wise purposes, which purposes are known unto the Lord.

Wherefore, I, Nephi, did make a record upon the other plates, which gives an account, or which gives a greater account of the wars and contentions and destructions of my people. And this have I done, and commanded my people what they should do after I was gone; and that these plates should be handed down from one generation to another, or from one prophet to another, until further commandments of the Lord.

And an account of my making these plates shall be given hereafter; and then, behold, I proceed according to that which I have spoken; and this I do that the more sacred things may be kept for the knowledge of my people. (1 Ne. 19:1–5)

Notice that the introduction to the plates specifically mentions that they were made of ore, linking this aside to the previous text that triggered this information. As with the first time Nephi$_1$ spoke of the plates, we are reminded that there are two sets of plates: one is themed for the political world, and the other, the small plates he was then writing on, for "ministry and the prophecies." It is also important that Nephi$_1$ makes explicit his intended audience for those small plates: they are "for the instruction of my people, who should possess the land." Although Nephi$_1$ has explicitly stated that he wasn't sure of the reason for the small plates, he had the logical assumption that it would be for an audience from his world and time.

The third time Nephi$_1$ mentions the purpose for his writing is also an unplanned insertion:

And it came to pass that not many days after his death, Laman and Lemuel and the sons of Ishmael were angry with me because of the admonitions of the Lord.

For I, Nephi, was constrained to speak unto them, according to his word; for I had spoken many things unto them, and also my father, before his death; many of which sayings are written upon mine other plates; for a more history part are written upon mine other plates.

And upon these I write the things of my soul, and many of the scriptures which are engraven upon the plates of brass. For my soul delighteth in the scriptures, and my heart pondereth them, and writeth them for the learning and the profit of my children. (2 Ne. 4:13–15)

This is a very brief aside and simply notes that there are two sets of plates, one with "a more history part," and one with "things of my soul."

The fourth mention is the one that was perhaps originally planned, as it is directly tied to when he produced his small plates:

> And thirty years had passed away from the time we left Jerusalem.
>
> And I, Nephi, had kept the records upon my plates, which I had made, of my people thus far.
>
> And it came to pass that the Lord God said unto me: Make other plates; and thou shalt engraven many things upon them which are good in my sight, for the profit of thy people.
>
> Wherefore, I, Nephi, to be obedient to the commandments of the Lord, went and made these plates upon which I have engraven these things.
>
> And I engraved that which is pleasing unto God. And if my people are pleased with the things of God they will be pleased with mine engravings which are upon these plates.
>
> And if my people desire to know the more particular part of the history of my people they must search mine other plates. (2 Ne. 5:28–33)

Again, Nephi$_1$ repeats the essential information: he made plates by commandment for future readers ("the Lord God said unto me: Make other plates"), and they contain "that which is pleasing unto God," while the other plates are for those who "desire to know the more particular part of the history of my people." Altogether, the four tangents, as well as the nature of his writing, suggest that Nephi$_1$ imagined a readership that was much closer in time and culture to his own than the eventual 1830 reception audience.[4]

Nephi$_1$ is less specific with the purpose of his larger dynastic records that were to be a storage repository for the acts of the kings and rulers. There is no stated audience for these records, and they may have simply been repositories that were not intended for a particular readership. Mormon would eventually use them as source material, but it is hard to find any explicit quotation from them. Unlike Nephi$_1$, Mormon's pur-

---

4. See, for example, Noel B. Reynolds, "The Political Dimension in Nephi's Small Plates," 15–37. 1 Nephi is an argument that legitimizes Nephi$_1$'s role as ruler and teacher of his new people and city. Although the original context has Nephi$_1$ ruling over his brothers, that never actually occurs. Nephi$_1$ may have been a ruler and teacher over his "brethren," but not Laman and Lemuel, his brothers.

poses in writing envisioned an audience that differed from any assumed audience of the large plates.

In the third mention above, Nephi₁ explicitly states that he was writing "for the learning and the profit of *my children*" (2 Ne. 4:10). This intended audience differs from the modern one that President Ezra Taft Benson and others have pointed to:

> The Book of Mormon . . . was written for our day. The Nephites never had the book; neither did the Lamanites of ancient times. It was meant for us. Mormon wrote near the end of the Nephite civilization. Under the inspiration of God, who sees all things from the beginning, he abridged centuries of records, choosing the stories, speeches, and events that would be most helpful to us.[5]

While it may be correct that the Lord intended the Book of Mormon to have an audience one and half millennia after Moroni had finished his father's record, this does not mean that those who wrote understood how far distant their audience would be, or more importantly, what the significant differences in cultural expectations would be. In particular, the implied audience of the large plates was a contemporaneous people, and then perhaps only the upper levels of society. Thus, while Mormon had a future audience in mind, he was adapting a record that had originally been written for those who had lived before him.

In his final farewell Mormon makes clear that *he* was writing to a future audience rather than a present one. Indeed, the destruction he witnessed at Cumorah made it painfully clear that he was not only writing to a future audience—but one which did not include his own:

> And now, behold, I would speak somewhat unto the remnant of this people who are spared, if it so be that God may give unto them my words, that they may know of the things of their fathers; yea, I speak unto you, ye remnant of the house of Israel; and these are the words which I speak:
>
> Know ye that ye are of the house of Israel.
>
> Know ye that ye must come unto repentance, or ye cannot be saved.
>
> Know ye that ye must lay down your weapons of war, and delight no more in the shedding of blood, and take them not again, save it be that God shall command you.
>
> Know ye that ye must come to the knowledge of your fathers, and repent of all your sins and iniquities, and believe in Jesus Christ, that he is the Son of God, and that he was slain by the Jews, and by the power of the Father he

---

5. Ezra Taft Benson, "The Book of Mormon—Keystone of Our Religion." See also Daniel H. Ludlow, "The Book of Mormon Was Written for Our Day," 265–67.

hath risen again, whereby he hath gained the victory over the grave; and also in him is the sting of death swallowed up. (Morm. 7:1–5)

As Mormon envisions those who would read his laboriously crafted work, he sees them as "the remnant of this people." They are a people who may have forgotten gospel essentials (that they are of the house of Israel and must repent), but he still sees them in the context of Lamanites and descendants of the house of Israel. Having just witnessed the violent destruction of the Nephites by the Lamanites, Mormon urges his future audience to "lay down your weapons of war, and delight no more in the shedding of blood" (v. 4)—pointing to his assumption that the nature of the people who had destroyed the Nephites might persist and still define his future reading audience.

Scriptures, Audience, and the Isaiah Chapters

When the long Isaiah chapters were included in the Book of Mormon, the nineteenth-century reception audience is the best indicator for why the King James Bible version of those chapters were included in the translation.[6] However, while that may explain the language of the translation, it does not explain the presence of the texts themselves. Why does the Book of Mormon cite entire chapters from Isaiah?[7] From the perspective of the nineteenth-century reception audience who would have likely had a Bible readily available, such wholesale inclusion of entire chapters seems unnecessary. Even though Nephi$_1$ uses themes from those chapters as he develops his prophecy for the future (2 Ne. 25–30), the modern audience had no need for Nephi$_1$ to provide the full text of them. For the reception audience, shorter references or quotation of specific verses would have been sufficient. In fact, outside of Nephi$_1$ and Jacob, the quoted sermons that invoke Isaiah interact with the texts without wholesale quotations;[8] and in all cases save 1 Nephi 20–21 and 2 Nephi 12–24, passages from Isaiah are used in dialogue or sermons and echo the way Raymond F. Person Jr. describes the use of scripture in Deuteronomy and Chronicles:

---

6. Royal Skousen, with Carmack, *The History of the Text of the Book of Mormon: The King James Quotations in the Book of Mormon*, 5.

7. 1 Ne. 20/Isa. 48; 1 Ne. 21/Isa. 49; 2 Ne. 12/Isa. 2; 2 Ne. 13/Isa. 3; 2 Ne. 14/Isa. 4; 2 Ne. 5/Isa. 5; 2 Ne. 16/Isa. 6; 2 Ne. 7/Isa. 7; 2 Ne. 18/Isa. 8; 2 Ne. 19/Isa. 9; 2 Ne. 20/Isa. 10; 2 Ne. 21/Isa. 11; 2 Ne. 22/Isa. 12; 2 Ne. 23/Isa. 13; 2 Ne. 24/Isa. 14.

8. 3 Ne. 16 interacts with much of Isa. 52; 3 Ne. 20–22 interacts with Isa. 54.

Texts in a primarily oral culture like ancient Israel are not static retrieval mechanisms that can be stored until they might be needed again, but are devices that facilitate the creative activity of remembering (not memorizing) the broader tradition so that it can continue to live in the oral-aural communication of ongoing performances.[9]

Questioning the audience is the best solution to understanding why so many Isaiah chapters are present in 1 and 2 Nephi. In both the Old World and the peoples of the Book of Mormon, there was a complex interplay between oral forms and literacy. In many cases, writing incorporated strategies from oral production, perhaps as a prelude to using the memorized text in an oral setting.[10] The way other scripture appears in the Book of Mormon generally follows the assumption of a present audience. However, that doesn't happen with most of the inserted Isaiah chapters. They have no explicit or even implicit contemporary audience. In fact, they are placed in the text without pretense to an audience.[11] A plausible explanation is that Nephi$_1$ understood that he was writing for a future generation, and it is for that unknown future audience that the Isaiah chapters in their entirety were included.

The reason for their inclusion may be found in a combination of two factors. First, as Jacob states: "Whatsoever things we write upon anything save it be upon plates must perish and vanish away" (Jacob 4:2). Given the likelihood that Nephi$_1$ discussed the importance and role of the small plates before handing them to his brother Jacob, we can assume that Nephi$_1$ also understood that preserving a text on metal plates best guaranteed its permanence. Second, Nephi$_1$ understood his audience to be temporally distant. He did not know them like he did his brothers or his

---

9. Raymond F. Person, Jr., "The Role of Memory in the Tradition Represented by the Deuteronomic History and the Book of Chronicles," 548–49.

10. Ernst R. Wendland, "Orality and its Implications for the Analysis, Translation, and Transmission of Scripture," 43–44.

11. It is interesting that Nephi$_1$ appears to have understood the problem of a known audience versus an unknown one. In 1 Nephi 20 and 21, he enters two whole chapters of Isaiah, but contextualizes them as something he taught his brothers because they had asked. I see that as framing fiction itself. There is no internal context, save that the addition of these chapters appears to have been an unplanned addition. To fit them into what had been, to that point, a remarkably structured account, Nephi$_1$ extends the idea of the immediate context of his brothers, even though it is unlikely that the brothers were the reason for the additional chapters. See Brant A. Gardner, *Labor Diligently to Write: The Ancient Making of a Modern Book*, 230–31.

own people. He knew that his future readers would have scripture (2 Ne. 29:3), but it is doubtful that he could have imagined a future population that was highly literate and had easy access to so many texts, including sacred books containing Isaiah's writings. Therefore, to ensure that his future audience would have the full text of Isaiah's prophecies that he found so important, he included them in their entirety on his plates.[12]

---

12. For one theological interpretation of these Isaiah chapters, see Joseph M. Spencer, *The Vision of All: Twenty-five Lectures on Isaiah in Nephi's Record*.

Chapter Eight

Interweaving Names and Narrative

The Book of Mormon presents the reader with one hundred and eighty-eight unique names.[1] That there should be a high number of personal names in a historical narrative is hardly unexpected. What is less expected is that many of the names may serve dual purposes in the narrative: they can both signify a person and provide a meaning that elucidates or complements the narrative context in which that person is named. Such a practice was common in Hebrew and Egyptian literature where names were often shortened forms of sentences or phrases descriptive of the person or the role they have in a narrative.[2] Take, for example, the first two named persons in the Bible: *Adam* is the Hebrew word of "man" (*'adam*) and is also a play on words, as he was formed from the ground (*adamah*); *Eve* is based on the Hebrew word for "to live" (*chava*), as she would be the mother of all living persons (Gen. 2:7, 3:20).

Matthew L. Bowen has found numerous examples of how names similarly function in the Book of Mormon. One example deals with one of the few women named in the Book of Mormon: Abish. That she is named is alone remarkable, as she was just a servant. Bowen's article on Abish is sufficiently complex in its analysis to recommend reading in its entirety. In short, Abish is named not just because she was part of the story, but because her name reprised the story. He concludes:

> Like the vision of her father that converted Abish (Alma 19:16), whose name suggests the meaning "father is a man," the theophanies that converted Lamoni from the tradition of his father (Alma 18:5) and later his wife and father from the traditions of their fathers were all indeed remarkable visions. Whatever the exact content of those visions, they conveyed the doctrinal truth that was revealed many years earlier in the remarkable vision of their fathers Lehi and Nephi: that Jesus Christ, the Divine Warrior and Eternal

---

1. Sharon Black and Brad Wilcox, "188 Unexplainable Names: Book of Mormon Names No Fiction Writer Would Choose," 128.

2. Matthew L. Bowen, *Name as Key-Word: Collected Essays on Onomastic Wordplay and the Temple in Mormon Scripture*, xlviii–xlvix. We see this to a lesser extent in modern names that retain the dual function of having meaning in the name as well as being used as a personal identifier. Thus, children today might be named *Faith*, *Charity*, or *Hope*, which intentionally invoke scriptural meanings.

Father (1 Nephi 11:21, original text), condescended to become man—i.e., to "come forth, and be born of a woman" and as Suffering Servant "redeem all mankind who believe on his name" (Alma 19:13).[3]

The narrative function of names that works only if we read them with a Hebrew background suggests the translation process created an intentional connection to that language. (Moroni claimed that he and his father could have written in Hebrew [Morm. 9:33], indicating that their oral language had retained a variation or New World dialect of Hebrew to that time.) The narrative use of names, however, also goes beyond Hebrew meanings. After all, the Nephites lived in a world previously inhabited by Jaredites and Mulekites, both of which had different languages.[4] The inheritance of names and meanings from those two cultures also colored the way Mormon used names. Gordon C. Thomasson first noticed the narrative function of naming in the Book of Mormon in places where Hebrew meaning is not required. He explained:

> *Metonymy* or *metonymic naming* involves "naming by association," a metaphoric process of linking two concepts or persons together in such a way as to tell us more about the latter by means of what we already know about the former. For example, to call a potential scandal a "Watergate" is to suggest volumes in a single word. Similarly, if we call an individual a Judas or a Quisling, rather than giving his or her proper name, we can in one word convey an immense amount of information about how we at least feel toward that person.[5]

The place where Thomasson examined metonymic naming is in a complex text that technically shouldn't be in the Nephite record. Alma 11 comes from Alma$_2$'s personal record and contains a complex description of comparative values of gold, silver, and barley with names and values for each (vv. 4–19). These details would have been common knowledge at the time, and Alma$_2$ shouldn't have had any reason to include them.

---

3. Bowen, 111.

4. The Mulekites have an origin story in Jerusalem and therefore in the Hebrew language. They spoke a different language from the Nephites at the time the Nephites arrived in Zarahemla (Omni 1:17). The Jaredites were sufficiently older that Hebrew would not have been their language, even if they shared the same linguistic family.

5. Gordon C. Thomasson, "What's in a Name? Book of Mormon Language, Names, and [Metonymic] Naming," 10.

However, these verses are marked by repetitive resumption, indicating that it was Mormon who inserted the text.[6] This opens the question of why Mormon thought it important enough to add. Returning to Thomasson:

> In Alma 11 we find a seeming digression from the topic of the text in the complex discussion of Nephite weights and units of measure and equivalents. Conspicuous, now, among the names of the units of value given is that of an ezrom (Alma 11:6, 12). It is a quantity of silver. Immediately after the discussion of money we find the person who is called Zeezrom. This appears to be a compound of the word Ze, which we can translate "This is an" as a prefix, and the word ezrom. Zeezrom is distinguished by having offered 10.5 ezrom of silver to Alma and Amulek if they would deny their testimonies. . . . His name would translate "this is a unit of silver." Besides linking him with his actions, the name links him into a typological complex with those who would sell their signs and tokens for money and to Judas's selling/betraying Christ for thirty pieces of silver. If this is not metonymic naming I am anxious to learn what it might be. Lest the likelihood of Zeezrom being a metonym be underrated, I subsequently noted that the largest Nephite weights and units of measure, the antion of gold (Alma 11:19), appears in later chapters of the text of Alma, first in referring to a chief ruler of Ammonihah—one Antionah (a big man in status and self-esteem, Alma 12:20)—and later to the big-money town or pride-in-wealth city of Antionum (Alma 31:3), home of the nouveau riche bourgeois Zoramites (note they take upon themselves the name of an ex-servant, Zoram).[7]

According to Thomasson, Mormon not only inserts a list of values so that modern readers might understand the value of the bribe, but he also does so that we would have the context to understand the intended connotations of names that Mormon used in his text. As Thomasson notes, "We often take names far too lightly. As a result, we miss much of what a truly polysemous text (having multiple meanings or significations) such as the Book of Mormon may communicate."[8] Interestingly (but as should be expected), this type of naming is absent in the more immediate, first-person narratives of the small plates. On the other hand, it is a literary technique Mormon used frequently, and it may very well be the case that nearly all the names that Mormon provided in his abridged history are not those that the individuals actually went by.[9] Thus, with the exception of

---

6. I use that specific example in Chapter 4.
7. Thomasson, "What's in a Name?," 15–16.
8. Thomasson, 8.
9. See the discussion of the order of the Nehors, in Brant A. Gardner, *Second Witness: Analytical and Contextual Commentary on the Book of Mormon*, 4:41–43.

his own name and that of his son Moroni (both of which are given in their own first-person writings), it is possible that all the names provided in Mormon's writings should be considered for a possible metonymic function rather than just taken as historically accurate.

Mormon understood, and made a point of highlighting, the divisions in Zarahemla that resulted from the uneasy merging of the peoples of Nephi and of Mulek—two different peoples with different languages, religions, and politics. The resulting conflict was certainly behind the civil war that would have been discussed in greater detail in the lost beginning of the book of Mosiah. During the reign of Mosiah$_2$, the people of Limhi and the people of Alma$_1$ returned to Zarahemla. Mormon notes: "And now all the people of Nephi were assembled together, and also all the people of Zarahemla, and they were gathered together in two bodies" (Mosiah 25:4). In the generation following King Benjamin's attempt to unify the people, the two different groups continued to gather with their own and not mix with each other.

These factions continued, and tensions in Zarahemla always tended to divide along those lines. This was a division that Mormon likely and subtly underscores by using metonymic personal names. The Hebrew root of the name Mulek was *mlk*, meaning "king." As Mormon provided names, he seems to have used those with a *mlk* root to signal to his readers that the bearer of the name was part of the anti-Nephite, pro-king faction in Zarahemla.

In Alma 46 we are introduced to Amalickiah:

> Now the leader of those who were wroth against their brethren was a large and a strong man; and his name was Amalickiah. And Amalickiah was desirous to be a king; and those people who were wroth were also desirous that he should be their king; and they were the greater part of them the lower judges of the land, and they were seeking for power. (vv. 3–4)

Amalickiah (AMaLicKiah) is based on the *mlk* root. Note that he is both "against their brethren," and that he was "desirous to be king."

More complicated is the interesting case of the Amlicites and Amalekites. Royal Skousen notes that Joseph Smith likely pronounced Amlicites as *Amlikites*. In fact, he points out that "the first two occurrences in [the Printer's Manuscript] of *Amlicites* (in Alma 2:11–12) are spelled *Amlikites*."[10] Skousen adds:

---

10. Royal Skousen, *Analysis of Textual Variants of the Book of Mormon*, 1605.

There is one additional Book of Mormon name, *Amalekite*, that could be included in the above list of names taking the form *am-l-k*. The printer's manuscript (and every published edition) uses the term *Amalekite(s)* to refer to a group of religious apostates, 14 times in Alma 21–27 and 5 times in Alma 43. Yet the original manuscript and other evidence suggests that these Amalekites were not an otherwise unidentified group of religious dissidents, but were in fact Amlici's own group, the Amlicites.[11]

J. Christopher Conkling accepts Skousen's suggestion and writes: "Chronologically, the Amlicites and Amalekites fit together perfectly; they never overlap."[12] However, Benjamin McMurtry provides a much more careful examination of the posited two different groups:

> The first textual reference to either of these groups is the appearance of Amlici in Alma 2:1. The rise of Amlici was in the commencement of the fifth year of the reign of the judges. Amlici gains a following, and they call themselves Amlicites (Alma 2:11). They do battle with the Nephite armies. Amlici is killed by the sword of Alma the Younger, and his followers are defeated and scattered. This all occurs in the fifth year of the judges.
>
> The first textual reference to the Amalekites occurs in Alma 21:2: "Now the Lamanites and the Amalekites and the people of Amulon had built a great city, which was called Jerusalem." We must not fall into the trap of thinking that because this story appears nineteen chapters after the story of the Amlicites that it takes place at a later time. The text reveals that Alma 21 takes place "when Ammon and his brethren separated themselves in the borders of the land of the Lamanites" (Alma 21:1). This separation took place "in the first year of the judges" (Alma 17:6). The Amalekites very likely existed long before the first year, due to the fact that their city was already "great" when it was first discovered by Aaron in the first year of the judges. They continued to be a distinct people until the eighteenth year of the judges (Alma 43:4, 6).[13]

McMurtry's solution is to posit the two as different peoples with similar names. Understanding the way Mormon used names, it is more likely that Mormon gave apostate groups a generic designation of *Amlicite/Amalekite* with at least the implied meaning of apostate-of-Mulekite-lineage.[14] Thus,

---

11. Skousen, 1606.

12. J. Christopher Conkling, "Alma's Enemies: The Case of the Lamanites, Amlicites, and Mysterious Amalekites," 111.

13. Benjamin McMurtry, "The Amlicites and Amalekites: Are They the Same People?," 270–71.

14. Mark A. Wright noticed this possibility and convinced me that it is the most plausible solution to the problems Skousen, Conkling, and McMurtry are attempting to resolve. It is the reason that they come to opposite conclusions

there were likely two different peoples, but they may have been designated with the same Mormon-created identifying name.

Mormon's use of *mlk*-root names for generic designations suggests that when we see "king-men" in Mormon's text, we are seeing the English translation of that *mlk*-root word. We should thus see king-men as a political party with roots in the descendants of Mulek. The specific use of this designation is intended to create a direct antithetical parallel with the Nephite-supporters, the "freemen":

> And it came to pass that those who were desirous that Pahoran should be dethroned from the judgment-seat were called *king-men*, for they were desirous that the law should be altered in a manner *to overthrow the free government and to establish a king over the land*.
>
> And those who were desirous that Pahoran should remain chief judge over the land took upon them the name of freemen; and thus was the division among them, for the *freemen* had sworn or covenanted *to maintain their rights and the privileges of their religion by a free government*. (Alma 51:5–6)[15]

Parallel to the implications of divisiveness that was inherited from the *mlk*-ites, Mormon also weaves in a theme of the destructive inheritance of the Jaredites among the Nephite nation. Assuming that the lost pages also mentioned the last Jaredite king, Coriantumr, coming to and living with the people of Zarahemla (as briefly mentioned in Omni 1:21), we can readily see how Mormon would want to connect that to a later account in the Book of Mormon: "And they came down again that they might pitch battle against the Nephites. And they were led by a man whose name was Coriantumr; and he was a descendant of Zarahemla; and he was a dissenter from among the Nephites; and he was a large and a mighty man" (Hel. 1:15).

A different type of subtle manipulation of names might be present in the unusual string of fathers and sons with identical names. The succession of

---

while examining the same data. It is probable that there were two different groups who left at different times. Both shared the characteristic of the Zarahemla/Mulekite heritage. For Mormon, that was all that needed to be highlighted. The actual names of those involved was not only superfluous but might have hidden the important connection that Mormon saw in them.

15. On a related note, notice that the freemen weren't concerned with the nature of government or the person, but with the "rights and the privileges of their religion." This is another confirmation to the close connection between religion and government, and why political differences were often expressed as religious differences, and vice versa.

Nephite dynasties, beginning with $Alma_2$, is quite complex. Continuation of the political line from father to son becomes rarer, and in 3 Nephi the government is completely dissolved, only to implicitly reappear in 4 Nephi. These dynastic/book changes are precisely the place where the most curious naming trend in the Book of Mormon occurs. At the end of the book of Mosiah, we have $Alma_1$. His son, $Alma_2$, begins the book of Alma, but it ends with his son $Helaman_1$ keeping the records. The book of Helaman begins with $Helaman_2$ and ends with his son, $Nephi_2$. The book of Nephi begins with $Nephi_3$—as does the book of 4 Nephi.

From a cultural standpoint, the succession of identically named fathers and sons is an anomaly, but within the Book of Mormon we have $Amos_2$, the son of $Amos_1$; the son of $Nephi_3$, the son of $Nephi_2$; the son of $Helaman_2$, the son of $Helaman_1$; and the son of $Alma_2$, the son of $Alma_1$. In the ancient world, it was not uncommon for a grandparent and grandchild to share a name, but it was rare for a parent and child to do so. In a world without surnames and without the concept of the clarifying junior or senior, having a parent and child with the same name would lead to too much confusion. Yet we have that precise issue not once, but four times with four sets of father and son pairs with the same name.

Joseph Spencer noticed an important pattern in these books and names:

> While each book in Mormon's history recounts a particular succession, each break between books also marks a succession. At the same time, Mormon softens the impact of these breaks by having all cross-book successions be those in which the successor shares his name with his father....
>
> That Mormon highlights dynastic continuity even at points of historical transition makes clear his interest in maintaining the essential progression of the trajectory of Christian preaching that underlies his history.[16]

The recognition of the pattern is important. Combined with the understanding that Mormon likely used names for textual purposes, this allows us to see a reason for the naming patterns that would otherwise be unattested in much of antiquity. After all, Mormon was not interested in history. He was interested in history teaching people to come to Jesus Christ, the Eternal God.

Spencer's insight shows that what Mormon is tracing is a dual system. On one line is the political succession, and on the other the religious succession. Even as the political dynasties undergo turmoil, the fact that

---

16. Joseph M. Spencer, *An Other Testament: On Typology*, 111.

the same-named religious figures straddle the dynastic changes allows Mormon to suggest that there was a continuation of the religious line.[17] Thus, these father and son names have a textual function greater than the use of a name to designate a historical person.

The appearance of the name Nephi in this sequence may also serve a particular textual function. Not only do we have Nephi$_2$ and Nephi$_3$ providing continuity across differently named books, but we also have them at an important ending and beginning. The change in book names might imply a discontinuity in the ruling line, but 3 Nephi makes it clear that there was not only a discontinuity; there was a dissolution. Nephi$_3$ lived during a time when the Nephite government ceased to exist and all who had been part of the larger government returned to the rule of their separate tribes. At the time Christ appears in Bountiful, we do not know how those people conceive their collective identity, but we do know that afterward there are "no manner of –*ites*" (4 Ne. 1:17). So then how do they become Nephites again after so long a period without *-ites*? It may be that Mormon established a narrative continuity of the Nephite religion by having the leader of that post-visitation people be named "Nephi." Thus, Nephi$_3$, the disciple of Christ, becomes not only the ruler for whom 4 Nephi is named but also by which the reconstituted people are known. (For more on 4 Nephi being named after Nephi$_3$, see Chapter 12.)

A final example of Mormon's possible manipulation of names comes from his inclusion of Alma$_2$'s final instructions to his three sons. These instructions, which have little historical significance and do not move Mormon's narrative along, were taken from Alma$_2$'s personal record. One reason for including them can be discerned from the names of the sons. Just as Zeezrom and Antionah referred to real people who probably were not known by those names, Mormon may have used metonyms for the names of Alma$_2$'s sons to reinforce a specific intended lesson for his readers (Alma 36–42).

The oldest son, Helaman$_1$, bears a name previously given to one of King Benjamin's sons (Mosiah 1:2). It is a good Nephite name. Helaman$_1$

---

17. "The first trajectory of continuous Nephite preaching is, however, coupled with a second trajectory—that, namely, of the progressive political collapse of the Nephite state. . . . For the moment it is only necessary to recognize that the initiation of Nephite preaching cannot be separated from the beginning of the collapse of the centuries-Old Nephite state—just as the culmination of Nephite Christian anticipation cannot be disentangled from the culmination of Nephite political deterioration." Spencer, 112.

received the plates from Alma$_2$, and nothing in the instructions his father gives him (Alma 36–37) suggests that he was less than a faithful Nephite.

The next son, Shiblon, shares an ambiguous name with one of the units of measure presented earlier by Mormon (Alma 11:15)—and therefore a possible positive connotation—as well as a Jaredite king (Ether 1:11–12)—whose reign was one of corruption and wickedness (Ether 11:4–9), and whose people and secret works Alma$_2$ had just warned Helaman$_1$ of (Alma 37:21–32). Shiblon seems to have basically been a good son, but in Alma$_2$'s final blessing, note the concern that he seems to have for his child:

> And now, as ye have begun to teach the word even so I would that ye should continue to teach; and I would that ye would be diligent and temperate in all things.
>
> See that ye are not lifted up unto pride; yea, see that ye do not boast in your own wisdom, nor of your much strength.
>
> Use boldness, but not overbearance; and also see that ye bridle all your passions, that ye may be filled with love; see that ye refrain from idleness.
>
> Do not pray as the Zoramites do, for ye have seen that they pray to be heard of men, and to be praised for their wisdom.
>
> Do not say: O God, I thank thee that we are better than our brethren; but rather say: O Lord, forgive my unworthiness, and remember my brethren in mercy—yea, acknowledge your unworthiness before God at all times. (Alma 38:10–14)

Right after the admonition to be diligent and temperate, Alma$_2$ lists the things that might tempt Shiblon to not be diligent or temperate. Those things are descriptions of apostasy and hallmarks of the Jaredite's downfall, indicating that Alma$_2$ was worried about his son possibly being tempted into apostasy.

The third son bears the name Corianton. That name is not otherwise attested in the Book of Mormon, but it seems clearly related to the Jaredite kings Coriantum (Ether 1:13–14) and Coriantor (vv. 6–7). And, of course, there is also Coriantumr, which was the name of both the last Jaredite king (12:1) and a prominent Nephite dissenter (Hel. 1:15). As suggested by his name, Corianton is the son who did apostatize for a time. Alma$_2$ tells Corianton that one of the things he did wrong was that "thou didst go on unto boasting in thy strength and thy wisdom" (Alma 39:2). That doesn't seem so bad, but it is also the very thing Alma$_2$ warned Shiblon against (38:11). As the child with the most obvious Jaredite name, it is unsurprising that Corianton was the one to cause the greatest problem and to become an actual apostate, rather than only have the potential to become one as is suggested for Shiblon.

The names of Alma$_2$'s sons so directly correspond with the information we read about them that it would require an incredible coincidence to have those be the names their parents gave them. Given that we see Mormon intentionally creating names in other places, and even including a description of weights and measures so that we might understand them, it is best to see these names for their metonymic function.

These subtle but important aspects of the use of names in Mormon's text are not present in the small plates, nor should they be. The small plates were holographic. Mormon's text was intentionally edited. The stated nature of the two types of texts explains the reason for the difference in naming.

Chapter Nine

Preserved Orality in Nephite Literature

The Book of Mormon is undeniably and adamantly literate. Where the Bible shows evidence of an oral stage behind many of the books of the Old Testament (and parts of the New), the Book of Mormon declares that it was founded in written texts. There is no indication that any book in the Book of Mormon was oral before it was written down. Indeed, the book of Omni's multiple writers make it clear that they are dealing with a physical record and the need to write upon it. Nevertheless, there is evidence that the Book of Mormon is a written artifact that came from a primarily oral culture and that its "oral world often pervades . . . written expression."[1]

The New World had few literate cultures. All of them were concentrated in the area known as Mesoamerica. Among those, literacy was concentrated in the ranks of the elite.[2] The majority of people in the New World literate societies would have relied upon the oral transmission of information rather than texts. This situation mirrors most ancient literate cultures in the Old World. Thus, William Eggington suggests: "Lehi and his descendants functioned in a society which exhibited strong oral residual culture characteristics: they had access to print as a technology but retained many features of a nonprint culture."[3] Without the benefit of editors, the Nephites should have produced evidence not only of their oral style but of their primary dependence upon oral communication—even as they wrote.[4]

The presence of Nephite literacy in an environment that continued to be highly oral provides the context for understanding why elements

---

1. William M. Schniedewind, *How the Bible Became a Book*, 13. Schniedewind is speaking of the Bible here and makes no mention of the Book of Mormon.
2. Don S. Rice, "Historical Contexts and Interpretive Themes," 5, notes that the extant examples of writing concentrate on the concerns of the elite. See also Allen J. Christenson, "The Use of Chiasmus by the Ancient K'iche' Maya," 333.
3. William G. Eggington, *"Our Weakness in Writing": Oral and Literate Culture in the Book of Mormon*, 2.
4. Hugh W. Pinnock, *Finding Biblical Hebrew and Other Ancient Literary Forms in the Book of Mormon*, 1, indicates his belief that the written forms were based on earlier oral forms.

of oral literature persisted in the written text.[5] That persistence contrasts with the general absence of those forms in nineteenth-century literature. Where vocabulary and King James–style language can be explained by the influence of the publication era of the Book of Mormon, these oral elements point to the persistence of a very different type of literature.

The following sections do not intend to exhaustively present the cases representing each oral form. The intent is to establish the category and provide sufficient examples for understanding. More exhaustive work can, and probably should, be done.

Privileging Orality within Texts

An artifact of cultures transitioning from oral to written traditions can be found in the writer's apparent distrust of writing as a means of effective communication. This is typically not explained but is implicit in statements that writers make about their own writing. For example, William M. Schniedewind found that "early Christian writers were often apologetic about their own writing."[6] He further notes that "Pliny the Elder emphasized the importance of the oral transmission as opposed to books: 'the living word (*viva vox*), as the common saying has it, is much more effective.'"[7]

The reason for this hesitation to trust writing came from the recognition that it is divorced from any real-time audience or the ability of the communicator to assure that the message is correctly understood. (This

---

5. "In societies today that are characterized by a vibrant, 'persistent' orality, that is, those which have been exposed to, but have not fully accepted, adapted to, or adopted writing and print, many functionally effective verbal modes and manners of expression commonly found in strictly oral discourse will find their way also into dynamic literary compositions of all types." Ernst R. Wendland, "Orality and its Implications for the Analysis, Translation, and Transmission of Scripture," 16–17.

6. Schniedewind, *How the Bible Became a Book*, 15.

7. Schniedewind, 14. He provides a further example:

> Writing is not necessarily considered a universal good. For example, in an interesting vignette involving Pharaoh and the god Thoth, Plato criticized the Egyptian god and inventor of writing: "You have invented an elixir not of memory, but of reminding; and you offer your pupils the appearance of wisdom, not true wisdom, for they will read many things without instruction and will therefore seem to know many things, when they are for the most part ignorant and hard to get along with, since they are not wise, but only appear wise." (p. 114)

should be easy to understand by anyone today who has had their attempt at sarcasm in a text message or social media post be misunderstood.) In turning to the issue that Schniedewind noted for the early church Fathers, Werner Kelber highlights that there was a documented

> reluctance and anxiety even expressed by the early church Fathers with regard to their own writing. Their seemingly awkward apologies arose out of fear that writing might compromise the Christian gospel. Far from taking writing for granted, they did not perceive it as a process of stabilizing oral impermanence, but rather as a more or less questionable means of releasing words from their normative, oral management. As long as words transpired in the oral medium, speakers remained in charge of the seed they had sown. But language divorced from human contexts and transposed into textuality has fallen outside the control of speakers. It is entirely up to readers, devoid of speaking contacts, to determine the meaning of worlds.[8]

William Eggington notes this tendency in the Book of Mormon:

> Some authors of the Book of Mormon knew the linguistic constraints and difficulties they faced as they constructed their texts. The oft quoted scripture of Ether 12:27, "and if men come unto me, I will show unto them their weakness," derives from counsel given to Moroni because Moroni was disturbed by his and other writers' weaknesses in writing. They admit to "stumbling because of the placing of [their written] words" (Ether 12:26), even though they acknowledge that their spoken words were powerful.[9]

It is an attitude we see as early as Nephi$_1$: "And now I, Nephi, cannot write all the things which were taught among my people; neither am I mighty in writing, like unto speaking; for when a man speaketh by the power of the Holy Ghost the power of the Holy Ghost carrieth it unto the hearts of the children of men" (2 Ne. 33:1). That is a classic statement of a person who is literate but still living in a primarily oral culture. It is easily missed in a modern culture so deeply imbued with texts.

The difference for Nephi$_1$ was the presence of his audience. When physically present, the Holy Ghost communicated above and beyond words. Although we believe the same to be available through texts, that was not the ancient perception. Walter Ong explains why this lack of an audience was such an issue for those coming from a highly oral society: "Extratextual context is missing not only for readers but also for the

---

8. Werner H. Kelber, *The Oral and the Written Gospel: The Hermeneutics of Speaking and Writing in the Synoptic Tradition, Mark, Paul, and Q*, 92–93.

9. Eggington, *Weakness in Writing*, 5–6.

writer. Lack of verifiable context is what makes writing normally so much more agonizing an activity than oral presentation to a real audience."[10]

Perhaps the difficulty in understanding what a non-present audience might need to know underlies the complaint we see that a Book of Mormon writer cannot write everything. Jacob cannot write "a hundredth part of the proceedings of this people" (Jacob 3:13). Mormon also bemoans that he cannot write "the hundredth part" (W of M 1:5; Hel. 3:14; 3 Ne. 5:8, 26:6). While it is very true that any written text cannot tell everything that occurs, the complaints about the efficacy of writing place these sentiments in a culture that is still heavily oral. (In the Bible it occurs only once, at Nehemiah 5:11, where the context is items to be restored and not information that cannot be written.[11])

During Moroni's day, Nephites apparently still considered their oral performance more powerful than the written record:

> And I said unto him: Lord, the Gentiles will mock at these things, because of our weakness in writing; for Lord thou hast made us mighty in word by faith, but thou hast not made us mighty in writing; for thou hast made all this people that they could speak much, because of the Holy Ghost which thou hast given them;
>
> And thou hast made us that we could write but little, because of the awkwardness of our hands. Behold, thou hast not made us mighty in writing like unto the brother of Jared, for thou madest him that the things which he wrote were mighty even as thou art, unto the overpowering of man to read them. (Ether 12:23–24)

Reading Moroni's declaration as an indication of the primacy of oral communication might be strengthened by the Nephite prophecy of Joseph Smith's role, which declares that for Joseph it will be the text rather than the oral communication that is more spiritually powerful:

> And the Lord hath said: I will raise up a Moses; and I will give power unto him in a rod; and I will give judgment unto him in writing. Yet I will not loose his tongue, that he shall speak much, for I will not make him mighty in speaking. But I will write unto him my law, by the finger of mine own hand; and I will make a spokesman for him. (2 Ne. 3:17)

Nephi$_1$'s vision of the future prophecies is an inversion of his contemporary expectations. Nephi$_1$ was mighty in speaking but weak in writing.

---

10. Walter J. Ong, *Orality and Literacy*, 100.

11. "Restore, I pray you, to them, even this day, their lands, their vineyards, their oliveyards, and their houses, also the hundredth *part* of the money, and of the corn, the wine, and the oil, that ye exact of them" (Neh. 5:11).

The one who would come would not be important for his speaking but rather for what was written.

It is not surprising to discover elements of orality in written culture. There is no firm dividing line between oral cultures and literate ones. Orality and literacy can, and do, co-exist and co-evolve.[12] Rosalind Thomas notes, "The historian Herodotus is also analysed as an 'oral writer' on the grounds of his style. Fluent and leisurely, it has certain archaic features (like ring composition [another term for chiasmus]) which some have seen as specifically 'oral.'"[13] She concludes, "But what seems to deserve more critical questioning is whether these stylistic features can simply be attributed to 'orality,' the 'oral context,' the prevalence of performance—all fairly vague terms—or to the literary and stylistic tradition then dominant."[14]

There are two things to be noted in the oral elements of the Book of Mormon discussed below. First, although many of these oral elements are found in the Bible, they are not exclusively Hebrew.[15] Second, the persistence of those forms required a continued emphasis and appreciation of them. Moroni wrote around a thousand years after Nephi$_1$. A thousand years is a long time to preserve a tradition if it is no longer valued. We continue to see orally influenced techniques throughout the Book of Mormon because orality continued to be a dominant cultural force tying the text to those forms, rather than evolving away from them as modern literature has done.

Evidence of Memorized Texts

One of the effects of a reliance on texts is that there is less stress on memory. Referring to a text takes the place of consulting memory.[16] The ability to consult libraries not only frees memory, it provides access to even more information than one person could remember. As memory is off-loaded onto a written medium, one need no longer remember *what* if

---

12. Cynthia L. Miller-Naudé and Jacobus A. Naudé, "The Intersection of Orality and Style in Biblical Hebrew: Metapragmatic Representations of Dialogue in Genesis 34," 60. Also Paul S. Evans, "Creating a New 'Great Divide': The Exoticization of Ancient Culture in Some Recent Applications of Orality Studies to the Bible," 751–53.

13. Rosalind Thomas, *Literacy and Orality in Ancient Greece*, 102.

14. Thomas, 102.

15. Robert F. Smith, *Egyptianisms in the Book of Mormon and Other Studies*, 76.

16. Raymond F. Person, Jr., "The Role of Memory in the Tradition Represented by the Deuteronomic History and the Book of Chronicles," 348.

one can remember *where*. (For this same reason it is not uncommon for a person today to not know the phone number of their spouse, as they just need to know it is on the contact list of their smart phone.)

According to Rosalind Thomas, for cultures that were literate but heavily oral, "the written word was more often used in the service of the spoken."[17] For example, there was an "immense importance of memorization and the trained memory to the learned and literate in the Middle Ages; memorization was not made redundant by the presence of books, but on the contrary, books were regarded as only one way to remember and therefore to retain knowledge."[18] It was the same for Hebrew texts.[19]

The Book of Mormon does not explicitly speak of memorized scriptures. It simply records instances where scripture is quoted where it would be highly unusual (if not impossible) for a physical written text to have been consulted. As translator, Joseph Smith's cultural assumption that a text would be *read* tends to camouflage some of these occasions.

When Aaron, one of the sons of Mosiah$_2$, is preaching before the king of the Lamanites, Mormon records:

> And it came to pass that when Aaron saw that the king would believe his words, he began from the creation of Adam, *reading the scriptures unto the king*—how God created man after his own image, and that God gave him commandments, and that because of transgression, man had fallen.
>
> And Aaron did expound unto him the scriptures from the creation of Adam, laying the fall of man before him, and their carnal state and also the plan of redemption, which was prepared from the foundation of the world, through Christ, for all whosoever would believe on his name. (Alma 22:12–13)

Aaron is relating scriptural stories from the brass plates. He certainly doesn't have the brass plates with him. Even carrying a perishable copy of the brass plates' text would constitute a rather large volume of material. It is also highly doubtful that he is reading from the Lamanite king's copy (in the unlikely case he had one). Indeed, the whole point is that this is new information for the king. Aaron is likely "reading" from memory.

This same issue occurs with Abinadi, who was apprehended in a public place and brought before King Noah's court, consisting of the king and his priest-advisors. While interrogating Abinadi the priests attempted to

---

17. Thomas, *Literacy and Orality in Ancient Greece*, 4.

18. Thomas, 23.

19. "Given the rather awkward nature of using the scrolls of lengthy Hebrew biblical texts for reading, memorization became a very important practice of the literate religious elite." Wendland, "Orality and its Implications," 40.

find fault in Abinadi's understanding of scripture and therefore pose questions of exegesis to him. Abinadi stood before the court and presented his defense. At one point, he said: "And now I *read* unto you the remainder of the commandments of God, for I perceive that they are not written in your hearts; I perceive that ye have studied and taught iniquity the most part of your lives" (Mosiah 13:11).

As with Aaron before the king of the Lamanites, it highly unlikely that Abinadi had a scriptural text before him, even though these priests certainly had access to a copy of the scriptures and had themselves read and studied them. Nevertheless, Abinadi indicated that he would "read." In this case if nothing else, it is a beautiful turn of the phrase because his "reading" of the commandments contrasts with an inability of Noah's priests to "read" because they did not have the scriptures "written in your hearts."

Karl van der Toorn reminds us that in biblical culture "the scroll served as a deposit box for the text; for daily use, people consulted their memory."[20] Even though Nephite scriptures clearly existed in a written form, and even though Aaron and Abinadi probably could read them in the written form, their typical use of the scriptures would have relied upon memory. Aaron and Abinadi were "reading" the scriptures that had already been "written in their hearts."

Discourse as Retention of Oral Sensibilities

In societies without written texts, complex arguments were often worked out in dialogue, with another person being required to assist in remembering and developing a complex theme. According to Robert Alter,

> A general trait of biblical narrative [is] the primacy of dialogue . . . so pronounced that many pieces of third-person narration prove on inspection to be dialogue-bound, verbally mirroring elements of dialogue that precede them or that they introduce. Narration is thus often relegated to the role of confirming assertions made in dialogue—occasionally . . . with an explanatory gloss.[21]

Walter Ong explains one of the reasons for the dependence upon dialogue:

> In the total absence of any writing, there is nothing outside the thinker, no text, to enable him or her to produce the same line of thought again or even to verify whether he or she has done so or not. *Aides-mémoire* such as notched sticks or a series of carefully arranged objects will not of themselves retrieve a complicated series of assertions. How, in fact, could lengthy, analytic solution ever be assembled in the first place? An interlocutor is virtually

---

20. Karel Van der Toorn, *Scribal Culture and the Making of the Hebrew Bible*, 23.
21. Robert Alter, *The Art of Biblical Narrative*, 81–82.

essential: it is hard to talk to yourself for hours on end. Sustained thought in an oral culture is tied to communication.[22]

There is an interesting difference between doctrinal exposition in Nephi$_1$ and Jacob and in Mormon's later writings. Both Nephi$_1$ and Jacob cite scripture and then provide explanations. Mormon, however, does not cite scripture (the brass plates). Instead, what he provides is narrative. When Mormon wants to teach a doctrinal point, he either provides a sermon or (as seen with Alma$_2$ and Amulek in Ammonihah) presents a dialogue that contains the doctrinal explanation.[23]

The influence of the dialogue form is so strong that even thoughts are expressed in speech as a quoted monologue.[24] Our modern habit of silent, internal prayer might see Nephi$_3$'s prayer as an internal monologue. It was not. It was said aloud and witnessed by passersby:

> And it came to pass that in this year Nephi did cry unto the Lord, saying:
>
> O Lord, do not suffer that this people shall be destroyed by the sword; but O Lord, rather let there be a famine in the land, to stir them up in remembrance of the Lord their God, and perhaps they will repent and turn unto thee.
>
> And it came to pass that the judges did say unto Nephi, according to the words which had been desired. And it came to pass that when Nephi saw that the people had repented and did humble themselves in sackcloth, he cried again unto the Lord, saying:
>
> O Lord, behold this people repenteth; and they have swept away the band of Gadianton from amongst them insomuch that they have become extinct, and they have concealed their secret plans in the earth.
>
> Now, O Lord, because of this their humility wilt thou turn away thine anger, and let thine anger be appeased in the destruction of those wicked men whom thou hast already destroyed.
>
> O Lord, wilt thou turn away thine anger, yea, thy fierce anger, and cause that this famine may cease in this land.
>
> O Lord, wilt thou hearken unto me, and cause that it may be done according to my words, and send forth rain upon the face of the earth, that she may bring forth her fruit, and her grain in the season of grain.

---

22. Ong, *Orality and Literacy*, 34.

23. The fact that Mormon represents more of an orally influenced written text, where Nephi$_1$ and Jacob provide a more textually based exposition, is probably related to Nephi$_1$ and Jacob being closer to the Judahite scribal tradition. Mormon lived about a thousand years later and that method of textual exposition may not have survived on the large plates, which were more dedicated to the political sphere.

24. Alter, *Art of Biblical Narrative*, 84.

> O Lord, thou didst hearken unto my words when I said, Let there be a famine, that the pestilence of the sword might cease; and I know that thou wilt, even at this time, hearken unto my words, for thou saidst that: If this people repent I will spare them.
>
> Yea, O Lord, and thou seest that they have repented, because of the famine and the pestilence and destruction which has come unto them.
>
> And now, O Lord, wilt thou turn away thine anger, and try again if they will serve thee? And if so, O Lord, thou canst bless them according to thy words which thou hast said. (Hel. 11:3–4, 9–16)

When Nephi$_1$ had a vision, that vision encoded the information as a dialogue with an angel:

> And it came to pass that I saw the heavens open; and an angel came down and stood before me; and he said unto me: Nephi, what beholdest thou?
>
> And I said unto him: A virgin, most beautiful and fair above all other virgins.
>
> And he said unto me: Knowest thou the condescension of God?
>
> And I said unto him: I know that he loveth his children; nevertheless, I do not know the meaning of all things.
>
> And he said unto me: Behold, the virgin whom thou seest is the mother of the Son of God, after the manner of the flesh. (1 Ne. 11:14–18)

This is a short sample of an instructive dialogue that continues for much longer in that chapter. It might be argued that this text is in dialogue because that is just the way it happened. However, the contrast between Nephi$_1$'s recounting of his father's dream strongly points to the literary effect of the dialogue. Nephi$_1$ could have simply described what he saw. Indeed, that is what he does with his father's vision. Nephi$_1$'s recounting of his father's dream mentions a guide (1 Ne. 6:7), but Nephi$_1$ only has Lehi describing what he sees. Other than the initial invitation to follow, the messenger does not speak. It is not a conversation. Nephi$_1$'s narrative intent emphasizes his own story, using his father as a launching point. When the emphasis is more focused on Nephi$_1$'s own vision, he elects to instead record it as a dialogue. Those are the conditions in which an orally influenced society might turn to dialogue.

The connection between orally influenced texts and dialogue may reach further than the evidence from the Bible. Maya literature shows a continuation from glyphic records to modern times where the primary means of reproducing that literature is oral. Allen J. Christenson found that one marker of orality (chiasmus, discussed below) is linked to dialogue:

Surprisingly, the most important characteristic of the texts that contain chiasms seems to be the presence of dialogue. Without exception, all of the texts that utilized chiasmus also included passages of dialogue. Frequently, the dialogue was itself arranged as a chiasm. . . . With only one exception, the texts that do not contain chiasms also do not contain passages of dialogue.[25]

The example of the Maya should not be seen as suggesting that they learned the technique from the Nephites or that the Nephites learned it from the Maya. The importance is that it existed and continued to be valued in the Maya culture. That places the concept in the plausible cultural context of the Nephites and provides the environment in which that technique would continue to be valued.

Redundancy in Orality

An element of orality that is present in biblical literature is repetition. Jack R. Lundbom notes that "the importance of repetition in Hebrew rhetoric can hardly be overstated. Repetitions express the superlative ('holy, holy, holy' in Isa. 6.3), provide emphasis (*epanalepsis*), give structure to psalms, prophetic oracles, and other compositions."[26]

The basic reason has to do with the stress oral production places on the memory. Walter Ong explains:

> The public speaker's need to keep going while he is running through his mind what to say next also encourages redundancy. In oral delivery, though a pause may be effect, hesitation is always disabling. Hence it is better to repeat something, artfully if possible, rather than simply to stop speaking while fishing for the next idea. Oral cultures encourage fluence, fulsomeness, volubility. Rhetoricians were to call this *copia*. They continued to encourage it, by a kind of oversight, when they had modulated rhetoric from an art of public speaking to an art of writing. Early written texts, through the Middle Ages and the Renaissance, are often bloated with 'amplification,' annoyingly redundant by modern standards.[27]

Despite the difficulties of engraving a text on metal plates, the Book of Mormon displays significant repetition and redundancy.[28] For example, consider the following italicized repetitions from 1 Nephi:

---

25. Christenson, "Use of Chiasmus," 332.
26. Jack R. Lundbom, *Biblical Rhetoric and Rhetorical Criticism*, 4.
27. Ong, *Orality and Literacy*, 40–41.
28. "The Book of Mormon contains numerous examples of topic development through repetition." Eggington, *Weakness in Writing*, 13.

And it came to pass that he returned to his own house at Jerusalem; and he cast himself upon his bed, *being overcome with the Spirit* and the things which he had seen.

And *being thus overcome with the Spirit*, he was carried away in a vision, even that he saw the heavens open, and he thought he saw God sitting upon his throne, surrounded with numberless concourses of angels in the attitude of singing and praising their God. (1:7–8)

And it came to pass that he called the name of the river, Laman, and *it emptied into the Red Sea;* and the valley was in the borders near the mouth thereof.

And when my father saw that the waters of the river *emptied into the fountain of the Red Sea*, he spake unto Laman, saying: O that thou mightest be like unto this river, continually running into the fountain of all righteousness! (2:8–9)

And I, Nephi, and my brethren took our journey in the wilderness, with our tents, to go *up to the land of Jerusalem*.

And it came to pass that when *we had gone up to the land of Jerusalem*, I and my brethren did consult one with another. (3:9–10)

Therefore I did obey the voice of the Spirit, and took Laban by the hair of the head, *and I smote off his head with his own sword*.

And after I had smitten off his head with his own sword, I took the garments of Laban and put them upon mine own body; yea, even every whit; and I did gird on his armor about my loins. (4:18–19)

And if it so be that we are faithful to him, we shall obtain the land of promise; and ye shall know at some future period that the word of the Lord shall *be fulfilled concerning the destruction of Jerusalem*; for all things which the Lord hath spoken *concerning the destruction of Jerusalem must be fulfilled*. (7:13)[29]

A triple repetition is seen in Helaman 10:2–3:

And it came to pass that Nephi went his way towards his own house, *pondering upon the things* which the Lord had shown unto him.

And it came to pass *as he was thus pondering*—being much cast down because of the wickedness of the people of the Nephites, their secret works of darkness, and their murderings, and their plunderings, and all manner of iniquities—and it came to pass *as he was thus pondering in his heart*, behold, a voice came unto him saying . . .

The repetition is not simply in the words; at times it may be used to structure the text. In the case of Nephi₁'s vision in 1 Nephi 11, the dialogue between the Spirit and Nephi₁ is characterized by the Spirit's

---

29. I have borrowed these examples from: Jeff Lindsay, "Why is the Book of Mormon so Wordy?"

repetitious questions that lead to the informative explication of the vision. At the beginning, the Spirit establishes *what* Nephi₁ wants. The question is repeated: "what desirest thou?"

> And the Spirit said unto me: Behold, *what desirest thou?* (v. 2)
>
> And he said unto me: *What desirest thou?* (v. 10)

When the information is given, the repeated phrase is "Look! And I looked."

> And it came to pass that the Spirit said unto me: *Look! And I looked* and beheld a tree; and it was like unto the tree which my father had seen; and the beauty thereof was far beyond, yea, exceeding of all beauty; and the whiteness thereof did exceed the whiteness of the driven snow. (v. 8)
>
> And it came to pass that he said unto me: *Look! And I looked* as if to look upon him, and I saw him not; for he had gone from before my presence. (v. 12)
>
> And after he had said these words, he said unto me: *Look! And I looked*, and I beheld the Son of God going forth among the children of men; and I saw many fall down at his feet and worship him. (v. 24)
>
> And it came to pass that the angel spake unto me again, saying: *Look! And I looked*, and I beheld the heavens open again, and I saw angels descending upon the children of men; and they did minister unto them.
>
> And he spake unto me again, saying: *Look! And I looked*, and I beheld the Lamb of God going forth among the children of men. And I beheld multitudes of people who were sick, and who were afflicted with all manner of diseases, and with devils and unclean spirits; and the angel spake and showed all these things unto me. And they were healed by the power of the Lamb of God; and the devils and the unclean spirits were cast out.
>
> And it came to pass that the angel spake unto me again, saying: *Look! And I looked* and beheld the Lamb of God, that he was taken by the people; yea, the Son of the everlasting God was judged of the world; and I saw and bear record. (vv. 30–32)

A similar repetition of phrases that bind concepts together can be seen in Jacob's sermon to the Nephites in 2 Nephi 9:30–54:

> But *wo unto* the rich, who are rich as to the things of the world. For because they are rich they despise the poor, and they persecute the meek, and their hearts are upon their treasures; wherefore, their treasure is their god. And behold, their treasure shall perish with them also.
>
> And *wo unto* the deaf that will not hear; for they shall perish.
>
> *Wo unto* the blind that will not see; for they shall perish also.
>
> *Wo unto* the uncircumcised of heart, for a knowledge of their iniquities shall smite them at the last day.

Wo unto the liar, for he shall be thrust down to hell.

Wo unto the murderer who deliberately killeth, for he shall die.

Wo unto them who commit whoredoms, for they shall be thrust down to hell.

Yea, *wo unto* those that worship idols, for the devil of all devils delighteth in them.

And, in fine, wo unto all those who die in their sins; for they shall return to God, and behold his face, and remain in their sins.

O, my beloved brethren, remember the awfulness in transgressing against that Holy God, and also the awfulness of yielding to the enticings of that cunning one. Remember, to be carnally-minded is death, and to be spiritually-minded is life eternal.

O, my beloved brethren, give ear to my words. Remember the greatness of the Holy One of Israel. Do not say that I have spoken hard things against you; for if ye do, ye will revile against the truth; for I have spoken the words of your Maker. I know that the words of truth are hard against all uncleanness; but the righteous fear them not, for they love the truth and are not shaken.

O then, my beloved brethren, come unto the Lord, the Holy One. Remember that his paths are righteous. Behold, the way for man is narrow, but it lieth in a straight course before him, and the keeper of the gate is the Holy One of Israel; and he employeth no servant there; and there is none other way save it be by the gate; for he cannot be deceived, for the Lord God is his name. And whoso knocketh, to him will he open; and the wise, and the learned, and they that are rich, who are puffed up because of their learning, and their wisdom, and their riches—yea, they are they whom he despiseth; and save they shall cast these things away, and consider themselves fools before God, and come down in the depths of humility, he will not open unto them. But the things of the wise and the prudent shall be hid from them forever—yea, that happiness which is prepared for the saints.

O, my beloved brethren, remember my words. Behold, I take off my garments, and I shake them before you; I pray the God of my salvation that he view me with his all-searching eye; wherefore, ye shall know at the last day, when all men shall be judged of their works, that the God of Israel did witness that I shook your iniquities from my soul, and that I stand with brightness before him, and am rid of your blood.

O, my beloved brethren, turn away from your sins; shake off the chains of him that would bind you fast; come unto that God who is the rock of your salvation. Prepare your souls for that glorious day when justice shall be administered unto the righteous, even the day of judgment, that ye may not shrink with awful fear; that ye may not remember your awful guilt in perfectness, and be constrained to exclaim: Holy, holy are thy judgments, O Lord God Almighty—but I know my guilt; I transgressed thy law, and my transgressions are mine; and the devil hath obtained me, that I am a prey to his awful misery.

But behold, my brethren, is it expedient that I should awake you to an awful reality of these things? Would I harrow up your souls if your minds were pure? Would I be plain unto you according to the plainness of the truth if ye were freed from sin? Behold, if ye were holy I would speak unto you of holiness; but as ye are not holy, and ye look upon me as a teacher, it must needs be expedient that I teach you the consequences of sin. Behold, my soul abhorreth sin, and my heart delighteth in righteousness; and I will praise the holy name of my God.

Come, my brethren, every one that thirsteth, come ye to the waters; and he that hath no money, come buy and eat; yea, come buy wine and milk without money and without price. Wherefore, do not spend money for that which is of no worth, nor your labor for that which cannot satisfy. Hearken diligently unto me, and remember the words which I have spoken; and come unto the Holy One of Israel, and feast upon that which perisheth not, neither can be corrupted, and let your soul delight in fatness.

Behold, my beloved brethren, remember the words of your God; pray unto him continually by day, and give thanks unto his holy name by night. Let your hearts rejoice. And behold how great the covenants of the Lord, and how great his condescensions unto the children of men; and because of his greatness, and his grace and mercy, he has promised unto us that our seed shall not utterly be destroyed, according to the flesh, but that he would preserve them; and in future generations they shall become a righteous branch unto the house of Israel.

And now, my brethren, I would speak unto you more; but on the morrow I will declare unto you the remainder of my words. Amen.

That is a lot of repetition, and in a modern text it might be seen as redundant. In the Book of Mormon it is an example of intentional parallelisms for literary purposes.

Leitwort

A special case of repetition that serves the same function in oral literature is *leitwort* (leading word), the use of a particular word that is intentionally replicated to enrich the experience of the reader.[30] Nevertheless, it must be noted that not all word repetitions will be *leitworter* because the nature of the text or subject matter might have a certain word appear more than once.[31] There are, however, multiple passages in the Book of

---

30. Racheli Moskowitz, Moriyah Schick, Joshua Waxman, "*Leitwort* Detection, Quantification and Discernment," 173.

31. Moskowitz, Schick, and Waxman, 173.

Mormon where the repetition is sufficiently numerous and meaningful that it can be seen as such.

For example, Ronald D. Anderson has pointed out the extensive use of "remember" in Helaman$_2$'s discourse to his sons Nephi$_2$ and Lehi$_2$ in Helaman 5.[32] Notice how the term is invoked fifteen times to emphasize to the readers the importance of consciously retaining God in our hearts and minds:

> For *they remembered the words* which their father Helaman spake unto them. And these are the words which he spake:
>
> Behold, my sons, I desire that ye should *remember* to keep the commandments of God; and I would that ye should declare unto the people these words. Behold, I have given unto you the names of our first parents who came out of the land of Jerusalem; and this I have done that when you *remember* your names ye may *remember* them; and when ye *remember* them ye may *remember* their works; and when ye *remember* their works ye may know how that it is said, and also written, that they were good.
>
> Therefore, my sons, I would that ye should do that which is good, that it may be said of you, and also written, even as it has been said and written of them.
>
> And now my sons, behold I have somewhat more to desire of you, which desire is, that ye may not do these things that ye may boast, but that ye may do these things to lay up for yourselves a treasure in heaven, yea, which is eternal, and which fadeth not away; yea, that ye may have that precious gift of eternal life, which we have reason to suppose hath been given to our fathers.
>
> O *remember, remember*, my sons, the words which king Benjamin spake unto his people; yea, *remember* that there is no other way nor means whereby man can be saved, only through the atoning blood of Jesus Christ, who shall come; yea, *remember* that he cometh to redeem the world.
>
> And *remember* also the words which Amulek spake unto Zeezrom, in the city of Ammonihah; for he said unto him that the Lord surely should come to redeem his people, but that he should not come to redeem them in their sins, but to redeem them from their sins.
>
> And he hath power given unto him from the Father to redeem them from their sins because of repentance; therefore he hath sent his angels to declare the tidings of the conditions of repentance, which bringeth unto the power of the Redeemer, unto the salvation of their souls.
>
> And now, my sons, *remember, remember* that it is upon the rock of our Redeemer, who is Christ, the Son of God, that ye must build your foundation; that when the devil shall send forth his mighty winds, yea, his shafts in

---

32. Ronald D. Anderson, "Leitworter in Helaman and 3 Nephi," 242.

the whirlwind, yea, when all his hail and his mighty storm shall beat upon you, it shall have no power over you to drag you down to the gulf of misery and endless wo, because of the rock upon which ye are built, which is a sure foundation, a foundation whereon if men build they cannot fall.

And it came to pass that these were the words which Helaman taught to his sons; yea, he did teach them many things which are not written, and also many things which are written.

And they did remember his words; and therefore they went forth, keeping the commandments of God, to teach the word of God among all the people of Nephi, beginning at the city Bountiful. (vv. 5–15)

The word "remember" serves as the *leitwort* throughout Helaman$_2$'s discourse. In these verses, he intentionally emphasizes the word by repeating it a total of thirteen times, with Mormon contextually bookending the discourse as words *remembered* by Nephi$_2$ and Lehi$_2$. As impressive as the repetition is through the whole set of verses, it is verses 6 and 7 that are highly structured as well as emphasize "remember" as a *leitwort*:

> Behold, my sons,
>   I desire that ye should remember to keep the commandments of God;
>   and I would that ye should declare unto the people these words.
>   Behold, I have given unto you the names of our first parents who came out of the land of Jerusalem;
>   and this I have done that when you *remember your names* ye *may remember them*;
>   and *when ye remember them* ye may *remember their works*
>   and when ye *remember their works* ye may know
>   how that it is said, and also written, *that they were good*.
>   Therefore, my sons, *I would that ye should do that which is good*,
>   that it may be *said of you, and also written*,
>   even as it has been *said and written of them*.

This is an intricate set of parallels that create a moving theme. The use of "remember" ties the theme together as it builds and amplifies from remembering to doing good. The artistry here may build upon themes used in orality but best reflect an editor having worked these words before recording them.

Another important example of a *leitwort* is seen in Nephi$_1$'s use of "murmur" in several texts. Nephi$_1$ often undergirded his themes with references to events in the brass plates, and the whole journey of his family from Jerusalem to the New World can be seen as echoing the Exodus.[33]

---

33. See S. Kent Brown, "The Exodus Pattern in the Book of Mormon," 111–26; Terrence L. Szink, "Nephi and the Exodus," 39–42; Thomas R. Valletta,

One of the ways Nephi₁ develops that connection is by using "murmur" to associate Laman and Lemuel with wayward Israel. The model of Israel is found in the book of Exodus:

> And in the morning, then ye shall see the glory of the Lord; for that he heareth your *murmurings* against the Lord: and what are we, that ye *murmur* against us?
>
> And Moses said, This shall be, when the Lord shall give you in the evening flesh to eat, and in the morning bread to the full; for that the Lord heareth your *murmurings* which ye *murmur* against him: and what are we? your *murmurings* are not against us, but against the Lord. (Ex. 16:7–8)

Nephi₁ intentionally invokes the *leitwort* "murmur," and he likely expects that his readers will understand it in the context of the Exodus:

> Now this he spake because of the stiffneckedness of Laman and Lemuel; for behold they did *murmur* in many things against their father, because he was a visionary man, and had led them out of the land of Jerusalem, to leave the land of their inheritance, and their gold, and their silver, and their precious things, to perish in the wilderness. And this they said he had done because of the foolish imaginations of his heart.
>
> And thus Laman and Lemuel, being the eldest, did *murmur* against their father. And they did *murmur* because they knew not the dealings of that God who had created them. (1 Ne. 2:11–12)

> And now, behold thy brothers *murmur*, saying it is a hard thing which I have required of them; but behold I have not required it of them, but it is a commandment of the Lord. (3:5)

> And after the angel had departed, Laman and Lemuel again began to *murmur*, saying: How is it possible that the Lord will deliver Laban into our hands? Behold, he is a mighty man, and he can command fifty, yea, even he can slay fifty; then why not us? (3:31)

> Now when I had spoken these words, they were yet wroth, and did still continue to *murmur*; nevertheless they did follow me up until we came without the walls of Jerusalem. (4:4)

> And now my brethren, if ye were righteous and were willing to hearken to the truth, and give heed unto it, that ye might walk uprightly before God, then ye would not *murmur* because of the truth, and say: Thou speakest hard things against us. (16:3)

> And it came to pass that Laman and Lemuel and the sons of Ishmael did begin to *murmur* exceedingly, because of their sufferings and afflictions in the wilderness; and also my father began to murmur against the Lord his God;

"The Exodus: Prophetic Type and the Plan of Redemption," 178–90.

yea, and they were all exceedingly sorrowful, even that they did *murmur* against the Lord. (16:20)

And it came to pass that the daughters of Ishmael did mourn exceedingly, because of the loss of their father, and because of their afflictions in the wilderness; and they did *murmur* against my father, because he had brought them out of the land of Jerusalem, saying: Our father is dead; yea, and we have wandered much in the wilderness, and we have suffered much affliction, hunger, thirst, and fatigue; and after all these sufferings we must perish in the wilderness with hunger.

And thus they did *murmur* against my father, and also against me; and they were desirous to return again to Jerusalem. (16:35–36)

And when my brethren saw that I was about to build a ship, they began to *murmur* against me, saying: Our brother is a fool, for he thinketh that he can build a ship; yea, and he also thinketh that he can cross these great waters. (17:17)

And we know that the people who were in the land of Jerusalem were a righteous people; for they kept the statutes and judgments of the Lord, and all his commandments, according to the law of Moses; wherefore, we know that they are a righteous people; and our father hath judged them, and hath led us away because we would hearken unto his words; yea, and our brother is like unto him. And after this manner of language did my brethren *murmur* and complain against us. (17:22)

And it came to pass that I, Nephi, said unto them that they should *murmur* no more against their father; neither should they withhold their labor from me, for God had commanded me that I should build a ship. (17:49)

Nevertheless, I did look unto my God, and I did praise him all the day long; and I did not *murmur* against the Lord because of mine afflictions. (18:16)

Yea, they did *murmur* against me, saying: Our younger brother thinks to rule over us; and we have had much trial because of him; wherefore, now let us slay him, that we may not be afflicted more because of his words. For behold, we will not have him to be our ruler; for it belongs unto us, who are the elder brethren, to rule over this people. (2 Ne. 5:3)

Outside of these, "murmur" appears only seven other times in the entire Book of Mormon, but each of those are independent of the other and do not function as a *leitwort*.[34]

---

34. Mosiah 21:6; 27:1; Alma 17:28; 19:19; 58:35; 60:4; 3 Nephi 27:4.

Chiasmus

The discussion of parallelisms in the Book of Mormon should begin with the recognition that chiasmus is a technique that appears in many oral cultures, and afterward in their literary traditions. Although such parallelisms are an aspect of the Hebrew Bible, they are not unique to the Hebrew Bible and are not, in and of themselves, a demonstration that there was an inherently Hebrew origin to the various parallel forms.[35]

Walter Ong describes the reasons we see patterning in so many texts from so many originally oral cultures:

> In a primary oral culture, to solve effectively the problem of retaining and retrieving carefully articulated thought, you have to do your thinking in mnemonic patterns, shaped for ready oral recurrence. Your thought must come into being in heavily rhythmic, balanced patterns, in repetitions or antitheses, in alliterations and assonances, in epithetic and other formulary expressions, in standard thematic settings (the assembly, the meal, the duel, the hero's "helper," and so on), in proverbs which are constantly heard by everyone so that they come to mind readily and which themselves are patterned for retention and ready recall, or in other mnemonic forms. Serious thought is intertwined with memory systems.[36]

One of those memory systems that appears in multiple cultures is chiasmus—a form of inverted parallel that takes one of two simplified forms: ABBA, or ABCBA. When John W. Welch announced the discovery of chiasmus in the Book of Mormon, he concluded:

> This article has attempted to introduce one concept of formal analysis into Book of Mormon studies. The form which has proven particularly useful has been chiasmus, a basic element of ancient Hebrews. Even though all knowledge of this form lay dormant for centuries, it was rediscovered in the nineteenth century when formal criticism became popular. But by that time the Book of Mormon had long been in print. Since the Book of Mormon

---

35. "The significant religious books written using Hebrew forms are the Old Testament and the Book of Mormon." Hugh W. Pinnock, "Finding Biblical Hebrew and Other Ancient Literary Forms in the Book of Mormon," 2. Similarly, Donald Parry writes: "Because the Book of Mormon emerged from the world of the Old Testament and some form of Hebrew was used by the Nephites, it makes sense that, at least in part, the book would read like and ancient Hebrew book—even in English translation." *Preserved in Translation: Hebrew and Other Ancient Literary Forms in the Book of Mormon*, xvii.

36. Ong, *Orality and Literacy*, 34.

contains numerous chiasms, it thus becomes logical to consider the book a product of the ancient world and to judge its literary qualities accordingly.[37]

Following John W. Welch's lead, Donald W. Parry and Hugh W. Pinnock have elaborated chiastic structures found in the Book of Mormon. One such example is from Mosiah 2:5–6:

A And it came to pass that when they came up to the *temple*,
  B they *pitched their tents* round about,
    C every man according to his *family*,
      D consisting of his wife, and his *sons*, and his *daughters*,
      D and their *sons*, and their *daughters*, from the eldest down to the youngest,
    C every *family* being separate one from another.
  B And they *pitched their tents*
A round about the *temple*.[38]

Although popularized as a possible proof of the antiquity of the Book of Mormon, chiasms are now recognized in many languages and literatures.[39] Allen J. Christenson found examples of chiasms in Maya literature and suggested that it might indicate origins of those texts in oral literature.[40] The importance of chiasmus in the Book of Mormon is not so much its ability to demonstrate that the Book of Mormon is ancient, but rather to show that the Book of Mormon behaves like a text from antiquity that retained oral elements. Although the ultimate origin of chiasmus in Nephite literature may have been the Old World, only the continued appreciation of the form in the New World would have preserved the form from Nephi$_1$'s time to Mormon's.

Literary Parallelisms

In addition to the chiastic reversed parallels, the Book of Mormon uses a larger number of simpler parallels. Donald W. Parry notes that the most common literary form in the Bible is parallelism. As he defines it, "a parallelism generally consists of two lines, with each line having features or expressions that parallel or correspond with the other."[41] He notes some of the parallels found in the Book of Mormon:

---

37. John W. Welch, "Chiasmus in the Book of Mormon," 83.
38. Parry, *Preserved in Translation*, 4.
39. Parry, 5, quoting David Noel Freedman.
40. Christenson, "Use of Chiasmus," 318.
41. Parry, *Preserved in Translation*, 13.

> Pray unto him continually by day,
> And give thanks unto his holy name by night. (2 Ne. 9:52)
>
> For their works were works of darkness,
> And their doings were doings of abominations. (2 Ne. 25:2)
>
> Yea, my heart sorroweth because of my flesh;
> My soul grieveth because of mine iniquities. (2 Ne. 4:17)[42]

Sometimes, the parallel lines reverse the idea:

> Ye are swift to do iniquity
> But slow to remember the Lord your God. (1 Ne. 17:45)
>
> Remember, to be carnally-minded is death,
> And to be| spiritually-minded is life eternal. (2 Ne. 9:39)
>
> And I would not that ye think that I know of myself—
> Not of the temporal but of the spiritual,
> Not of the carnal mind but of God. (Alma 36:4)[43]

A fascinating case of parallelisms is the set of verses in 2 Nephi 4 commonly referred to as the Psalm of Nephi, which Richard Dilworth Rust says has "the dominant poetic feature of . . . parallelism."[44] This long set of poetic parallelisms was not part of Nephi$_1$'s planned text.[45] The majority of Nephi$_1$'s writing is narrative and reflective of the typical story-telling style; thus, we there find only brief and scattered parallelisms. However, in the case of the Psalm of Nephi, we see Nephi$_1$ departing from his planned text and intimately expressing himself on the plates, resulting in a more direct indication of his oral style committed to text. That orality is likely the reason that there is an abundance of parallelisms and an absence of any overall structure. This is spontaneous speech somehow recorded without losing that spontaneity.

The following reformatting of the Psalm of Nephi$_1$ highlights the literary parallels. At times, words in brackets add implied parallels that may have been explicit in the original but did not make it into the translation. Bolded type indicates recurring thematic words. These form a *leitmotif* throughout the poem. Italics indicate words forming the parallels in the same set of phrases. In order to flavor the scansion with a more ancient

---

42. Parry, 16.
43. Parry, 20.
44. Richard Dilworth Rust, "Poetry in the Book of Mormon," 101.
45. Brant A. Gardner, *Labor Diligently to Write: The Ancient Making of a Modern Book*, 237.

feeling, the name *Yahweh* (transliterated as *Jehovah* in the King James Bible) is used rather than the more oblique reference to "the Lord."

My **soul** *delighteth* in the scriptures, and
My **heart** *pondereth* them, and
[My heart/soul] *writeth* them for the learning and the profit of my children. Behold,
My **soul** *delighteth* in the things of Yahweh; and
My **heart** *pondereth* continually upon the things which I have seen and heard.

Nevertheless, notwithstanding the great goodness of Yahweh, in showing me his *great* and marvelous works,

My **heart** *exclaimeth*: O wretched man that I am! Yea,
My **heart** *sorroweth* because of my flesh;
My **soul** *grieveth* because of mine iniquities.

I am encompassed about, because of the temptations and the sins which do so easily beset me.
And when I desire to *rejoice*,
My **heart** *groaneth* because of my sins;

Nevertheless, I know in whom I have trusted.
My God hath been my support
[My God] hath *led me* through mine afflictions in the *wilderness*; and
[My God] hath *preserved me* upon the waters of the *great deep*.
[My God] hath *filled me with his love*, even unto the consuming of my flesh.
[My God] hath *confounded mine enemies*, unto the causing of them to quake before me. Behold,
[My God] hath heard my *cry by day*, and
[My God] hath given me knowledge by *visions in the nighttime* and
By *day* have I waxed bold in mighty prayer before him;

yea, my voice have I *sent up* on high;
and angels *came down* and ministered unto me.
And upon the wings of his *Spirit*
hath my *body* been carried away upon exceedingly high mountains.

And mine *eyes* have beheld great things, yea, even too great for man;
Therefore, I was bidden that I should not **write** them. O then,
If I have seen so great things,
If Yahweh in his condescension unto the children of men hath visited men in so much mercy,
Why should my **heart** *weep* and
[Why should] my **soul** *linger* in the valley of sorrow, and
[Why should] my **flesh** *waste away*, and
[Why should] my **strength** *slacken*,

Behold, my sons, I desire that ye should *remember* to keep the commandments of God; and I would that ye should declare unto the people these words. Behold, I have given unto you the names of our first parents who came out of the land of Jerusalem; and this I have done that when you *remember* your names ye may *remember* them; and when ye *remember* them ye may *remember* their works; and when ye *remember* their works ye may know *how that it is said, and also written*, that they were good.

In addition to the reference to what "is said," the word "remember" appears six times, and Helaman$_2$ uses that in conjunction with his sons' names to tie them to the deeds of those for whom they were named. We have both the repetition and recognition of a saying that point to an oral stylistic form.

Stereotyping

Just as repeated words could provide internal structures and learning through repetition, the Book of Mormon presents us with another typical ancient mode of expression: stereotypes. Michael Shermer defines a stereotype as "the tendency to assume that a member of a group will have certain characteristics believed to represent the group without having actual information about that particular member."[47] That is the simple expression of the meaning, but the function and use of stereotypes is more complex. Carol Tavris and Elliot Aronson explain what stereotypes do for us:

> Cognitive psychologists view stereotypes as energy-saving devices that allow us to make efficient decisions on the basis of past experiences; they help us quickly process new information, retrieve memories, identify real differences between groups, and predict, often with considerable accuracy, how others will behave or think. . . .
>
> That's the upside. The downside is that stereotypes flatten out differences within the category we are looking at and exaggerate differences between categories.[48]

The problem with stereotypes is that they are typically applied to the category of "not-us." It is typical that once we see ourselves as part of a group, we establish ill will towards those who are "other."[49] Once es-

---

47. Michael Shermer, *The Believing Brain:. From Ghosts and Gods to Politics and Conspiracies—How We Construct Beliefs and Reinforce Them as Truths*, 275.

48. Carol Tavris and Elliot Aronson, *Mistakes Were Made (But Not by Me): Why We Justify Foolish Beliefs, Bad Decisions, and Hurtful Acts*, 75.

49. Andrew Newberg and Mark Robert Waldman, *Born to Believe: God, Science, and the Origin of Ordinary and Extraordinary Beliefs*, 89.

tablished, stereotypes can remain stable over years.⁵⁰ The problem with persisting stereotypes is that they often hide incorrect information.⁵¹

The books of Nephi₁ are intent on establishing the categories of Nephite and Lamanite. It intentionally defines being Lamanite as "not-us." That *otherness* was expressed in judgmental terms early, and many of those stereotypes persist throughout the Book of Mormon. While stereotyping is clearly not unique to oral traditions, the differences among the otherwise similar Lamanite stereotype points to ideas that are passed on orally rather than a text that has been intentionally quoted. For example, note how Nephi₁'s description of the Lamanites is repeated generations later by his descendants:

> And because of their cursing which was upon them they did become an idle people, full of mischief and subtlety, and did seek in the wilderness for beasts of prey. (2 Ne. 5:24)

> Therefore it came to pass, that after we had dwelt in the land for the space of twelve years that king Laman began to grow uneasy, lest by any means my people should wax strong in the land, and that they could not overpower them and bring them into bondage.
>
> Now they were a lazy and an idolatrous people; therefore they were desirous to bring us into bondage, that they might glut themselves with the labors of our hands; yea, that they might feast themselves upon the flocks of our fields. (Mosiah 9:11–12)⁵²

> They were a wild, and ferocious, and a blood-thirsty people, believing in the tradition of their fathers, which is this—Believing that they were driven out of the land of Jerusalem because of the iniquities of their fathers, and that they were wronged in the wilderness by their brethren, and they were also wronged while crossing the sea. (Mosiah 10:12)

> And assuredly it was great, for they had undertaken to preach the word of God to a wild and a hardened and a ferocious people; a people who delighted in murdering the Nephites, and robbing and plundering them; and their hearts were set upon riches, or upon gold and silver, and precious stones; yet they sought to obtain these things by murdering and plundering, that they might not labor for them with their own hands. (Alma 17:14)

---

50. Jan Vansina, *Oral Tradition as History*, 21.
51. Vansina, 146. See also Tavris and Aronson, *Mistakes Were Made*, 83–84.
52. Note that this account of the Lamanites by Zeniff comes after him initially spying on the Lamanites and refusing to attack them after seeing "that which was good among them" (Mosiah 9:1).

> Now, the more idle part of the Lamanites lived in the wilderness, and dwelt in tents; and they were spread through the wilderness on the west, in the land of Nephi; yea, and also on the west of the land of Zarahemla, in the borders by the seashore, and on the west in the land of Nephi, in the place of their fathers' first inheritance, and thus bordering along by the seashore. (Alma 22:28)
>
> Now these dissenters, having the same instruction and the same information of the Nephites, yea, having been instructed in the same knowledge of the Lord, nevertheless, it is strange to relate, not long after their dissensions they became more hardened and impenitent, and more wild, wicked and ferocious than the Lamanites—drinking in with the traditions of the Lamanites; giving way to indolence, and all manner of lasciviousness; yea, entirely forgetting the Lord their God. (Alma 47:36)
>
> And they have been handed down from one generation to another by the Nephites, even until they have fallen into transgression and have been murdered, plundered, and hunted, and driven forth, and slain, and scattered upon the face of the earth, and mixed with the Lamanites until they are no more called the Nephites, becoming wicked, and wild, and ferocious, yea, even becoming Lamanites. (Hel. 3:16)

We even see the stereotype when missionaries go to the Lamanites to convert them:

> Now those priests who did go forth among the people did preach against all lyings, and deceivings, and envyings, and strifes, and malice, and revilings, and stealing, robbing, plundering, murdering, committing adultery, and all manner of lasciviousness, crying that these things ought not so to be. (Alma 16:18)
>
> And assuredly it was great, for they had undertaken to preach the word of God to a wild and a hardened and a ferocious people; a people who delighted in murdering the Nephites, and robbing and plundering them; and their hearts were set upon riches, or upon gold and silver, and precious stones; yet they sought to obtain these things by murdering and plundering, that they might not labor for them with their own hands.
>
> Thus they were a very indolent people, many of whom did worship idols, and the curse of God had fallen upon them because of the traditions of their fathers; notwithstanding the promises of the Lord were extended unto them on the conditions of repentance. (Alma 17:14–15)

Even when the goal is to make the Lamanites into believing Nephites, the emphasis is on their otherness.

Of course, Joseph Smith's information environment also stereotyped Native Americans, and the Nephite stereotype is not dissimilar from Joseph's contemporary stereotyping. The reason for ascribing this to something ancient is that the evidence of the text belies the stereotype. When we get a glimpse of Lamanite culture during the sons of Mosiah$_2$'s journey to their lands, the Lamanite culture is large, complex, and utterly contradictory to the stereotype. Far from being uncivilized, they have a complex political structure with a hierarchy of kings, suggesting something even more sophisticated than anything described for the Nephites. We also see large building projects and at least the implications of formal ritual visits between kings. There is no evidence whatsoever of the uncivilized stereotype that persists throughout Nephite history.[53] If the modern stereotype had driven the textual descriptions of the Lamanites, we would expect the descriptions to support rather than contradict the stereotype. That contradiction is, however, consonant with an ancient stereotype that depicted experience belied.

Dyadic Pairs

There are two types of word pairs that are similar but distinct: dyadic pairs and diphrastic kennings. As with other types of parallelism, it is suggested that these dyadic pairs were part of oral performances that were then incorporated into written texts.[54]

Dyadic pairs are parallels where two words often appear as a set but do not appear to have any meaning beyond the paired words. After discussing dyadic pairs in the bible, Kevin L. Barney turned to the Book of Mormon:

> If the Book of Mormon had as a part of its origin the writings of a Hebrew-speaking people from preexilic Jerusalem, we might expect to find examples of word pairs within its pages. For although the Book of Mormon is predominantly a prose work, it does contain passages that may be classified

---

53. Brant A. Gardner, *Traditions of the Fathers: The Book of Mormon as History*, 157–58.

54. Kevin L. Barney, "Poetic Diction and Parallel Word Pairs in the Book of Mormon," 19. On the use of couplets among the Maya, Nicholas A. Hopkins and J. Kathryn Josserand write, "Perhaps the most common verbal device marking peak events is the couplet, a pair of lines that are sometimes identical and sometimes only structurally or semantically parallel. The couplet is the hallmark of forma speech in Mayan languages and is one of the distinctive features that distinguishes one genre of speech from another. Prayers, the most formal of the speech genres, may consist of nothing but couplets." Nicholas A. Hopkins and J. Kathryn Josserand, "The Narrative Structure of Chol Folktales, One Thousand Years of Literary Tradition," 28–29.

as poetry, as well as numerous isolated instances of parallelism of various types.[55]

Barney gives the example of the pairing of *anger/fierce anger:*

> except ye repent I will visit this people in mine *anger;*
> yea, and I will not turn my *fierce anger* away. (Alma 8:29)

> A I will visit them
>   B in my *anger,*
>   B yea, in my *fierce anger*
> A will I visit them. (Mosiah 12:1)

> A yea, he will visit you
>   B in his *anger,*
>   B and in his *fierce anger*
> A he will not turn away. (Alma 9:12)[56]

Alma 8:29 presents the basic pair. The first line gives a condition marked with *anger.* The second line is the consequence, with *fierce anger.* The fact that *fierce anger* is always the second element of the dyad points to the intensification in the repetition.

The next two examples (from Mosiah and Alma) are short chiasms. In the paired A lines of Mosiah 12:1, the lines are virtually the same. In the Alma 9:12 example, the paired A lines show a parallel concept in different words (visit/not turn away). In both cases, the B pairs serve to provide the intensifying impact by pairing *anger* with *fierce anger.*

A very poetic dyad is seen with *hear cries / answer prayers,* a pairing not found in the Bible.

> And God did *hear our cries and did answer our prayers*; and we did go forth in his might; yea, we did go forth against the Lamanites, and in one day and a night we did slay three thousand and forty-three; we did slay them even until we had driven them out of our land. (Mosiah 9:18)

> Nevertheless, after much tribulation, the Lord did *hear my cries, and did answer my prayers,* and has made me an instrument in his hands in bringing so many of you to a knowledge of his truth. (Mosiah 23:10)

> And not many days hence the Son of God shall come in his glory; and his glory shall be the glory of the Only Begotten of the Father, full of grace, equity, and truth, full of patience, mercy, and long-suffering, quick to *hear the cries of his people and to answer their prayers.* (Alma 9:26)

---

55. Barney, "Poetic Diction and Parallel Word Pairs," 23–24.
56. Barney, 33–34. I have moved Alma 8:29 to the first example rather than the second where Barney presented it.

Diphrastic Kennings

Kerry M. Hull defines the second type of paired words: "Diphrastic kenning [is] the pairing of two distinct elements to produce a metaphorical, more abstract third concept."[57] One such pairing in the Book of Mormon is *gold/silver*. The words typically appear in that order, and often as "gold and silver."[58] Although it is possible for gold and silver to appear as simply the metals themselves,[59] they typically have an additional metaphorical meaning of wealth.[60] For examples, in Jacob 1:11, Jacob says of his people, "Yea, and they also began to search much *gold and silver*, and began to be lifted up somewhat in pride"; Amulek is described as "having forsaken all his *gold, and his silver*, and his precious things" (Alma 15:11); and Nephi$_3$ laments, "O, how could you have forgotten your God in the very day that he has delivered you? But behold, it is to get gain, to be praised of men, yea, and that ye might get *gold and silver*. And ye have set your hearts upon the riches and the vain things of this world, for the which ye do murder, and plunder, and steal, and bear false witness against your neighbor, and do all manner of iniquity" (Hel. 7:20–21). In each, "gold and silver" are symbolic of wealth that come from and inspires unrighteousness.

---

57. Kerry M. Hull, "Poetic Tenacity: A Diachronic Study of Kennings in Mayan Languages," 73.

58. 1 Ne. 3:16, 13:7; Jacob 1:15; Mosiah 11:9, 22:12; Alma 15:16, 17:14; Hel. 7:21; 3 Ne. 24:3; 4 Ne. 1:46; Ether 10:12, 10:23.

59. In the following verses, it appears that gold, silver, and copper are mentioned in the context of creating the plates. Those metals are the ones combined to create *tumbaga*, which is suggested as the alloy used for the golden plates:

> And it came to pass that we did find upon the land of promise, as we journeyed in the wilderness, that there were beasts in the forests of every kind, both the cow and the ox, and the ass and the horse, and the goat and the wild goat, and all manner of wild animals, which were for the use of men. And we did find all manner of ore, both of gold, and of silver, and of copper.
>
> And it came to pass that the Lord commanded me, wherefore I did make plates of ore that I might engraven upon them the record of my people. And upon the plates which I made I did engraven the record of my father, and also our journeyings in the wilderness, and the prophecies of my father; and also many of mine own prophecies have I engraven upon them. (1 Ne. 18:25–19:1)

60. Parry, *Preserved in Translation*, 41–42, sees both *heart/soul* and *gold/silver* as simple dyadic pairs. I believe they are better understood as kennings.

Another pair is *heart/soul*, which is used to spiritually represent the whole person:

> Behold, my *soul* is rent with anguish because of you,
> and my *heart* is pained. (1 Ne. 17:47)

> And now that my *soul* might have joy in you,
> and that my *heart* might leave this world with gladness because of you. (2 Ne. 1:21)

A final example is one that is important in understanding Nephite political issues. The pair is *murder/plunder*, and it functions as a metaphorical description of wars to establish tribute in the Book of Mormon.[61] It is a pairing first seen in King Benjamin's discourse, telling his people what he had not made them do:

> Neither have I suffered that ye should be confined in dungeons, nor that ye should make slaves one of another, *nor that ye should murder, or plunder*, or steal, or commit adultery; nor even have I suffered that ye should commit any manner of wickedness, and have taught you that ye should keep the commandments of the Lord, in all things which he hath commanded you. (Mosiah 2:13)

The very idea that a king might be able to force or encourage someone to murder suggests that we are seeing a metaphorical meaning. That meaning is reinforced by other locations where we find the *murder/plunder* pair.

- The Lamanites are said to teach that their children "should hate [the Nephites], and that they *should murder them*, and that they should rob *and plunder them*, and do all they could to destroy them; therefore they have an eternal hatred towards the children of Nephi." (Mosiah 10:17)
- After his conversion, the king of the Lamanites sends a proclamation to his people. Among other things, "that they ought *not to murder, nor to plunder*." (Alma 23:3)
- One version of the Gadianton robbers found that "there was no way to that they could subsist save it were to *plunder* and rob and *murder*." (3 Ne. 4:5)

Of course, it is possible to read these terms separately, but they appear together with such frequency that they form some type of pairing. The identification as a diphrastic kenning comes from the fact that murdering is hardly advantageous to an entire people. The act of murdering itself

---

61. Gardner, *Traditions of the Fathers*, 237–38.

does not add to subsistence, but the concept of taking over territory by force does.

Such reading is enhanced by the assumption that the Book of Mormon took place in Mesoamerica, where diphrastic kennings were an element of Maya oral literature for centuries.[62] Once again, this does not suggest that there was any causal connection between the Book of Mormon and Maya literature. What it indicates is that these oral techniques continued to be present in the region that is argued to be the land in which the Nephite story took place. It is the continued appreciation of those features that suggests the reason that they would be seen throughout the long Nephite history.

---

62. Hull, "Poetic Tenacity."

Chapter Ten

Blocks of Time

Certain elements of time are tied to the physical world. Night and day are visible distinctions with connecting liminal periods. Seasons repeat but vary according to how closely a land is to the equator. The movement away from the equator turns two seasons (rainy and dry) into four (spring, summer, fall, winter). The visible movement of the sun along the horizon allows cultures to recognize a repetition and renewal of the sun that defines a year.

While modern cultures are most familiar with a solar year, historical Israel also used the shorter lunar year. It is that lunar calendar that arguably underlies the Nephite definition of a year. Randall P. Spackman lays out the problem encountered if we simply assume that a Nephite year consisted of a solar year:

> The descendants of Lehi counted precisely 600 years between his departure from Jerusalem and the time when they viewed the heavenly signs that immediately preceded and followed the Lord's birth (see 3 Nephi 1:1–22). If the calendar used to measure those years was a solar calendar, it would place the Lord's birth in A.D. 3 or 4 at the earliest. This seems contrary to scriptural and historical sources, which indicate that Jesus Christ was born in the spring of 5 B.C.[1]

He suggests that the most parsimonious explanation would be that the prophecy followed an Old World practice of using lunar years:

> If the Nephites measured the 600-year period preceding Christ's birth with a lunar calendar composed of twelve "moons," there is no discrepancy at all in the counting of 600 years. A twelve-moon calendar averages only 354.367 days per year, eleven days fewer than a solar calendar, which averages 365.2422 days per year. Between 597 B.C. and 5 etc., ample time existed for this lunar calendar to measure all 600 years.[2]

There is a second parallel possibility. From Mormon's perspective of nearly a thousand years of Nephite history in the Mesoamerica, the inherited Old World lunar calendar would likely have merged with a

---

1. Randall P. Spackman, "The Jewish/Nephite Lunar Calendar," 50.
2. Spackman, 51.

Mesoamerican calendar that bore similarities to the lunar calendar. John L. Sorenson suggests:

> Among the lowland Maya, whose calendar is the one we know best in southern Mesoamerica, at least three kinds of "years" were calculated: (1) the tzolkin or sacred year of 260 days (thirteen months of twenty days each), (2) the haab, which was 365 days long (eighteen months of twenty days each, plus a closing "month" of five "unlucky" days), (3) the tun of 360 days. The tun was used for most calendrical calculations. . . .
>
> The prophesied "six hundred years" in that reckoning would constitute precisely one and one half baktuns (thirty katuns), a neat total of 216,000 days. But this count of 600 tun "years" would be about 3,156 days shorter than the total using our sidereal year today (approximately 365 days, 6 hours, 9 minutes, and 9.54 seconds long). In other words, "600 years" by the Maya tun method of calculating time would turn out 8.64 years shorter than "600 years" in today's conventional sense. If we mark off 600 tun years from Zedekiah's first year, 597–596 B.C., 216,000 days brings us into the year overlapping 5–4 B.C., an acceptable date for Christ's birth.[3]

Regardless of the calendar used to calculate the fulfillment of this prophecy, Mormon's use of sets of years corresponds more to a Mesoamerican model than that of the Old World. Our modern world uses a base-10 mathematic system. We collect years into groups that reflect some multiple of 10. We mark 100 years and 1,000 years. Since those are larger numbers, we also mark half of those, placing importance on 50 (or 500) as a significant milestone. These number sets also get their own vocabulary. We have the terms *decade, century,* and *millennium* to describe the large conceptual units; these became the basis for other extended periods of time as well—such as *sesquicentennial* describing a period of 150 years.

Furthermore, these number sets develop a cultural meaning beyond simply counting the passage of time. For example, the conceptual units based on the decimal system led to the cultural importance of the year AD 2000, which triggered millennial expectations of some kind of end of the world at worst, or at least an end to anything depending upon computers.

Rather than a decimal system, the Book of Mormon more closely represents number sets that are important in a base-20 (vigesimal) system that underlay Mesoamerican math. One of the most important number sets in this system consisted of 400 years. For Maya scholars, the word for that number set is *baktun*, which has a conceptual impact analogous to our millennium. The word *katun* designates twenty years and has the

---

3. Sorenson, *An Ancient American Setting for The Book of Mormon,* 273.

conceptual impact of a *decade*. As with our base-10 system, divisions of those larger-named units were also significant. Thus, in base-10, a 500-year period may not have a unique name, but it is nevertheless an important conceptual unit. Similarly, in a base-20 system, 200 years is also an important division.

Ending Chapters on Five-Year Intervals

One of the most intriguing non-modern concepts behind Mormon's chapter endings is the interplay between the counts of the years and Mormon's chapters. When Mormon began writing the book of Alma, he had a new conceptual structure—the reign of the judges—to help him organize events by tying them to specific years.[4] Previously, the small plates and the book of Mosiah only sporadically offered dates, often leaving out specific ones that would be very helpful to modern readers attempting to correlate the Book of Mormon text into a historical framework.

The frequent inclusion of dates beginning with the book of Alma is obvious to any reader. Less obvious is how those dates affected the way Mormon ended some of his chapters. As discussed previously, Mormon used a hierarchy of features that triggered the end of chapters, the most important being a testificatory "amen." Another feature that could trigger the end of a chapter was the end of an inserted sermon. When Mormon had no other reason to end a chapter, he elected to end his chapters on a five-year boundary.

Mark A. Wright noticed that Mormon was very sensitive to units of five years.[5] An interesting feature of this sensitivity is that it influenced chapter endings and beginnings but was adapted to the particulars of the history Mormon related. Depending upon the story being told, at times the chapter ended after the fifth-year boundary with the next year beginning with the sixth, Sometimes it ended after the fourth year and began the next chapter on the fifth.

Scholars use the Maya language-based term *hotun* to label sets of five years. Although a five-year period does not necessarily indicate that it comes from a base-20 system, the way that unit is used in Mormon's writings follows the cultural use of the five-year collective *hotun*. For the Maya, the *hotun* was particularly important for historical records. They would erect a stela (standing carved stone) on *hotun* anniversaries. The stela summarized or commemorated the important events for the previous five

---

4. See "Chronological Organization" in Chapter 12 for more details.
5. Mark A. Wright, personal communication.

years.[6] We must caution against the temptation to suggest that the Maya *hotun* stelae provided the conceptual model that influenced Mormon's attention to five-year, or *hotun* periods, in his text. This does not necessarily suggest a causal relationship, but rather one that would come from people in the same cultural area sharing similar conceptual worlds.

The first original chapter break in Alma comes between chapters I (1–3) and II (4) and at a five-year division between the end of the fifth year and the beginning of the sixth:

> And *thus endeth the fifth year of the reign of the judges.*
>
> [Chapter Break]
>
> Now it came to pass *in the sixth year of the reign of the judges* over the people of Nephi, there were no contentions nor wars in the land of Zarahemla. (3:27–4:1)

The transition between Mormon's chapter V (7) and VI (8) differs in that it was generated by a testificatory "amen" (Alma 7:27). Mormon adds the narrative that ends the arc from chapter V (7) to the beginning of chapter VI (8). However, he also wants to note a *hotun*, so we are also given a year-ending and year-beginning, this time between the ninth and tenth years:

> And now, may the peace of God rest upon you, and upon your houses and lands, and upon your flocks and herds, and all that you possess, your women and your children, according to your faith and good works, from this time forth and forever. And thus I have spoken. *Amen.*
>
> [Chapter Break]
>
> And now it came to pass that Alma returned from the land of Gideon, after having taught the people of Gideon many things which cannot be written, having established the order of the church, according as he had before done in the land of Zarahemla, yea, he returned to his own house at Zarahemla to rest himself from the labors which he had performed.
>
> And *thus ended the ninth year of the reign of the judges* over the people of Nephi.

---

6. Mark Alan Wright, "Nephite Daykeepers: Ritual Specialists in Mesoamerica and the Book of Mormon," 253. According to Sylvanus Griswold Morley, "The Maya monuments, and especially those of the stela type, seem to have been used, perhaps primarily, to mark the passage of time, stelae being erected at intervals of every hotun (1,800 days) or multiples thereof as every lahuntun (3600 days) or katun (7200 days) throughout the Old Empire, approximately 200 to 600 AD." Sylvanus Griswold Morley, "The Hotun as the Principal Chronological Unit of the Old Maya Empire," 201.

> And it came to pass *in the commencement of the tenth year of the reign of the judges* over the people of Nephi, that Alma departed from thence and took his journey over into the land of Melek, on the west of the river Sidon, on the west by the borders of the wilderness. (7:27–8:3)

Mormon has the new narrative arc beginning at the start of the tenth year. While here the end of a year and a beginning of a new one are documented after the chapter break due to the chapter-ending "amen," it is more typical that Mormon pays attention to *hotun* periods and uses them as chapter divisions/beginnings when there are no other higher priority markers.

A cleaner break marking the tenth and eleventh years occurs between Alma X (13:10–15) and Alma XI (16):

> And *thus ended the tenth year of the reign of the judges* over the people of Nephi.
> [Chapter Break]
> And it came to pass *in the eleventh year of the reign of the judges* over the people of Nephi, on the fifth day of the second month, there having been much peace in the land of Zarahemla, there having been no wars nor contentions for a certain number of years, even until the fifth day of the second month in the eleventh year, there was a cry of war heard throughout the land. (15:19–16:1)

The change from Alma XI (16) to Alma XII (17–20) presents an interesting case. Alma XI (16) ends in the fourteenth year (Alma 16:21), but Alma XII (17–20) doesn't mark the beginning with a year. Instead, the history shifts to "An account of the sons of Mosiah . . . according to the record of Alma," which Mormon previously promised to return to in Mosiah 28:8 and is covered in Alma XII–XV (21–29). It is within that account that Mormon notes the end of the fifteenth year:

> And now, after the church, having been established throughout all the land, having got the victory over the devil, and the word of God being preached in its purity in all the land, and the Lord pouring out his blessings upon the people—*And thus ended the fourteenth year of the reign of the judges over the people of Nephi.*
> [Chapter Break]
> *An account of the sons of Mosiah, which rejected their rights to the kingdom for the word of God and went up to the land of Nephi to preach to the Lamanites. Their sufferings and deliverance. According to the record of Alma. . . .*
> . . . And *thus ended the fifteenth year of the reign of the judges* over the people of Nephi.
> And this is the account of Ammon and his brethren their journeyings into the land of Nephi, their sufferings in the land—their sorrows and their afflictions, and their incomprehensible joy—and the reception and safety of

the brethren in the land of Jershon. And now may the Lord, the redeemer of all men, bless their souls forever.

And this is the account of the wars and contentions among the Nephites, and also the wars between the Nephites and the Lamanites. *And the fifteenth year of the reign of the judges is ended.* (16:21, 27:7–9)

Alma XV (27–29) ends the 11–15-year *hotun*, and Alma XVI (30–35) begins with the sixteenth year. However, as just noted, the end of the fifteenth year is mentioned earlier in the middle of the chapter before Mormon provides additional commentary, then includes without introduction a prayer by Alma$_2$ that closes his account of the sons of Mosiah (29:1–17). Similar to the break between Alma V and VI, Mormon creates a break after Alma$_2$'s testificatory "amen" that closes his prayer. Chapter XVI (30–35) then begins with recalling some key events of the fifteenth year before shifting to the sixteenth:

> And now, may God grant unto these, my brethren, that they may sit down in the kingdom of God. Yea, and also all those which are the fruit of their labors, that they may go no more out, but that they may praise him forever. And may God grant that it may be done, according to my words, even as I have spoken. *Amen.*
>
> [Chapter Break]
>
> Behold, now it came to *pass that after the people of Ammon were established in the land of Jershon, yea, and also after the Lamanites were driven out of the land, and their dead were buried by the people of the land* [events of the fifteenth year] . . .
>
> And it was *in the sixteenth year of the reign of the judges* over the people of Nephi, there began to be continual peace throughout all the land. Yea, and the people did observe to keep the commandments of the Lord; and they were strict in observing the ordinances of God, according to the law of Moses. For they were taught to keep the law of Moses until it should be fulfilled. And thus the people did have no disturbance in all the sixteenth year of the reign of the judges over the people of Nephi.
>
> And it came to pass that in the commencement of the seventeenth year of the reign of the judges, there was continual peace.
>
> But it came to pass in the latter end of the seventeenth year, there came a man into the land of Zarahemla, and he was Anti-Christ, for he began to preach unto the people against the prophecies which had been spoken by the prophets, concerning the coming of Christ. (29:17–30:6)

The remainder of the book of Alma continues the relative pattern. The break between Alma XXI (45–49) and Alma XXII (50) comes between the end of the nineteenth year (49:29–30) and the beginning of the twentieth year (50:1); the break between Alma XXII and XXIII (51) comes between the end of the twentieth year (50:40) and the beginning of the twenty-fifth year (51:1); the break between Alma XXII (51) and XXIV (52) comes between the end of the twenty-fifth year (51:37) and beginning of the twenty-sixth year (52:1); the break between Alma XXIV and (52–53) and XXV (54) comes between the end of the twenty-eighth year (53:23) and the beginning of the twenty-ninth year (54:1); the break between Alma XXV (54) and XXVI (56) comes between the end of the twenty-ninth year (55:35) and the beginning of the thirtieth (56:1); and finally the break between Alma XXIX (62) and its final chapter XXX (63) comes between the end of the thirty-fifth year (62:52) and the beginning of the thirtieth-sixth year (63:1). Mormon thus used the *hotun* concept loosely, sometimes breaking before the beginning of a five-year period and sometimes at the end.

The final chapter of Alma ends in the thirty-ninth year (63:16–17), and Helaman begins in the fortieth year (1:1). It is highly likely that this is intentional, as we don't have Helaman$_2$ as the ruler—the reason for the book name change—until the forty-second year (Hel. 2:1–2).[7] The beginning of the book of Helaman was seemingly backdated to begin at a more auspicious *katun* of the reign of judges.[8]

Time-sets and Prophecy

In Mormon's text, we see *hotun* sets more often than larger numbers because they mark shorter periods. However, we also see *katun* sets (twenty years) and *baktun* sets (four hundred years). Mormon does not force these numbers onto his narrative, but he sometimes bends time and narration to have the numbers and text align in significance. One place to see this is in the use of time-sets in prophetic predictions.

The underlying prophecy for Nephite society was: "Yea, even six hundred years from the time that my father left Jerusalem, a prophet would the Lord God raise up among the Jews—even a Messiah, or, in other words, a Savior of the world" (1 Ne. 10:4). Although that prophecy was given in the Old World (and originally would have been understood in Old World terms), it nevertheless fell into a recognizable pattern for Mesoamerican oracles. It was one and one-half *baktuns*.

A *baktun* period was particularly important in the Maya mental world. Similar to the way modern Western cultures saw the importance of the

---

7. Mark A. Wright, personal communication.
8. Two periods of twenty years.

turn of the millennium, the turn from one *baktun* to the next was a significant liminal period and thus often tied to prophecy. David Stuart tells the story of the Itzá, the last remaining unconquered Maya nation at the end of the Spanish conquest. The conquest that Itzá faced was primarily conversion rather than military conflict.

> In their written account, Orbita and Fuensalida vividly describe how the Itzá king responded: "It is not yet time to abandon our gods. . . . Now is the age of Three Ahaw." Kanek' went on to explain. "The prophecies tell us the time will yet come to abandon our gods, years from now, in the age of Eight Ahaw. We will speak nor more of this now."[9]

Each *katun* bore a name, and Three Ahaw was the name of the then current *katun* (1618 in our calendar). Eighty years later, in 1695, the situation changed, and the Itzá allowed their conversion. Prophecy and time were intricately bound together, and when the prophesied time arrived, the Itzá accepted their fate. Stuart clarifies the Maya expectation:

> Based on what we can discern about Maya notions of prophecy, the Itzá probably foresaw the turn of the cycle more as a *recurrence* of some previous historical era or experience, familiar and predestined according to the patterns of native history. The prophecy of the katun called 8 Ahaw was shaped by the events and characteristics of earlier katuns, from centuries in the past, bearing the same name.[10]

The importance of full sets of time arguably makes an appearance in the Book of Mormon. There is an interesting timing of the way years were counted when the Nephites moved from the reign of the judges to anchoring years in the birth of the Messiah:

> And thus did pass away the ninety and sixth year; and also the ninety and seventh year; and also the ninety and eighth year; and also the ninety and ninth year;
>
> And also an hundred years had passed away since the days of Mosiah, who was king over the people of the Nephites.
>
> And six hundred and nine years had passed away since Lehi left Jerusalem.
>
> And nine years had passed away from the time when the sign was given, which was spoken of by the prophets, that Christ should come into the world.
>
> Now the Nephites began to reckon their time from this period when the sign was given, or from the coming of Christ; therefore, nine years had passed away. (3 Ne. 2:4–8)

---

9. David Stuart, *The Order of Days: The Maya World and the Truth about 2012*, 6–7.
10. Stuart, 19–20.

It is not unexpected that the Nephites, a Christ-believing people, would mark the beginning of a new set of years with the timing of Christ's birth. What is interesting is that they waited nine years to do it. Verse 6 notes that the six-hundred-year prophecy had been fulfilled nine years earlier. When did they finally change? Mark A. Wright noticed that they changed when the years following Mosiah$_2$, or the beginning of the book of Alma, reached a full set of one hundred years (or one-fourth *baktun*; as noted earlier, multiples or divisions by four were also conceptually important). Only then did they backdate their new way of keeping time.[11]

Nephi$_1$ had ominously prophesied at the very beginning of his Nephite history that his people would eventually "dwindle in unbelief" (1 Ne. 12:21–23). When it was finally turned into a specific prophecy, it came as a *baktun* prophecy:[12]

> Behold, I, Samuel, a Lamanite, do speak the words of the Lord which he doth put into my heart; and behold he hath put it into my heart to say unto this people that the sword of justice hangeth over this people; and *four hundred years* pass not away save the sword of justice falleth upon this people. (Hel. 13:5)

We see another plausible vigesimal system time-set in Samuel the Lamanite's prophecy of the coming birth of the Messiah. It was a *hotun* prophecy:

> Behold, I give unto you a sign; for *five years* more cometh, and behold, then cometh the Son of God to redeem all those who shall believe on his name. (Hel. 14:2)

---

11. Mark A. Wright, personal communication.

12. Perhaps it is significant that the named period does not occur until Mormon's writing. Nephi$_1$ lived at the beginning of the Nephite time in the New World and may not have yet adapted to the Mesoamerican dating concepts. Mormon was certainly living at a time when those concepts would have worked their way into the Nephite mental worldview.

Section III:
Nephite Writers and Their Sources

Chapter Eleven

Reconstructing the Final Nephite Archive

When Ammaron placed the Nephite archive in the hill Shim, it consisted of "all the sacred records which had been handed down from generation to generation, which were sacred" (4 Ne. 1:48). Those sacred records contained the writings of nearly a thousand years' worth of Nephite archivists. Given the physical size of the set of plates Moroni delivered to Joseph, there must have been at least hundreds of perhaps similarly sized sets of plates.

Mormon describes some of the contents of the archive during the time of Helaman$_2$:

> And now there are many records kept of the proceedings of this people, by many of this people, which are particular and very large, concerning them.
>
> But behold, a hundredth part of the proceedings of this people, yea, the account of the Lamanites and of the Nephites, and their wars, and contentions, and dissensions, and their preaching, and their prophecies, and their shipping and their building of ships, and their building of temples, and of synagogues and their sanctuaries, and their righteousness, and their wickedness, and their murders, and their robbings, and their plundering, and all manner of abominations and whoredoms, cannot be contained in this work.
>
> But behold, there are many books and many records of every kind, and they have been kept chiefly by the Nephites.
>
> And they have been handed down from one generation to another by the Nephites. (Hel. 3:13–16)

When the twenty-four-year-old Mormon took the plates of Nephi but left the remainder in the hill Shim (Morm. 1:4), we understand that he took the current Nephite record, not the entire archive. When we see the term *plates of Nephi* in Mormon's writings, we should understand the phrase as a collective term for the entire archive of the people of Nephi rather than any specific single set of plates.

Mormon consistently wrote that he took his record from the plates of Nephi (large plates). Nevertheless, he included other records that he indicated were different sources separate from the large plates. Thus, the archive was akin to a library with different types of records included in the collection.

Large and Small Plates

Nephi₁ was the first Nephite record keeper and the founder of the Nephite tradition of record keeping. He originally intended to create a single record tradition, but the Lord's command caused him to create a second record that had an entirely different purpose and transmission line:

> And now, as I have spoken concerning these plates, behold they are not the plates upon which I make a full account of the history of my people; for the plates upon which I make a full account of my people I have given the name of Nephi; wherefore, they are called the plates of Nephi, after mine own name; and these plates also are called the plates of Nephi.
>
> Nevertheless, I have received a commandment of the Lord that I should make these plates, for the special purpose that there should be an account engraven of the ministry of my people.
>
> Upon the other plates should be engraven an account of the reign of the kings, and the wars and contentions of my people; wherefore these plates are for the more part of the ministry; and the other plates are for the more part of the reign of the kings and the wars and contentions of my people.
>
> Wherefore, the Lord hath commanded me to make these plates for a wise purpose in him, which purpose I know not. (1 Ne. 9:2–5)

As perhaps an indication that Nephi₁ did not foresee the two sets of plates existing in the same place, he gave both sets the name "the plates of Nephi." With two different sets of plates both bearing the same name, Latter-day Saint tradition has distinguished between the two by calling the set containing the record of reigns of the kings the "large" plates of Nephi, and the second set, comprising 1 Nephi through Omni, the "small" plates of Nephi. The adjectives large and small should be understood to represent the quantity of plates rather than the physical size of any given plate.[1]

We do not have any explicit evidence that Nephi₁ directed the continuation of the large plates, but we do know that they were passed down through the official record keepers from Nephi₁'s time to Mormon himself. In contrast, we have Jacob's explicit recognition of the command to continue the small plates record:

---

1. The brass plates may have served as the conceptual and physical model for Nephi₁'s plates. As the one who created the plates, we may assume that Nephi₁ did not create plates of different sizes. There was no reason to. The addition of the small plates to the Mormon's plates suggests that there had been a "Nephite standard size" for archival plates. See Brant A. Gardner, *Second Witness: Analytical and Contextual Commentary on the Book of Mormon*, 1:13.

> For behold, it came to pass that fifty and five years had passed away from the time that Lehi left Jerusalem; wherefore, Nephi gave me, Jacob, a commandment concerning the small plates, upon which these things are engraven.
>
> And he gave me, Jacob, a commandment that I should write upon these plates a few of the things which I considered to be most precious; that I should not touch, save it were lightly, concerning the history of this people which are called the people of Nephi.
>
> For he said that the history of his people should be engraven upon his other plates, and that I should preserve these plates and hand them down unto my seed, from generation to generation. (Jacob 1:1–3)

Nephi$_1$ established two different transmission lines for the two different sets of plates he created. The two sets of records were physically separated when Nephi$_1$ died. The large plates went to the unnamed next king of the Nephites and continued through all the dynastic changes until the entire archive was entrusted to Mormon. The small plates were in a different location; they were not representative of the government, and as we read what subsequent writers recorded, they were obviously disconnected from the seats of Nephite power.

The way the records came back together is important. The small plates appear to end when there is no more space left to write on them, with the last author, Amaleki, declaring, "these plates are full" (Omni 1:30). As Jacob's descendants were not connected to the seats of power, they may have been unable to make more plates (or it may be that they were unable to add more plates to Nephi$_1$'s set). With the small plates nearly filled, Amaleki informs his readers: "And it came to pass that I began to be old; and, having no seed, and knowing king Benjamin to be a just man before the Lord, wherefore, I shall deliver up these plates unto him" (v. 25).

Both sets of plates became part of the whole Nephite archive, which Ammaron eventually sequestered in the hill Shim, making it possible for Mormon to later discover and add the small plates to his own (Morm. 4:23). (See Chapter 15 below for the timing and reason for the discovery of the small plates.)

Brass Plates

It is probable, but not certain, that the Nephite archive also contained the brass plates, as they clearly fit the definition of important records. When King Benjamin conferred the kingship upon his son Mosiah$_2$, he passed along several sacred objects, including the brass plates, that had been held and passed down for generations:

> And moreover, he also gave him charge concerning the records which were engraven on the plates of brass; and also the plates of Nephi; and also, the sword of Laban, and the ball or director, which led our fathers through the wilderness, which was prepared by the hand of the Lord that thereby they might be led, every one according to the heed and diligence which they gave unto him. (Mosiah 1:16)

Gordon Thomasson suggests that these objects formed a royal treasure, and Don Bradley similarly argues that they were collected and held as temple relics that have analogues to the stone tablets, sword of Goliath, and other relics held in the Israelite temple.[2]

Plates of Ether

The book of Ether was undoubtedly contained in the Nephite archive. When Mosiah$_2$ created the reign of the judges, he passed the sacred records to Alma$_2$:

> Therefore he took the records which were engraven on the plates of brass, and also the plates of Nephi, and all the things which he had kept and preserved according to the commandments of God, after having translated and caused to be written the records which were on the plates of gold which had been found by the people of Limhi, which were delivered to him by the hand of Limhi. . . .
>
> And now, as I said unto you, that after king Mosiah had done these things, he took the plates of brass, and all the things which he had kept, and conferred them upon Alma, who was the son of Alma; yea, all the records, and also the interpreters, and conferred them upon him, and commanded him that he should keep and preserve them. (Mosiah 28:11, 20)

At the beginning of the reign of the judges, we have a list of the separate records that were included in the Nephite archive: the brass plates, the plates of Nephi (including the small plates, even though not mentioned), and the plates of Ether. Writing in Mosiah 28:11–19, Mormon said that he would later give the story of the Jaredites. He left the fulfillment of that promise to Moroni, but in order for Moroni to accomplish it with the plates of Ether, or at least Mosiah$_2$'s translation of them, it had to be included in the archive.

---

2. Gordon C. Thomasson, "Mosiah: The Complex Symbolism and Symbolic Complex of Kingship in the Book of Mormon," 27–32. Don Bradley, *The Lost 116 Pages: Reconstructing the Book of Mormon's Missing Stories*, 148–55.

Record of Zeniff

The Record of Zeniff contained the history of Nephites who had left Zarahemla to reclaim the land of Nephi from the Lamanites. They were separated from Zarahemla by both distance and a Lamanite cultural and political boundary. Their first king, Zeniff, began his own dynastic record documenting the reigns of himself, his son Noah, and his grandson Limhi.

That record included a first-person record of Zeniff, which Mormon included in its entirety (Mosiah VI [9–10]). The record continued after the part that Mormon copied, providing information on the reigns of Noah and Limhi. It is not known if those two wrote in the first person, and it may be more likely that they had scribes keep the record for them. The record of Zeniff entered the Nephite archive when Limhi's people returned to Zarahemla (Mosiah 25:5).

Record of $Alma_1$

We meet the story of $Alma_1$ in the header to Mosiah XI (23–27). In general, Mormon kept the information from $Alma_1$'s record in this labeled section. Of course, some of $Alma_1$'s story had to be part of the record of Zeniff, when $Alma_1$ sat with Noah's priests holding court on Abinadi. Nevertheless, after $Alma_1$ left, he created a separate record that Mormon used as another source for $Alma_1$'s story. There is no record of the medium on which the record was created. The fact that this was a personal record created in a small and separated group argues against it being on plates. It entered the archive when $Alma_1$'s people returned to Zarahemla (Mosiah 25:6).

Personal Record of $Alma_2$

When King $Mosiah_2$ instituted the reign of the judges, $Alma_1$'s son, also named Alma (disambiguated as $Alma_2$), was made Chief Judge and keeper of the Nephite archive. That he kept the archive is not clear until after $Alma_2$ stepped away from his political role to focus on his religious duties, making Nephihah the new chief judge (Alma 4:20). We learn much later in the story that Nephihah had refused the sacred records, which is why they were still in $Alma_2$'s possession before he entrusted them to his son $Helaman_1$ (50:38).

The story of the records becomes a little confusing at this point because, as the first chief judge, the record of his dynasty on the large plates was named after $Alma_2$. In addition to that official book of Alma, Mormon makes it clear that he had access to a second, personal record that $Alma_2$ kept. The header to Alma V (7), which was included on Mormon's plates, reads: "The words of Alma which he delivered to the people in Gideon, according to *his own* record."

Although it would be possible to read this as a reference to the book of Alma on the large plates, this would be redundant since the rest of Alma$_2$'s history was taken from that book. The only reason for Mormon to denote this record is to highlight it as separate from that of the large plates. (As discussed in the previous chapter, Mormon notes in a header that Alma XII–XV (21–29), which contains the accounts of the sons of Mosiah$_2$, are also from Alma$_2$'s separate record.) Furthermore, because Mormon so rarely directly quotes from the large plates, the extensive inclusion of sermons from Alma$_2$'s personal life and ministry (Alma 5, 7, 10–13, 29, 32–34, 36–37, 38, 39–42, 45) points to them also coming from an account distinct from the large plates' book of Alma. It is also probable that the original for this personal record was on a more perishable medium than the plates, although obviously preserved in the archive where Mormon could find it.

Personal Record of Nephi$_3$

There is a complicated story behind the two books commonly known as 3 Nephi and 4 Nephi. That topic is considered in the next chapter. At this point, it is important to note that Mormon tells his readers that he is taking much, if not most, of his 3 Nephi book from a "shorter but true account" (3 Ne. 5:9). Although Mormon does not explicitly name him, we understand it was Nephi$_3$'s personal record:

> And now it came to pass that according to our record, and we know our record to be true, for behold, it was a just man who did keep the record—for he truly did many miracles in the name of Jesus; and there was not any man who could do a miracle in the name of Jesus save he were cleansed every whit from his iniquity. (8:1)

The nature of the 3 Nephi suggests that it was not based on a named book on the large plates. Instead, it was sourced by Mormon from a separate, personal record. As with the other personal records it may have been on a perishable medium and stored with the archive.

Chapter Twelve

The Structure of the Large Plates

When Mormon discovered the small plates, he expressed his desire to include them with his record:

> And the things which are upon these plates pleasing me, because of the prophecies of the coming of Christ; and my fathers knowing that many of them have been fulfilled; yea, and I also know that as many things as have been prophesied concerning us down to this day have been fulfilled, and as many as go beyond this day must surely come to pass—Wherefore, I chose these things, to finish my record upon them. (W of M 1:4–5)

Mormon included these plates with his own record, but unlike his abridged account of the Nephites, he did not edit or alter them in any way. Thus, we know precisely what the content of the small plates was, according to their translation. We know less about the large plates of Nephi, save that they were Mormon's main source of the historical framework from which he built his message.

Even though the large plates formed the backbone of Mormon's story, Mormon quoted them little. King Benjamin's sermon at the beginning of Mormon's extant writing must have been included on the large plates, given its role in the transfer of power from Benjamin to his son Mosiah$_2$ (Mosiah 1:10). That is the only sure quotation from the large plates in the Mormon-edited books. After that, however, quotations of sermons and teachings appear to have come from secondary records.

Understanding that the majority of the historical information came from the large plates, what other influence did the large plates have upon the way Mormon constructed his text? Chapter 6 examined some features of the way Mormon constructed chapters, including the use of book and chapter headers that he may have been emulating from the large plates. Interestingly, Mormon's synoptic headers seem to only deal with the information taken from the large plates and do not address information that that may have come from alternate sources.

Mormon was consistent in creating new chapters when there was a new source, but he did not particularly mark his return to the large plates text as wrote. For example, after he finished copying from Alma$_2$'s personal record, we can see Mormon returning to the large plates in chapter XX

(43–44). After two verses that provide the necessary transition between the text from Alma$_2$'s personal record and the political history from the large plates, Mormon specifically states: "And now I return to an account of the wars between the Nephites and the Lamanites, in the eighteenth year of the reign of the judges" (Alma 43:3). While he returns to this account, he does not indicate the source for it. Mormon likely assumed that his readers would understand that it was the large plates.

Typically Mormon gives no indication that he was shifting between sources. For example, Mormon used Alma$_2$'s personal record beginning with Alma III (5), again in Alma X (13:10–15:19), and also for Alma XII (17–20), which begins with a header. Between them, chapter XI (16) is instead from the large plates, but it has no header or explicit statement indicating that. The only way to identify the source here is to note the type of information Mormon provides, as well as the inclusion of year markers, which are not provided within sermons or more personal records. That type of information comes from the large plates. (Similarly, Nephi$_1$'s small plates lack organizational year markers.)

Chronological Organization

The fact that Mormon was using history as the overarching model for his purposes requires that his text appear in mostly chronological order. The exceptions are the flashback chapters in the book of Mosiah that discuss the events related to the Nephites who left Zarahemla to return to the land of Nephi (taken from the record of Zeniff) and the story of the missionary efforts of the sons of Mosiah (taken from Alma$_2$'s personal record), both of which Mormon includes in his history after writing about their reception within the large-plates timeline. The historical nature of the large plates is thus the obvious source for all dates in the Mormon-edited books in the Book of Mormon.

While the dates can be assigned to the large plates, there is also an important change to the way dates were handled that altered the way Mormon presented his history. In the book of Mosiah, we are given a few dates, but many that would be helpful to know (such as when Zeniff left for the land of Nephi) are simply not provided. That changes with the very first verse in the book of Alma: "Now it came to pass that in the first year of the reign of the judges over the people of Nephi" (Alma 1:1). From this point on, Mormon's text is permeated with the marking of years.

John L. Sorenson describes this organizational feature:

The fundamental format of the plates of Nephi was that of annals. Annals are yearly summaries of salient events. This format is clearly reflected at many points in the Book of Mormon, for example in Helaman 6:15: "And it came to pass that in the sixty and sixth year of the reign of the judges, behold, Cezoram was murdered by an unknown hand as he sat upon the judgment-seat. And it came to pass that in the same year, that his son, who had been appointed by the people in his stead, was also murdered. And thus ended the sixty and sixth year." That is how Mormon chose to summarize the record for that year.

Generally these annalistic entries were succinct. As an example, Mormon's record for the twenty-six years documented in Helaman, chapters 2 through 6, averages fewer than seven verses per year.[1]

The pervasive annalistic organization in Mormon's editing indicates that it is a feature of his large-plate source. Once begun, the large plates continued to use years as an organizational structure through to Mormon's time. The very first verse of 4 Nephi repeats this annalistic organization, this time based on the years since the New World signs of Jesus's birth (3 Ne. 2:7–8): "And it came to pass that the thirty and fourth year passed away, and also the thirty and fifth" (4 Ne. 1:1).

This annals format is also found in later Mesoamerican texts. For example, the "Annals of Cuauhtitlan" is a historical document originally written in Nahuatl, the Aztec language. The extant copy is a transcription from an earlier document that dates as early as 1590 BCE.[2] The entire document is organized around years, and just as we see in 4 Nephi 1:6, there are several years listed where no event accompanies the year. In the following excerpt from the history of the fall of Tollan (an important city state from around 900 BCE), the years are noted according to the Mesoamerican method of designating years. In the following, 2 Flint, 3 House, 4 Rabbit, etc. are years as represented in the Mesoamerican system:

[The fall of Tollan: A.D. 896–1070]

2 Flint. 3 House. 4 Rabbit. 5 Reed. 6 Flint. 7 House. 8 Rabbit. 9 Reed.

10 Flint. 11 House. 12 Rabbit. 13 Reed. 1 Flint. 2 House. 3 Rabbit.

4 Reed. 5 Flint. 6 House. 7 Rabbit. 8 Reed. 9 Flint. 10 House.

11 Rabbit. 12 Recd. 13 Flint. 1 House. 2 Rabbit. 3 Reed. 4 Flint.

5 House. 6 Rabbit. 7 Reed. 8 Flint. 9 House.

---

1. John L. Sorenson, "Mormon's Sources," 4.

2. John Bierhorst, trans., *History and Mythology of the Aztecs: The Codex Chimalpopoca*, 12.

> 10 Rabbit [A.D. 930]. Ayauhcoyotzin, ruler of Cuauhtitlan, died in that year. He had ruled for fifty-five years. Matlacxochitzin, ruler of Tollan, also died then, and Nauhyotzin was inaugurated, succeeding him as Tollan's ruler.
>
> 11 Reed [931]. The Cuauhtitlan ruler Necuamexochitzin was inaugurated in that year. His palace was in Tepotzotlan Miccacalco. The reason it was called Miccacalco [At the House of the Dead] is that lightning struck there, killing noblemen and ladies, and so they changed residence. Nothing was left standing but the Chichimec rulers' straw-house. They did not dare go back to their palace.
>
> 12 Flint. 13 House. 1 Rabbit. 2 Reed. 3 Flint. 4 House. 5 Rabbit.
>
> 6 Reed. 7 Flint. 8 House. 9 Rabbit. 10 Reed. 11 Flint.
>
> 12 House [945]. It was the year the Cuauhtitlan ruler called Necuamexochitzin died. He had ruled for fifteen years. Also at that time the Tollan ruler, Nauhyotzin, died, and Matlaccoatzin was inaugurated, succeeding him.
>
> 13 Rabbit [946]. In that year Mecellotzin was inaugurated as ruler of Cuauhtitlan. His palace was built in a place called Tianquizzolco Cuauhtlaapan.[3]

The second document is from further south and is from the Maya rather than the Aztec. Written in the Cakchiquel Maya language, "The Annals of the Cakchiquels" shows a similar structure, but in this case is listed by days rather than years:

> A little less than two years after the death of the Tukuchés, the Zutuhils were killed in *Zahcab* on the day 1 Ah-mak [July 10, 1495]. The Zutuhils were killed and annihilated, and their chiefs *Nahtihay* and *Ahquibihay* surrendered. Only the lord Voo Caok, the Ahtziquinahay, did not surrender, but his heart was full of evil intentions toward the Cakchiquels.
>
> On the day 5 Ah [July 27, 1495] ended the second year after the revolution.
>
> On the day 2 Ah [August 30, 1496] ended the third year after the revolution.
>
> On the day 3 Queh [September 13, 1946, or May 31, 1497] there was a revolt in the Quiché. The Tukuchés went to take part in it there in the Quiché.
>
> On the day 12 Ah [October 4, 1497] ended the fourth year after the revolution.
>
> During the fifth year those of *Mixcu* died, subjects of the king Cablahuh Tihax, who wished to assume power. On the day 7 Camey [December 16, 1497] the warriors fell on the city of those of Mixcu and annihilated them.

---

3. Bierhorst, 37. The Mesoamerican calendar rotated a set of named days through numbers. The nature of the cyclical repetition was such that a certain number and day could only occur once every 260 days.

Then the Yaquis of *Xivicu* died who had joined the king Voo Caok, lord of the Akahals, when the Akahal people revolted, wishing to take command of that place.[4]

The obvious difference between the Nephite annals and the examples from the Annals of Cuauhtitlan or the Annals of the Cakchiquels is that the latter two had extremely abbreviated entries. Mormon clearly had more to work with. Nevertheless, all three mark years in which no events are listed. Both the Annals of the Cakchiquels and Mormon's abridgement often note the ending of a year. Interestingly, in the Annals of the Cakchiquels, there is a count from a specific event rather than a fixed date ("the second year after the revolution" and "the third year after the revolution").

The pervasive use of annals from Alma to 4 Nephi did not dominate the book of Mosiah. Instead, Mosiah follows a pattern more similar to the small plates, which only sporadically enters the number of years from the departure from Jerusalem. For example, in Mosiah 6:4, Mormon dates the beginning of Mosiah's reign as "about four hundred and seventy-six years from the time that Lehi left Jerusalem."

Mark A. Wright has suggested that it could be related to the adoption of the *long count* among the Maya that occurred about this time.[5] The Maya had always kept time and records, but the long count initiated an ancestral (and perhaps mythological) date from which all subsequent dates would be measured. This is conceptually similar to the Christian world's use of the birth of Christ as a foundation for dating (which the Nephites adopted nine years after Jesus's birth, but the Old World did not adopt until over five centuries later). Whether or not the change was related to a long count, it is plausible that it occurred due to external cultural pressures.

If the Book of Mormon occurred in Mesoamerica, the regional emphasis on the yearly dating would be a reasonable explanation for the change at the beginning of the book of Alma. What it does not indicate is why the change occurred at that precise time. That might be explained by Wright's hypothesis that it is temporally correlated to the change to the long count.

As a final note on the chronological organization, the nearly one thousand years of Nephite record keeping requires that there be multiple sets of plates. Perhaps there was a single set for each book, but since the book

---

4. Dionisio José Chonay and Delia Goetz, trans., *Annals of the Cakchiquels and Title of the Lords of Totonicapan*, 110.

5. Based on personal conversation with Wright.

of Lehi covered at least four hundred years, it is unlikely that all those records would be bound as a single unit. When the Nephite archivists kept the plates, it is a reasonable assumption that the plate sets would have been ordered chronologically. However, when Mormon retrieved the archive from the hill Shim, it was at a time that he was retreating and likely had little time to take care to keep the records organized as they were. The later disorganized state of the records may explain why Mormon was "search[ing] among the records" following his abridgment up to the reign of King Benjamin when he discovered the small pates (W of M 1:3).

Individual Named Books within the Book of Mormon

The most recognizable organizational structure of the Book of Mormon is the division of the text into books that bear a person's name. Evidence from the Original Manuscript indicates that these book divisions were part of the dictated text and therefore represent organizational structures that existed on Mormon's plates. Although we do not have the complete original manuscript, there are places where we can see how the transition to a new book was handled during dictation. For example, at the transition from the book of Alma to the book of Helaman, Oliver Cowdery continued to write on the same page. However, he drew a solid horizontal line covering most of the page between the books. This line is above the slightly indented title "The Book of Helaman," which is followed by a roughly centered "Chapter I" in the next line of text. After that comes the chapter synopsis.[6] The solid line indicates the beginning of a new book and hints at some sort of marking or distinction on the plates that signaled an end to a book.[7] While Cowdery used it to identify the break, there is nothing beyond it suggesting that Joseph told him to

---

6. *The Original Manuscript of the Book of Mormon*, 436–37.

7. Royal Skousen, "Critical Methodology and the Text of the Book of Mormon," 137. While there are no other book markers preserved in the Original Manuscript for Mormon's text, there are two more examples in the 1 Nephi to Omni section. The extant manuscript preserves the change from 1 Nephi to 2 Nephi and a damaged page where Jacob changes to Enos. Neither of those two book breaks employs the horizontal line divider. This evidence tells us that there was something in the small Plates of Nephi that indicated a book change as well as in Mormon's text. However, with so little information, we cannot suggest that the line used on the one instance extant from the large Plates of Nephi indicates a different type of book marker, or simply that Oliver's convention changed over time.

add one. It may just be that Joseph indicated the break in some way, and Cowdery elected to use a line.

All of this points to the separate book names being part of Mormon's larger book, and it is a reasonable suggestion that the large plates of Nephi also had these book divisions. However, that is a suggestion that requires qualification. We cannot immediately assume that books that appear in the Book of Mormon were on the large plates. For example, the book of Mormon, book of Moroni, and book of Ether were all created separately from the large plates and were therefore not represented on those plates. There are other questions to be answered.

Books of the Small Plates

As modern readers approach the Book of Mormon, we are met with book names that fit the assumptions we formed from the Old and New Testament. The original names of the books of the small plates in the Printer's Manuscript are:

- The Book of Nephi: His Reign and Ministry
- The Book of Nephi
- The Book of Jacob, the Brother of Nephi
- The Book of Enos
- The Book of Jarom
- The Book of Omni

As with the Old and New Testament, these are associated with the writer of the books. The exception is the Book of Omni. There, additional authors declined to create a new book and instead mostly contributed only a paragraph each. The final writer, Amaleki, added significantly more to the small book (providing 19 of Omni's 30 verses), but he elected to give the small plates to King Benjamin once he had filled up the remaining space on them (Omni 1:25, 30).

The use of numbers to differentiate between the two books of Nephi is a later addition to the text and was not part of Mormon's plates. The way Nephi$_1$ separated them is interesting because he declares that it is about his "reign and ministry." That it should contain an account of his ministry is unsurprising, as within that book Nephi$_1$ writes:

> Nevertheless, I have received a commandment of the Lord that I should make these [small] plates, for the special purpose that there should be an account engraven of the ministry of my people.
>
> Upon the other [large] plates should be engraven an account of the reign of the kings, and the wars and contentions of my people; wherefore

these plates are for the more part of the ministry; and the other plates are for the more part of the reign of the kings and the wars and contentions of my people. (1 Ne. 9:3–4)

The surprising part is that his book title indicates that it would also discuss his *reign*, even though he declared that his other large plates would contain the record "of the reign of the kings." While not intending it to be a thorough record of his and his descendant's reigns, 1 Nephi is nevertheless profoundly interested in establishing a political justification for the new people.[8] A repeated theme in 1 Nephi is showing how Nephi$_1$ fulfilled the promise that he would be a ruler over his brothers. The prophecy was declared early in Nephi$_1$'s story: "And inasmuch as thou shalt keep my commandments, thou shalt be made a ruler and a teacher over thy brethren" (1 Ne. 2:22).

The Reigns of Kings and Judges

Mormon makes clear that he did not use the small plates to write his early Nephite history, as he did not discover them until he was working on King Benjamin, the second Nephite king in Zarahemla (W of M 1:3). Although there are references in Mormon's writings that might be seen as quotations of small plate texts, it is more likely that Mormon was quoting text from the large plates that had parallel information or language.

In addition to not using the small plates, the book names that Mormon used were taken from the large plates and clearly followed a different logic from what we see on the small plates. The books that Mormon intended to form his Book of Mormon were:

- [The Book of Lehi][9]
- The Book of Mosiah
- The Book of Alma, the Son of Alma
- The Book of Helaman
- The Book of Nephi, the Son of Nephi, which was the Son of Helaman

---

8. An early examination of this idea is Noel B. Reynolds, "The Political Dimension in Nephi's Small Plates." See also Brant A. Gardner, *Traditions of the Fathers*, 175–80.

9. Joseph Smith, "Preface," *Book of Mormon*, 1: "I would inform you that I translated, by the gift and power of God, and caused to be written, one hundred and sixteen pages, the which I took from the Book of Lehi, which was an account abridged from the plates of Lehi, by the hand of Mormon." Note that the facsimile reprint shows this page as 1, but the next page as iv. The First Book of Nephi begins on page 5.

- The Book of Nephi, which is the Son of Nephi, One of the Disciples of Jesus Christ
- The Book of Mormon
- [The Book of Ether]

In his analysis of the nature of the Nephite record, John L. Sorenson suggests:

> Nephi could not have anticipated how many metal plates this secular history would eventually require, so blank sheets of hammered metal must have been added periodically to his original set to accommodate the writings of later generations of historians; but the name of the record, "the plates of Nephi," was retained for the enlarged set in honor of the founder of the tradition.
>
> There is reason to believe that when successive portions of the master record were added, they were labeled "the book of so-and-so" even though they were integral parts of "the plates of Nephi." While named after the principal individual who began each section, they sometimes also included records kept by that person's descendants (e.g., Alma 63:17, "the account of Alma, and Helaman his son, and also Shiblon, who was his son").[10]

Sorenson's suggestion is a commonly held assumption: the books were named for the "principal individual who began each section." However, that does not adequately explain what is happening with the book names in Mormon's text, which he took from the large plates. What it cannot answer is why there was ever a new name on the record. If the record changed names when the first person wrote, there would have been no reason to have a new name. The prime example of this problem comes as we understand the book of Lehi.

The book of Lehi was the first named book in Mormon's golden plates. It was fully lost when Martin Harris mishandled the initial transcription

---

10. Sorenson, "Mormon's Sources," 5. Sorenson continues: "It seems reasonable that each of the component books represented a number of metal plates manufactured at the onset of the named scribe's tenure; these would have been filled up by him and his descendants, after which a new major writer would craft new plates and begin another installment of the ongoing historical record." I would disagree with that statement. Certainly, scribes created a number of plates, but there was no reason to worry about the number of the plates. With ties to the government, new plates could be created as needed, and one must suppose that even had they been bound with metal rings, those rings might be opened to add or remove plates as might be needed. It is doubtful, for example, that there were blank plates at the end of one record that remained blank because the next scribe created a new set of empty plates.

pages. Nevertheless, we have no indication that there was any named book following Lehi save for the book of Mosiah (named for Mosiah$_1$ the father of Benjamin, not Mosiah$_2$ the son of Benjamin). This means that the book of Lehi covered between four hundred and four hundred fifty years of Nephite history,[11] involving multiple generations of kings. (Jacob notes that there was a king who followed Nephi$_1$ [Jacob 1:9], and he possibly lived to see yet another or more [v. 11].)

The Book of Mosiah lists three kings in the record. The book was named for Mosiah$_1$ (whose history in the opening chapters of the book of Mosiah had been lost with the book of Lehi). We then have a portion of King Benjamin's reign (although the conflict leading to his great sermon was also lost). Finally, the book ends not only with Mosiah$_2$ but also with the end of Nephite kings as he transferred leadership to judges.

The book of Alma begins with the seating of Alma$_2$ as the Chief Judge. After abdicating the position to Nephihah rather than one of his sons (Alma 4:16–17), Alma$_2$ continued to "keep record of this people . . . on the plates of Nephi," then commanded his son Helaman$_1$ to do the same (37:1–2).

The book of Helaman is named for Helaman$_2$, who was the son of Helaman$_1$ and was made the Chief Judge. Following his death, his son Nephi$_2$ was made chief judge (Hel. 3:37). Like his great-grandfather, Alma$_2$, Nephi$_2$ also abdicated the position to focus on his ministry with his brother Lehi$_2$.

Looking at these changes in the book names, the common thread that explains them is a change in dynasty. Thus, rather than being written to represent a person, they were part of the large plate records of the kings. Thus, the book of Lehi is named after the founder of the peoples of the promised land;[12] the book of Mosiah is named after Mosiah$_1$, "who was made king over the land of Zarahemla" (Omni 1:12);[13] the book of Alma is named after Alma$_2$, "the first and chief judge over the people of Nephi" (Alma book header); and the book of Helaman is named after Helaman$_2$, who was made Chief Judge after the murder of his predecessors, Pahoran

---

11. The chronology is not completely clear at this point. It is a problem with dating through the end of the book of Mosiah. When Alma begins with a new annalistic outline, the dating becomes much more accurate.

12. It may be the case that Nephi$_1$ chose this name to establish his own claim as the legitimate successor to his father in his history.

13. Bradley, *The Lost 116 Pages*, 241–73. For the reasons given above, I disagree with Bradley's argument that this book was originally titled "The Book of Benjamin" (275–78).

and Pacumeni (Hel. 2:2). (Of note, Helaman$_2$ was the first Chief Judge descended by Mosiah$_1$ after Alma$_2$ stepped away from the position to focus on his ministry.) It is highly probable that these were the names on the large plates, and Mormon simply replicated the dynastic collection under the name of the king or Chief Judge who began the dynasty.

The Books of 3 and 4 Nephi

As recorded in 3 Nephi 7:1–4, the dynastic Nephite political structure collapsed:

> Now behold, I will show unto you that they did not establish a king over the land; but in this same year, yea, the thirtieth year, they did destroy upon the judgment-seat, yea, did murder the chief judge of the land.
>
> And the people were divided one against another; and they did separate one from another into tribes, every man according to his family and his kindred and friends; and thus they did destroy the government of the land.
>
> And every tribe did appoint a chief or a leader over them; and thus they became tribes and leaders of tribes.
>
> Now behold, there was no man among them save he had much family and many kindreds and friends; therefore their tribes became exceedingly great. (3 Ne. 7:1–4)

The dissolution of the government creates an important backdrop for the next two books Mormon includes. Were the two books of Nephi included on the large plates? Mormon clearly indicates the termination of his source for the book of Helaman: "and thus ended the book of Helaman, according to the record of Helaman and his sons" (Hel. 16:25). What we expect is that early in the book of 3 Nephi, there should be an indication that the writer is a ruler and beginning a new dynasty. We don't get that. What we get are some unusual statements about the text.

The first unusual aspect of 3 Nephi is the synoptic book header. These typically tell us something about the contents of the book. For example, the header of the book of Alma informs that it includes the accounts of Alma$_2$, the reign of the judges, and both wars among the Nephites and with the Lamanites. However, the book header for 3 Nephi states: "And Helaman was the son of Helaman, who was the son of Alma, who was the son of Alma, being a descendant of Nephi who was the son of Lehi, who came out of Jerusalem in the first year of the reign of Zedekiah, the king of Judah." The header is unusual in its content, and that may be due to nineteenth-century compositor John Gilbert's decision to create a book header similar to that of previous books. Thus, it may be that what we have typeset as a header was intended to be a long continuation of the title. As Mark A. Wright has suggested, Mormon's title for the book may have been:

> The book of Nephi, the son of Nephi, who was the son of Helaman. And Helaman was the son of Helaman, who was the son of Alma, who was the son of Alma, being a descendant of Nephi who was the son of Lehi, who came out of Jerusalem in the first year of the reign of Zedekiah, the king of Judah.[14]

Such a long and unusual title serves two purposes. First, it signals a shift in the way Mormon is sourcing his material. A book name change has previously signaled a change in dynasty, but this book does not. Indeed, it is in 3 Nephi that we see that "in the thirty and first year that they [the Nephites] were divided into tribes, every man according to his family, kindred and friends" (3 Ne. 7:14). The book represents a people whose overarching governmental structure has been dissolved. Rather than using the plates of Nephi as his primary source and including secondary material, it seems that here Mormon used $Nephi_3$'s personal record for his primary source—at least insofar as the descriptions of Christ's appearance are concerned—and consulted the large plates for additional information.

Furthermore, an additional purpose for this unique title is that rather than denoting a change in dynasty, it emphasizes both genealogy and continuation. It appears that the unusual replication of names with Nephi, son of Nephi; son of Helaman, son of Helaman; and Alma, son of Alma has a narrative function to indicate the religious continuity among political turmoil.[15]

Not only does this title reinforce such a continuation, but the very name "Nephi" creates an intentional connection to the beginning of the Nephite nation, which we see recreated by 4 Nephi. After the people who experienced the Savior at Bountiful formed the basis for a new government, it was then that there were no longer any *-ites* (4 Ne. 1:17). Thus, there were no *Nephites*. It may be then that this renewed Nephite people took their name from $Nephi_3$, the disciple of Christ. It may also be that the book simply titled "The Book of Nephi" did not originally carry the name "Nephi." As discussed in Chapter 8, Mormon seems to have played with names in his text. Because he was ultimately telling the story of the Nephites, he may have taken the book from the large plates but given it the name Nephi to create the continuation of the story.

---

14. Mark A. Wright, personal email in my possession.
15. Joseph M. Spencer, *An Other Testament: On Typology*, 112–13.

Chapter Thirteen

Nephi₁'s and Jacob's Use of Source Texts[1]

Not only does Nephi₁'s account of the retrieval and importance of the brass plates directly tie the Nephite tradition of keeping records to that of the Old World, it also places Nephi₁ and his father within an Old World scribal tradition.[2] Nephi₁'s role and abilities as a scribe are normally taken for granted, as he is the first author that readers encounter in the published Book of Mormon, as well as the creator of the plates of Nephi that generations of record keepers maintained. However, in Nephi₁'s account, it is his father Lehi₁ who models record keeping for Nephi₁ by reading and learning from the brass plates as soon as they were recovered (1 Ne. 5:10). He also maintained his own record for which Nephi₁ does not "make a full account of the things which [his] father hath written" (1:16). When Lehi₁'s family arrived in the New World, they would have carried with them two different records: the brass plates and Lehi's personal record. While various prophets quoted from the brass plates throughout our Book of Mormon, only Nephi₁ used his father's writings.

S. Kent Brown undertook the task of understanding what parts of Lehi's writings made an appearance in Nephi₁'s writings. He suggests:

> The structure of the early verses of 1 Nephi 1 shows Nephi's dependence on his father's account, preserving the opening of Lehi's record itself. As a matter of custom, ancient prophets introduced an account of their divine callings near the beginning of their record, coupling it with a colophon about the year of the reign of the local king—precisely what we find in 1 Ne. 1:4–15. Directly after Nephi's opening remark about himself (1:1–3) there is a notation that the story began during the first year of king Zedekiah's reign (1:4). Next, as expected, we read of God commissioning the prophet (1:5–15). But

---

1. Some of this chapter has previously appeared in Brant A. Gardner, *Labor Diligently to Write*.

2. Noel B. Reynolds specifically elaborates that tradition as a Manassite scribal school. Noel B. Reynolds, "Lehi and Nephi as Trained Manassite Scribes," 161–216. See also Brant A. Gardner, "Nephi as Scribe," 45–55.

it I not the call of Nephi; it is Lehi's call. In this light, I believe that Nephi inserted the opening of his father's book into 1 Ne. 1:4–15.[3]

Not only do the structure and content of those verses hint that they were essentially copied from Lehi's record, but Nephi₁ directly references Lehi's written record:

> And now I, Nephi, do not make a full account of the things which my father hath written, for he hath written many things which he saw in visions and in dreams; and he also hath written many things which he prophesied and spake unto his children, of which I shall not make a full account. (1 Ne. 1:16)

Nephi₁, however, complicates the matter by adding:

> But I shall make an account of my proceedings in my days. Behold, I make an abridgment of the record of my father, upon plates which I have made with mine own hands; wherefore, after I have abridged the record of my father then will I make an account of mine own life. (v. 17)

At issue is here what Nephi₁ means when he writes that he is making an "abridgment" of his father's record. Today, that term typically describes a new text that retains much of the original while being edited it to be shorter. (For example, abridgments of lengthy works of fiction—such as Victor Hugo's *Les Miserables*—are commonly created by an editor cutting what they deem filler or unnecessary.) However, this is not what Nephi₁ intends; rather, the term is being used here to describe Mormon's own efforts at abridging the millennium-long Nephite historical record—that is, a shortened account that does not necessarily cite the original.[4]

Thus, Nephi₁ here referred to a shift of focus rather than an entire change in source material. Because Nephi₁'s story begins with his father's prophetic call, he had to include his father's story for readers to understand the family's journeying and the Lord's guidance that brought the family to the New World.

Besides his father's record, the oldest record in Nephi₁'s possession was the brass plates, which Nephi₁ obviously quoted from, as did his brother Jacob. However, no other writer on the small plates appears to have consulted or quoted the brass plates in their writings.

---

3. S. Kent Brown, *From Jerusalem to Zarahemla. Literary and Historical Studies of the Book of Mormon*, 30.

4. The first meaning in Webster's 1828 dictionary entry for "abridgment" is "an epitome; a compend, or summary of a book."

Nephi₁'s Use of Scripture

Nephi₁ used the scriptures in two ways. The first involved knowing and understanding scriptural narratives to exhort others, such as his brothers. Nephi₁ admonishes them to complete their mission to retrieve the brass plates:

> Therefore let us go up; let us be strong like unto Moses; for he truly spake unto the waters of the Red Sea and they divided hither and thither, and our fathers came through, out of captivity, on dry ground, and the armies of Pharaoh did follow and were drowned in the waters of the Red Sea.
>
> Now behold ye know that this is true; and ye also know that an angel hath spoken unto you; wherefore can ye doubt? Let us go up; the Lord is able to deliver us, even as our fathers, and to destroy Laban, even as the Egyptians. (1 Ne. 4:2–3)

In this example, Nephi₁ references a scriptural story to make his point to his brothers. That this happens before they acquired the brass plates shows that Nephi₁ had already learned the stories well enough to reference them. Not only that, but his brothers too had to have known the stories in order for Nephi₁'s efforts to be effective.

Nephi₁'s second use of scripture is more complex and points to his having some scribal training. After mastering the fundamental texts, a scribal student would then be trained in the exegesis of those texts.[5] Robert Wiseman explains how this aspect of the scribal industry functioned in the Dead Sea Scrolls:

> A *pesher* is a commentary—at Qumran, a commentary on a well-known biblical passage, usually from the Prophets, but also from Psalms and sometimes even other biblical books like Genesis, Leviticus, or Deuteronomy. The important thing is that the underlying biblical passage being interpreted should be seen as fraught with significance in relation to the ideology or history of the Scroll Community. Often this takes the form of citing a biblical passage or quotation out of context or even sometimes slightly altered, followed by the words, "*pesher*" or "*pesher ha-diver*," meaning "its interpretation" or "the interpretation of the passage is." The text then proceeds to give an idiosyncratic interpretation having to do with the history or ideology of the group, with particular reference to contemporary events.[6]

This description sounds like a much more academic explanation of what Nephi₁ stated more simply:

---

5. Van der Toorn, *Scribal Culture and the Making of the Hebrew Bible*, 58.
6. Robert Eisenman, *James the Brother of Jesus*, 81.

And I did read many things unto them which were written in the books of Moses; but that I might more fully persuade them to believe in the Lord their Redeemer I did read unto them that which was written by the prophet Isaiah; for I did *liken* all scriptures unto us, that it might be for our profit and learning. (1 Ne. 19:23)

As John W. Welch has noted, Nephi$_1$ and Jacob are the two writers who most often cite Isaiah, particularly in large passages.[7] Garold N. Davis also noticed that not only are the long citations of Isaiah confined to Nephi$_1$ and Jacob, but references to the house of Israel (and the synonymous house of Jacob) are almost exclusively found in their writings.[8] This is not a coincidence; it is part of the conscious selection of themes that Nephi$_1$ wanted to emphasize.

For example, Davis highlights Nephi$_1$'s summary of Isaiah 48–49 that he read to his brothers after their father's discourse on his vision:

Nephi returns from having been "carried away in the spirit" (1 Nephi 15:1) to find his brothers engaged in a dispute because they cannot understand Lehi's words concerning the scattering of Israel and the subsequent gathering through the fulness of the gentiles (see verses 7, 13). Nephi's explanation of these concepts follows the same pattern as that noted above in 1 Nephi 10:3–14: the house of Israel will be scattered (see verses 12, 17, 20), the Messiah "shall be manifested in body unto the children of men" (verse 13), and "at that day shall the remnant of our seed known that they are of the house of Israel, and that they are the covenant people of the Lord" (verse 14). Nephi then reveals that he used the prophet Isaiah as his scriptural support for these teachings: "I did rehearse unto them the words of Isaiah, who spake concerning the restoration of the Jews, or of the house of Israel; and after they were restored they should no more be confounded, neither should they be scattered again" (verse 20).[9]

The way that Nephi$_1$ and Jacob use Isaiah suggests that they both had a particular type of concern for the new people of Nephi. First, they were concerned that this new people see themselves as a continuation of the house of Israel, and they made certain to connect their people to those promises of the past through Isaiah and the brass plates. Second, Nephi$_1$ and Jacob were also interested in the future of their new people and used

---

7. John W. Welch, "Getting Through Isaiah with the Help of the Nephite Prophetic View," 19.

8. Garold N. Davis, "Pattern and Purpose of the Isaiah Commentaries in the Book of Mormon," 279.

9. Davis, 282–83.

the Lehite exodus to identify the New World people with scattered Israel, thus linking them to the promises of the gathering of Israel. The people of Nephi might have been separated from the rest of Israel, but Nephi₁ and Jacob wanted them to understand that they could be redeemed through their faithfulness to God's covenant with Israel.

The interesting prophetic step in this is the role of the Gentiles. Just as the emphasis on the house of Israel is localized primarily in Nephi₁ and Jacob, so too is any discussion of those not of Israel.[10] A modern reader of Nephi₁'s and Jacob's references to the Gentiles might see themselves in this role of saving the Lehite descendants. However, that is not likely to have been the reason that Nephi₁ and Jacob would have spoken about them. We must remember that the idea of the *pesher* was to liken the scriptures to the current population, and the events that modern readers might recognize were still in the far distant future for Nephi₁ and his people. Instead, we approach this prophetic use of scripture from Nephi₁'s contemporaneous context; the most likely explanation is that for Nephi₁ and his people, the Gentiles were a non-Israelite population that was already present in the New World when they arrived.[11]

Both Nephi₁ and Jacob had important and immediate reasons for using Isaiah to teach their people, and they did it in a way that differs from the modern tendency to proof text a short passage from the scriptures. As Grant Hardy has pointed out, "Nephi's general pattern for interpreting scripture is to follow a direct quote—often rather lengthy—with a discussion that incorporates a few key phrases but does not provide a comprehensive or detailed commentary."[12]

Nephi₁'s Introduction to Isaiah in 2 Nephi

The insertion of thirteen complete chapters of Isaiah in 2 Nephi led to four (original) chapters that flowed from themes included in the Isaiah chapters. It was following their inclusion in 2 Nephi 25:1–8 that Nephi₁ explains why he did so, which is presented in Table 13 with interpretive commentary on the right.

---

10. Davis, 281.
11. Brant A. Gardner, "A Social History of the Early Nephites."
12. Grant Hardy, *Understanding the Book of Mormon*, 65.

Table 13

Verse	Comment
1 Now I, Nephi, do speak somewhat concerning the words which I have written, which have been spoken by the mouth of Isaiah. For behold, Isaiah spake many things which were hard for many of my people to understand; for they know not concerning the manner of prophesying among the Jews.	Nephi introduces his own take on Isaiah's words. He underlines the idea that his people find Isaiah difficult because they "know not concerning the manner of prophesying among the Jews." It is tempting to see this as a reference to the specific training Nephi would have had in the scribal school.
2 For I, Nephi, have not taught them many things concerning the manner of the Jews; for their works were works of darkness, and their doings were doings of abominations.	Although Nephi clearly links works of darkness to the Jews in the Old World, his vision of the future will see his own people succumbing to the "works of darkness rather than light" (2 Ne. 26:10).
3 Wherefore, I write unto my people, unto all those that shall receive hereafter these things which I write, that they may know the judgments of God, that they come upon all nations, according to the word which he hath spoken.	Nephi writes to his people and likens the works of darkness of the Old World to those that will happen in the New. It is for that reason that he declares that "the judgments of God" will "come upon all nations." The Nephites will be one of those nations.
4 Wherefore, hearken, O my people, which are of the house of Israel, and give ear unto my words; for because the words of Isaiah are not plain unto you, nevertheless they are plain unto all those that are filled with the spirit of prophecy. But I give unto you a prophecy, according to the spirit which is in me; wherefore I shall prophesy according to the plainness which hath been with me from the time that I came out from Jerusalem with my father; for behold, my soul delighteth in plainness unto my people, that they may learn.	Nephi repeats the idea that Isaiah is hard to understand. However, he here claims that Isaiah is best understood through prophecy. Thus, Nephi's writing should not be read as exegesis, but as prophecy triggered by themes in Isaiah.

Table 13 continued

Verse	Comment
5 Yea, and my soul delighteth in the words of Isaiah, for I came out from Jerusalem, and mine eyes hath beheld the things of the Jews, and I know that the Jews do understand the things of the prophets, and there is none other people that understand the things which were spoken unto the Jews like unto them, save it be that they are taught after the manner of the things of the Jews.	This appears to be an oblique reference to his scribal training. The Jews understood these things, and Nephi understands them because he is also from Jerusalem. To know these things, one must be "taught after the manner of the things of the Jews."
6 But behold, I, Nephi, have not taught my children after the manner of the Jews; but behold, I, of myself, have dwelt at Jerusalem, wherefore I know concerning the regions round about; and I have made mention unto my children concerning the judgments of God, which hath come to pass among the Jews, unto my children, according to all that which Isaiah hath spoken, and I do not write them.	Nephi repeats the information from verse 2 that he has not taught his people after the manner of the Jews. He repeats the declaration from verse 5 that Nephi came from Jerusalem.
7 But behold, I proceed with mine own prophecy, according to my plainness; in the which I know that no man can err; nevertheless, in the days that the prophecies of Isaiah shall be fulfilled men shall know of a surety, at the times when they shall come to pass.	Nephi repeats the declaration from verse 4 that he will provide his own prophecy. In verse 4 he noted the plainness of his prophecy. He repeats that statement and declares that when the prophecies are fulfilled, people will recognize their fulfillment.
8 Wherefore, they are of worth unto the children of men, and he that supposeth that they are not, unto them will I speak particularly, and confine the words unto mine own people; for I know that they shall be of great worth unto them in the last days; for in that day shall they understand them; wherefore, for their good have I written them.	The prophecy will be of great worth because when they are fulfilled, people will understand them.

Most striking in these eight verses is the amount of repetition that has no literary function.[13] Strangest is perhaps the end of verse 4 and the beginning of 5:

> I shall prophesy according to the plainness which hath been with me from the time that *I came out from Jerusalem* with my father; for behold, my soul *delighteth in plainness* unto my people, that they may learn. Yea, and my soul *delighteth in the words of Isaiah, for I came out from Jerusalem.*

The delight in plainness might be a nice parallel to delighting in the words of Isaiah, except Nephi₁ has declared that Isaiah is hard to understand—not plain.

The lack of directness in discourse is something new for Nephi₁. Up to this point, repetitions have more likely been for poetic emphasis, but here we are seeing a stream of conscious writing that contrasts to the tightly planned text of 1 Nephi. At this point it appears that Nephi₁ is writing directly from the plates and without a specifically thought-out plan. Because of this, his clarity of expression suffers for lack of prior editing or planning. For example, as Nephi₁ begins his prophecy in plainness, he references the coming Messiah:

> But, behold, they shall have wars, and rumors of wars; and when the day cometh that the Only Begotten of the Father, yea, even the Father of heaven and of earth, shall manifest himself unto them in the flesh, behold, they will reject him, because of their iniquities, and the hardness of their hearts, and the stiffness of their necks.
>
> Behold, they will crucify him; and after he is laid in a sepulchre for the space of three days he shall rise from the dead, with healing in his wings; and all those who shall believe on his name shall be saved in the kingdom of God. Wherefore, my soul delighteth to prophesy concerning him, for I have seen his day, and my heart doth magnify his holy name. (2 Ne. 25:12–13)

After Nephi₁ finishes with his prophecy in plainness based on Isaiah, he begins a new chapter—in which he again seems to repeat himself:

> And now I, Nephi, make an end of my prophesying unto you, my beloved brethren. And I cannot write but a few things, which I know must surely come to pass; neither can I write but a few of the words of my brother Jacob.

---

13. Donald W. Parry, *Poetic Parallelisms in the Book of Mormon*, 109–10, provides several places where these verses can be formatted as different types of parallels. There is clearly a lot of repetition, but the attempt to format them as though they were intentional poetic forms obscures the murky unclarity of the text.

Wherefore, the things which I have written sufficeth me, save it be a few words which I must speak concerning the doctrine of Christ; wherefore, I shall speak unto you plainly, according to the plainness of my prophesying.

For my soul delighteth in plainness; for after this manner doth the Lord God work among the children of men. For the Lord God giveth light unto the understanding; for he speaketh unto men according to their language, unto their understanding.

Wherefore, I would that ye should remember that I have spoken unto you concerning that prophet which the Lord showed unto me, that should baptize the Lamb of God, which should take away the sins of the world. (2 Ne. 31:1–4)

The opening discussion of a prophecy in plainness is the same. The topic of the coming Messiah is the same. In this case, however, Nephi$_1$ is not teaching about resurrection but of atonement from sin. Both are aspects of the Messiah. The prophecy in plainness based on Isaiah will reprise themes from the vision that Nephi$_1$ and his father had about the future of the house of Israel and its struggles before its restoration. The prophecy in plainness in the last three original chapters of 2 Nephi is where Nephi$_1$ applies the mission of the Savior to the individual rather than to the greater society.

Nephi$_1$'s Prophetic *Pesher* on Isaiah in 2 Nephi

Nephi$_1$ uses specific phrases to help his readers understand that the prophecy of the Tree of Life he experienced can also be seen in Isaiah's teachings. Although subtle, the presence of similar phrasing allows readers to see the connections Nephi$_1$ made to Isaiah. Table 2A in Chapter 2 correlates verses from Nephi$_1$'s prophecy based on Isaiah with phrases or themes from his earlier vision in the Old World. Side by side, it is easy to see that Nephi$_1$ is not later presenting a new or different vision of the future; rather, this newer version is an affirmation of his prophetic vision of the tree based on Isaiah.

Jacob and Sources

We also see Jacob's use of Isaiah in the sermons Nephi$_1$ included in his small plates. Given his young age when they arrived in the New World, Jacob likely learned how to use scripture, and particularly Isaiah, from Nephi$_1$ rather than his elderly father, Lehi$_1$. Therefore, it is not surprising that Jacob used the Isaiah texts in the same way as did Nephi$_1$.

In his own book Jacob does not cite Isaiah, but the practice of citing a large amount of text to extract smaller segments to be emphasized was the same. A long inclusion of scripture comes when, in a sermon to his people, Jacob cites the prophet Zenos's olive tree allegory (Jacob 5, with the application following in Jacob 6). The length and horticultural accuracy of the Zenos allegory suggests that the long quotation in the small plates was directly copied from the brass plates; however, whether Jacob read the entire allegory to his audience or merely summarized it for them are equally plausible. In either case, the use of the long scriptural passage with an application to the current audience based on elements of the long passage follows the pattern Nephi$_1$ set for how scripture was to be used in teaching.

Chapter Fourteen

Mormon's Use of Source Texts

Mormon had two different experiences with writing history on plates. The earlier instance saw him become the official Nephite record keeper, where he was given charge of the entire Nephite archive and tasked with taking the (large) plates of Nephi and recording "all the things that ye have observed concerning this people" (Morm. 1:4). Mormon did just that. He recounts: "And upon the plates of Nephi I did make a full account of all the wickedness and abominations" (2:17–18). As the Nephite historian, his sources were his observations and experiences, not the records of others.

His second experience came much later in life when inspiration had him consult the Nephite archives to construct a spiritual history that became the Book of Mormon. This time his primary source was the large plates of Nephi, which formed the backbone of Mormon's history. However, he also utilized other records that had been kept for centuries (see Chapter 11), and those made up only a small fraction of what was available to him (Hel. 3:13–16). Furthermore, as an abridged and spiritual history, there were certainly stories on the large plates that Mormon elected not to tell. We cannot know what those stories and sources might have been. We have only what Mormon decided fit his agenda for his Book of Mormon.[1] From what he did decide to include, we can learn how Mormon used the sources available to him.

Mormon, Sources, and History

In his study of Mormon as an editor, Thomas W. Mackay points to Mormon's diligence in noting sources other than the large plates, remarking, "That Mormon scrupulously names his sources is a stunning feat."[2] (See more information in Chapter 6.) However, while Mormon makes

---

[1]. It is also important to remember that we have what Mormon deemed important from the reign of King Benjamin to the end. We do not know what secondary sources might have been available, or used, in the beginning of Mormon's work, which was lost.

[2]. Thomas W. Mackay, "Mormon as Editor: A Study in Colophons, Headers, and Source Indicators," 92. Also, Richard Neitzel Holzapfel, "Mormon, the Man and the Message," 119:

clear when he is beginning to pull from alternate sources (usually with a header), he simply assumes that readers would understand he is returning to the large plates as his source.

The most interesting of these transitions comes after Mormon had been using Alma$_2$'s personal record in Alma III–X (5–15). Alma III (5) begins with a header indicating that Mormon is quoting from "[t]he words which Alma . . . delivered to the people in their cities and villages throughout the land." Chapter XI (16), however, returns to the large plates source for its information without any explicit mention that the source of the information has changed. Instead, the return to the large plates must be discerned by the change in the type of information recorded as well as the marking of the year, the latter of which is nearly diagnostic for text coming from the large plates.[3] The next chapter, Alma XII (17–20), again includes a header indicating Mormon's use of the "record of Alma" as his secondary source.

While Mormon often directly and extensively quotes from secondary sources (such as the record of Zeniff, Alma$_2$'s personal record, and the Nephi$_3$'s personal record), he rarely does so from the large plates. With the exception of King Benjamin's sermon (which would have likely been recorded in the record of the kings, particularly due to the sermon being part of Mosiah$_2$'s coronation ceremony), all other sermons and theological expositions found in the Book of Mormon come from secondary records.

Mormon dealt with history, but he had no intention of being an historian.[4] Like many Old Testament writers, he saw history as the loom

---

Mormon used a range of introductory and inserted notations to guide his readers: such as the names of authors for records, speeches, and epistles that are quoted or abridged—imbedded source indicators; genealogical or other authenticating information about the authors; and brief or extended summaries of contents, including subheadings for complex inserts or documents. Mormon's contribution as editor like in the fact that he assiduously presents source documents and texts while retaining a unity of narrative flow in his historical account.

3. At least diagnostic beginning with the book of Alma, which is when the marking of individual years begins.

4. In this I appear to contradict Grant Hardy's reading of Mormon: "Perhaps the most striking difference between Nephi and Mormon is how much the latter sees himself as a historian, with a responsibility to tell the story of his civilization comprehensively and accurately." Grant Hardy, *Understanding the Book of Mormon: A Reader's Guide*, 91. I suspect that our differences lie mostly in emphasis rather than actual substance.

upon which the image of God's intent would appear as the warp and weft of time filled in the picture. As he concluded his work, Mormon wrote to the Lamanites as a remnant of the house of Israel and made clear his purpose in writing:

> Therefore repent, and be baptized in the name of Jesus, and lay hold upon the gospel of Christ, which shall be set before you, not only in this record but also in the record which shall come unto the Gentiles from the Jews, which record shall come from the Gentiles unto you.
>
> For behold, *this is written for the intent that ye may believe that*; and if ye believe that ye will believe this also; and if ye believe this ye will know concerning your fathers, and also the marvelous works which were wrought by the power of God among them. (Morm. 7:8–9)

Mormon used the backbone of Nephite history to frame the story he intended to tell but crafted it to meet this intent.[5] According to David B. Honey,

> The fact that the work has been edited out of various other records leads us to conclude that the redactor, Mormon, must have been guided by certain editorial principles by which he decided which records were important to copy, excerpt, or summarize and which data were judged either essential, superfluous, or unnecessary to include.[6]

The Book of Mormon is a tapestry created from the events of the past, designed to illustrate the future of God's plan for the house of Israel.[7]

Mormon's Two Overarching Purposes

Mormon himself was never explicit about why he wrote the Book of Mormon. Moroni, who understood what his father wanted to do, explicitly stated those purposes in the Title Page: (1) "to show unto the remnant

---

5. Grant Hardy, "Mormon as Editor," 25, notes that Mormon shows that "the bad things that happen are truly terrible, while the good things are wondrous indeed." However, there is mention of a third set of people in the environs whose fate is not discussed. Hardy suggests that the "answer is that these people did not fit into the pattern of 'the righteous prosper, the wicked suffer.'"

6. David B. Honey, "The Secular as Sacred: The Historiography of the Title Page," 95.

7. Honey, 97: "The next guideline defines just which type of events best portray the influence of the Lord: those events are most crucial for inclusion, whether from past Hebrew or contemporary Nephite history, that lead to 'the convincing of the Jew and Gentile that Jesus is the Christ, the Eternal God, manifesting himself unto all nations.'"

of the house of Israel what great things the Lord hath done for their fathers; and that they may know the covenants of the Lord, that they are not cast off forever"; and (2) "to the convincing of the Jew and Gentile that Jesus is the Christ, the Eternal God, manifesting himself unto all nations."

Mormon's method of fulfilling these purposes was not to declare them, but rather to show them. As Richard Dilworth Rust stated:

> One mark of great literature is that it *shows* a concept concretely and avoids telling or explaining it abstractly. Appropriately, then, the Book of Mormon purposes to "*show* unto the remnant of the House of Israel what great things the Lord had done for their fathers."[8]

Showing how these divine promises were, or would be, fulfilled guided the way Mormon interacted with his sources. He showed events from the large plates and quoted exegesis from his secondary sources—all in the service of showing that Jesus is the Christ, the Eternal God, as well as what great things God had done for the ancestral fathers.

Showing that Jesus Is the Christ, the Eternal God

Near the end of his ministry, Joseph Smith taught: "It is necessary for us to have an understanding of God himself in the beginning."[9] Nearly a millennium and a half earlier, Mormon understood this same principle and made it a focus of the Book of Mormon to show that Jesus is the Christ, the Eternal God.

To see how Mormon does this we must first recognize two crucial elements to the Nephite understanding of God. The first is that their God was the same who had made the covenant with the house of Israel, a covenant that crossed the seas and continued in the New World. That God was known as *Yahweh* (or *Jehovah*, as the name has been transliterated in the King James Bible).

The second element is that Yahweh himself would come to earth to perform the Atonement. Lehi$_1$ and Nephi$_1$ learned and taught that instead of an anticipated military deliverer like David, Jesus would be and is the

---

8. Richard Dilworth Rust, *Feasting on the Word. The Literary Testimony of the Book of Mormon*, 19. Norman F. Cantor, *In the Wake of the Plague: The Black Death and the World It Made*, 17. "The scientific method had not yet been invented. When faced with a problem, people in the Middle Ages found the solution through diachronic (as opposed to synchronic) analysis. The diachronic is the historical narrative, horizontally developing through time: 'Tell me a story.'"

9. "History, 1838–1856, volume E-1 [1 July 1843–30 April 1844]," The Joseph Smith Papers, 1968.

Christ *and* the Eternal God. In more time-appropriate language, Moroni declared in the Title Page that *Yahweh is the Messiah*. The Nephite God was Yahweh, who for much of Nephite history was promised and then, in spectacular fashion, fulfilled.

Thora Florence Shannon and Avram R. Shannon examined the connection between Jesus Christ and the law of Moses in the Book of Mormon. They note:

> Early in the Book of Mormon, the Lord begins to reveal to Lehi$_1$ and his family about his bodily coming to earth to save the world through his sacrificial blood atonement. Edward J. Brandt has shown that there are three separate revelational periods where Jesus Christ is specifically introduced by name to the Nephites before his post-resurrection appearances. These occasions are composed first of the grouped revelations of Lehi$_1$, Nephi$_1$, and Jacob. Then, when the specific knowledge of Jesus Christ and his atoning sacrifice appears to have been lost among the general Nephites, there are separate but roughly contemporaneous revelations, first in the book of Mosiah by King Benjamin, and then by Abinadi. *These revelations each explicitly connect with the law of Moses, because Jesus Christ and the atoning blood of his sacrifice are inextricably connected with the law of Moses.*[10]

Abinadi is perhaps most explicit in identifying the Messiah with God. In Mosiah 15:1 he taught: "I would that ye should understand that God himself shall come down among the children of men, and shall redeem his people." Earlier, he rhetorically asked, "For behold, did not Moses prophesy unto them concerning the coming of the Messiah, and *that God should redeem his people?* Yea, and even *all the prophets who have prophesied ever since the world began*—have they not spoken more or less concerning these things?" (13:33). Mormon includes a sermon by Amulek, emphasizing the sacrificial nature of Jesus's atonement:

> For it is expedient that there should be a great and last sacrifice; yea, not a sacrifice of man, neither of beast, neither of any manner of fowl; for it shall not be a human sacrifice; but it must be an infinite and eternal sacrifice. . . . And behold, this is the whole meaning of the law, every whit pointing to that great and last sacrifice; and that great and last sacrifice will be the Son of God, yea, infinite and eternal. (Alma 34:10, 14)

In the Book of Mormon, Mormon first showed the prophecies that declared that Yahweh himself would come down to be sacrificed and to redeem his people; then he showed how those prophecies were fulfilled.

---

10. Thora Florence Shannon and Avram R. Shannon, "'I Am the Law.' Jesus Christ and the Law of Moses in the Book of Mormon," 145–46; emphasis added.

Yahweh did indeed come down. The description of the event in 3 Nephi 11 captures some of the wonder of that event:

> And now it came to pass that there were a great multitude gathered together, of the people of Nephi, round about the temple which was in the land Bountiful; and they were marveling and wondering one with another, and were showing one to another the great and marvelous change which had taken place.
>
> And they were also conversing about this Jesus Christ, of whom the sign had been given concerning his death.
>
> . . . .
>
> And it came to pass, as they understood they cast their eyes up again towards heaven; and behold, they saw a Man descending out of heaven; and he was clothed in a white robe; and he came down and stood in the midst of them; and the eyes of the whole multitude were turned upon him, and they durst not open their mouths, even one to another, and wist not what it meant, for they thought it was an angel that had appeared unto them. (vv. 1–2, 8)

A glorious being undeniably came down. Those in Bountiful recognized that the being was sacred, but they did not yet perceive that being as their God. Instead, they assumed it was an angel or a divine messenger. To show that this descended divine being was indeed Yahweh *the Messiah*, they needed one more showing. According to Mark A. Wright,

> When Christ appeared to the Nephites, he may have been communicating with them according to their cultural language when he invited them to come and feel for themselves the wounds in his flesh. He bade them first to thrust their hands into his side, and secondarily to feel the prints in his hands and feet (3 Nephi 11:14). This contrasts with his appearance to his apostles in Jerusalem after his resurrection. Among them, he invited them to touch solely his hands and feet (Luke 24:39–40). Why the difference? To a people steeped in Mesoamerican culture, the sign that a person had been ritually sacrificed would have been an incision on their side—suggesting they had had their hearts removed—whereas for the people of Jerusalem in the first century, the wounds that would indicate someone had been sacrificed would have been in the hands and the feet—the marks of crucifixion.[11]

The difference was not simply in the type of wounds but in the way the wounds defined the person. The being who had appeared before the apostles in the Old World was standing before those gathered in Bountiful. As Wright points out, their experiences were similar but had what might

---

11. Mark A. Wright, "Axes Mundi: Ritual Complexes in Mesoamerica and the Book of Mormon," 90–91.

appear to be minor differences. Nevertheless, it is precisely in those differences that the message was conveyed.

In Jerusalem, Jesus's disciples had witnessed his hands and feet nailed to a cross as he suffered and died before them. What they needed to know following his resurrection was that the very Jesus they had seen crucified was now the man standing before them. The marks on the hands and feet of their resurrected Lord testified that it was that very Jesus who had died nailed to the cross and was now living again.

In Bountiful, the people knew that a heavenly being had descended. What *they* needed to know was that this glorious being before them had once died as a sacrifice. Marks in the hands and feet would not show them that, as they did not have crucifixion as a form of torture and death to give those marks meaning. The killing wound in the side, however, would, signifying his sacrificial death and atoning mission.

After Jesus demonstrated to the people that he was the very Yahweh the Messiah, it is unsurprising that when he commanded that his disciples should pray, that "they began to pray; and they did pray unto Jesus, calling him their Lord and their God" (3 Ne. 19:18). They got the message. Their God stood before them. Of course they prayed to him. They always had.

Having shown the fulfillment of the prophesied sacrificial atonement of their own God, Mormon had no more need to show that Jesus is the Christ, and after 3 Nephi he no longer entered sermons or discussions on that matter.

Showing Unto the Remnant of the House of Israel What Great Things the Lord Hath Done

Mormon showed that Jesus is Christ the Eternal God by presenting prophecy and then showing the fulfillment of prophecy. His other message for his future audience required a different method. The way that Mormon intended to show his purpose for the remnant of the house of Israel was to show "what great things the Lord hath done for their fathers." This relied upon a cyclical concept of history that looked to the past to understand the future.

Historical Consciousness and Things that Repeat

Mormon participated in a worldview that saw history as a thing that repeated. The cycles might be longer or shorter, but they were nonetheless cycles. This was a prominent idea in Mesoamerican cultures, as noted by David Stuart: "This cyclical system of time gave rise to the idea that history was forever based on familiar recurring patterns, and that 'prophecy,' at least in the Maya understanding of time, was but a reflection of events and trends of the past."[12] Time did not simply pass and disappear; it passed by only to pass by again.

The cyclicality of history may have also been inherited from Old World Israel.[13] Geoffrey F. Spencer describes that historical worldview:

> The genius of the Old Testament prophets was not that they produced oracles about future events but that they were inspired to understand God's action in their people's history and in the crises of their own days. Only in this context could they assert with confidence the plan of God's judgement and salvation in the time to come. History becomes prophetic because what God has done becomes the key to what he will do.[14]

Therefore, showing what great things God had done for the Lamanite fathers was an explicit promise that those great things could and would be done for Mormon's future audience. Inside that framework, Mormon showed the repeating patterns that would validate the promise for the future by creating thematic parallels where people or stories were intended to be seen as repetitions.[15] Thus, Richard Dilworth Rust observes: "Essentially every event or person in the Book of Mormon may well remind us of another event or person; the book is like a beautifully composed symphony with repeated themes and motifs."[16]

Although Mormon used the large plates as the backbone of his narrative, he was free to mold history into a shape that furthered his theological intent. Thematic parallels began with history but were written in ways that emphasized their similarities. Major differences that might have been recorded on the large plate record were simply ignored in favor of the parallel elements. When themes repeated, Mormon was showing a pattern that pointed to future promises.

Fully understanding Mormon's use of parallels hits an immediate wall, as we do not have his beginning to the Book of Mormon. While the replacement small plates ensure that readers have the essential early stories,

---

12. David Stuart, *The Order of Days: The Maya World and the Truth about 2012*, 20.

13. A. R. Millard, J. K. Hoffmeier, and D. W. Baker, *Faith Tradition and History*, 223, 318, describe a similar cyclical notion of history for Babylon and Canaan.

14. Geoffrey F. Spencer, "A Reinterpretation of Inspiration, Revelation, and Scripture," 24.

15. Mark D. Thomas, *Digging in Cumorah. Reclaiming Book of Mormon Narratives*, 14–15, discusses narrative formulas and repeating plots.

16. Rust, *Feasting on the Word*, 196.

Table 14A

Lehi₁ and Nephi₁	Mosiah₁
Lived in the land of Lehi₁'s inheritance. (1 Ne. 1:4)	Lived in the land of first inheritance, a common designation for the land of Nephi. (Mosiah 9:1)
God warned Lehi₁ that his life, and that of his family, was in danger. (1 Ne. 1:20, 2:1)	God warned Mosiah₁ that his and his people's lives were in danger. (Omni 1:12)
Fled with his family and left the land of his inheritance. (1 Ne. 2:3–4)	Fled with his people and left the land of their first inheritance. (Omni 1:12–13)
Arrived in a new land. (1 Ne. 18:23–24)	Arrived in a new land where he encountered a new people with a different religion and language. (Omni 1:13–17)
Nephi₁ became king over the newly established city. (2 Ne. 5:18)	Mosiah₁ became king over the newly united people in a new city. (Omni 1:19)

they were not composed by Mormon as part of his larger project. With the small plates we may have regained many of the stories, but the way that Mormon couched that early history remains lost.

Despite this loss, the prevalence of thematic parallels from Mosiah through 3 Nephi are sufficient to establish them as elements of Mormon's art and hint at likely parallels contained in those lost pages. For convenience in following the historical arcs, this examination will begin with those implied thematic parallels, begging patience as the concept becomes more established with further examples.

Thematic Parallels Beginning in the Lost Pages

Based on some of the limited history contained in the small plates, we can assume that Mormon saw a fundamental shift in Nephite history occurring between the books of Lehi and Mosiah. The arrival of the Nephites in the land of Zarahemla parallels the foundation of the Nephite nation in the New World and Mosiah₁'s new Nephite nation in Zarahemla, as shown in Table 14A.

It seems also safe to assume, based on his use of thematic parallels, that Mormon added meaning beyond history to these events in the lost pages. By writing the story of Mosiah₁ as a thematic parallel to the origin story of the Nephite nation, Mormon must have declared that there was a renewed Nephite nation in the land of Zarahemla. That renewal became explicit when king Benjamin called for a newly united people to adopt a new name and a renewed covenant with their God (Mosiah 4).

Positing this thematic parallel has an important implication. There is obviously no mention in Nephi$_1$'s record of meeting the people already inhabiting the New World, even though archaeology tells us that it was already populated when Lehi$_1$'s family arrived. However, if we read the beginning of the Nephite nation through this likely thematic parallel, the meeting with the Mulekites undoubtedly paralleled Lehi$_1$ and his family meeting of a new people who had a different language and religion. That point would have been important for Mormon's thematic parallel, but fell outside of Nephi$_1$'s intended scope of the small plates.[17]

Covering a much longer time period is the thematic parallel between Nephi$_1$'s creation of the Nephite nation and Nephi$_3$'s creation of a new Nephite nation in 4 Nephi. Prior to Christ's arrival, the Gadiantons succeeded in dissolving the Nephite nation into tribes (3 Ne. 7:14). Following Christ there were no -ites (4 Ne. 1:16–17). Thus, there were no Nephites. They were formed again, plausibly when Nephi$_3$ was made the ruler (and began the dynasty for which 4 Nephi is named—see Chapter 11).

Thematic Parallels Beginning in the Book of Mosiah

Just as the first part of the thematic parallel between Nephi$_1$ and Mosiah$_1$ was lost with the early manuscript, so too was our introduction to a story that would have been in the early chapters of the book of Mosiah. Were it not for the book of Omni, we would be unaware of the important pairing of Mosiah$_1$ and Mosiah$_2$. It is there that we learn that after Mosiah$_1$ arrived in Zarahemla, the Nephites had their first introduction to the Jaredites:

> And it came to pass in the days of Mosiah, there was a large stone brought unto him with engravings on it; and he did interpret the engravings by the gift and power of God. And they gave an account of one Coriantumr, and the slain of his people. And Coriantumr was discovered by the people of Zarahemla; and he dwelt with them for the space of nine moons. It also spake a few words concerning his fathers. And his first parents came out from the

---

17. Don Bradley makes a similar argument for Lehi$_1$'s family discovering an existing society, but instead looks to thematic parallels between them and the Joshua-led conquest of the Canaanites in the Hebrew Bible. Don Bradley, *The Lost 116 Pages: Reconstructing the Book of Mormon's Missing Stories*, 169–92.

Table 14B

Mosiah₁	Mosiah₂
King in Zarahemla. (Omni 1:19)	King in Zarahemla. (Mosiah 6:3–4)
Ruled over a newly united people. (Omni 1:19)	Ruled over a newly reunited people (after Benjamin renewed the covenant). (Mosiah 5:1–2)
Translated a Jaredite record that involved the last king, Coriantumr. (Omni 1: 20–22)	Translated a Jaredite record that ended with the last king, Coriantumr. (Mosiah 28:11–13, Ether 12:1)
Created a new government combining Nephites and Zarahemlaites under a single king. (Omni 1:19)	Created the reign of the judges. (Mosiah 29:38–41)

tower, at the time the Lord confounded the language of the people; and the severity of the Lord fell upon them according to his judgments, which are just; and their bones lay scattered in the land northward. (Omni 1:20–22)[18]

This is the first part of a larger thematic parallel between Mosiah₁ and Mosiah₂, which runs deeper than just their shared name,[19] as shown in Table 14B.

Among the several parallels that Mormon highlights between the two, the most important for his narrative was that each translated a Jaredite record. Although he did not include Ether's account himself (which his son Moroni would later do, perhaps after reading his father's history and recognizing its importance), Mormon used the Jaredites as the ultimate thematic exemplar of a destroyed nation. He blamed the Jaredite destruction on their secret combinations and drew parallels between that and the Gadianton Robbers. Just as the Jaredites fell through a group using secret combinations, the Nephites would fall by means of Gadianton's use of secret combinations.[20] Mormon made this parallel explicit in Helaman 2:12–14:

---

18. It is interesting that Omni's record speaks of the Jaredite origin story. That was information that Mosiah₁ translated, but it may not have been part of what Mormon told of that story. The parallel of the two Mosiahs translating was important, but Mormon was never interested in Jaredite beginnings, only their ending.

19. Perhaps Mormon manipulated their names so that his readers would more easily understand that they should see the two rulers as thematic parallels. (See Chapter 8.)

20. See Brant A. Gardner, *Second Witness. Analytical and Contextual Commentary on the Book of Mormon*, 5:11–29, for greater detail on the way Mormon wrote about the Gadianton robbers.

And more of this Gadianton shall be spoken hereafter. And thus ended the forty and second year of the reign of the judges over the people of Nephi. And behold, in the end of this book ye shall see that this Gadianton did prove the overthrow, yea, almost the entire destruction of the people of Nephi. Behold I do not mean the end of the book of Helaman, but I mean the end of the book of Nephi, from which I have taken all the account which I have written.

At the end of his own abridgement of the Jaredite history, Moroni would build on this thematic parallel by pairing the Jaredite hill Ramah with the Nephite hill Cumorah (Ether 15:11). Both hills saw the destruction of a people; according to Moroni, they were the very same hill.

Mormon Selecting Text to Introduce the Jaredite/Gadianton Thematic Parallel

Mormon's art in creating thematic parallels is displayed in the way he used the large plate source and a secondary source to tell the same story twice. It is a story that would have been in an early chapter of the book of Mosiah and entirely lost with the early manuscript had it not also been briefly recorded by Amaleki in the book of Omni:

> And now I would speak somewhat concerning a certain number who went up into the wilderness to return to the land of Nephi; for there was a large number who were desirous to possess the land of their inheritance. Wherefore, they went up into the wilderness. And their leader being a strong and mighty man, and a stiffnecked man, wherefore he caused a contention among them; and they were all slain, save fifty, in the wilderness, and they returned again to the land of Zarahemla.
>
> And it came to pass that they also took others to a considerable number, and took their journey again into the wilderness. And I, Amaleki, had a brother, who also went with them; and I have not since known concerning them. (Omni 1:27–30)

When Mormon returns to this event in his history, it receives only a brief mention since he would have already presented it in more detail:

> And now, it came to pass that after king Mosiah had had continual peace for the space of three years, he was desirous to know concerning the people who went up to dwell in the land of Lehi-Nephi, or in the city of Lehi-Nephi; for his people had heard nothing from them from the time they left the land of Zarahemla; therefore, they wearied him with their teasings. And it came to pass that king Mosiah granted that sixteen of their strong men might go up to the land of Lehi-Nephi, to inquire concerning their brethren. (Mosiah 7:1–2)

These two verses introduce the most complicated combination of narrative time and flashback, as it requires telling two stories that occurred simultaneously. Mormon's solution was to combine two texts: He followed the large plate text up to a point, and then inserted a completely different holographic account (the record of Zeniff).

The large plates timeline told the story of Ammon[21] and his company's departure to find the people who had been separated for so long. However, because their journey took place in a different land (and thus outside the purview of the large plates), Mormon must have relied on Ammon's own record of events, which is recounted in Mosiah V (7–8).[22] Faced with multiple contemporaneous and distinct histories, Mormon skipped any intervening Nephite history so that the focus remained on this expedition.

After recounting Ammon discovering Limhi and his people, Mormon then abruptly shifts both the source record and the timeline by inserting the record of Limhi's grandfather, Zeniff, directly quoting Zeniff (Mosiah VI [9–10]) and then abridging the rest (Mosiah VII–X [11–22]). The inserted story followed the Zeniffite timeline until the people of Limhi and Alma$_1$ both returned to Zarahemla and reentered the large plate timeline.

Why did Mormon elect to enter the Zeniffite record after Ammon's meeting with Limhi? The answer is inherently speculative, but the final event that Mormon recorded of Ammon's meeting with Limhi before his abrupt shift to a different record and time was the story of finding the Jaredite ruins and record. In the narrative based on Ammon's account, Limhi was anxious to have the Jaredite record translated and asked Ammon if there was one who could do so. Ammon answered that there was a seer in Zarahemla, "a man that can translate the records; for he has wherewith that he can look, and translate all records that are of ancient date" (Mosiah 8:13). There are many important stories Mormon told about the people of Zeniff—including Abinadi, and Alma$_1$'s conversion and creation of a church. However, before telling those stories, Mormon introduced the Jaredite record and Mosiah$_2$ as a translator.[23]

---

21. This Ammon was selected to lead the expedition to find the people of Zeniff. He should not be confused with the Ammon who was one of the sons of Mosiah$_2$.

22. Mosiah 25 declares that Mosiah$_2$ gathered his people together to tell their story. It is plausible that the recorded story of Ammon and Limhi occurred prior to that event when the king would have been informed prior to deciding that the whole people should know the tale.

23. In the Original Manuscript, Mosiah 21:28 reads: "And now Limhi was again filled with joy on learning from the mouth of Ammon that king Benjamin had a gift from God, whereby he could interpret such engravings; yea, and Ammon also did rejoice." This was changed in the 1847 edition to read Mosiah,

Mormon told no story without a reason, and he would not have haphazardly stopped right at the point where he both introduced the Jaredite record and established the second part of the thematic parallel between Mosiah$_1$ and Mosiah$_2$. In abridgement of the record of Zeniff, Mormon retells the story of finding the Jaredite plates. In this second telling of the story, he repeats the essentials:

> Now king Limhi had sent, previous to the coming of Ammon, a small number of men to search for the land of Zarahemla; but they could not find it, and they were lost in the wilderness. Nevertheless, they did find a land which had been peopled; yea, a land which was covered with dry bones; yea, a land which had been peopled and which had been destroyed; and they, having supposed it to be the land of Zarahemla, returned to the land of Nephi, having arrived in the borders of the land not many days before the coming of Ammon. And they brought a record with them, even a record of the people whose bones they had found; and it was engraven on plates of ore. (Mosiah 21:25–28)

The physical process of engraving upon plates had to have been laborious. Despite the labor, Mormon elected to tell this story twice in order to highlight the importance of that event.[24]

The Thematic Parallel between Jaredites and Mulekites

Unfortunately, we do not have Mormon's account of Mosiah$_1$'s meeting with the people of Zarahemla. However, later information tells us that Mormon saw the people of Zarahemla (descendants of Mulek) as a destructive force that he linked to the Jaredites. The strongest connection between the people of Zarahemla and the Jaredites comes when Mormon points out that they come from the same place:

> They [the Nephites] came to the land which they called Bountiful. And it bordered upon the land which they called Desolation, it being so far northward that it came into the land which had been peopled and been

---

which is the correct reading. Mormon was copying from the Zeniffite record, and this statement is importantly given as a quotation from Limhi. His people left when Benjamin was king and they may not have yet known that Mosiah$_2$ was the current king. Amaleki gave his record upon which he recorded to the departure of his brother to king Benjamin (W of M 1:10). Therefore, the last king known to the Zeniffites was King Benjamin.

24. Once again, it must be highlighted that Mormon made choices in what he wrote, and those choices were never dictated only because an event happened or that it was written on a record. In this case, we must understand that Mormon intentionally recorded the same story twice in order to emphasize its importance.

destroyed, of whose bones we have spoken, which was discovered by *the people of Zarahemla, it being the place of their first landing.* (Alma 22:29–30)[25]

Mormon reports that the people of Mulek first landed in Jaredite territory around the time that Lehi had landed further south.[26] When Mosiah$_1$ found the people of Zarahemla, they were no longer in the place where they landed and no longer in Jaredite lands. Nevertheless, they were tied to those lands by their own place of landing and by their connection to Coriantumr, the final Jaredite ruler who lived among them for several months.

For Mormon, that connection between the people of Zarahemla (as descendants of Mulek) and the Jaredite land of Desolation created a conceptual link to a dangerous potential enemy. Indeed, until the explicit appearance of the Gadiantons in the beginning of the book of Helaman, the greatest danger to the Nephite nation comes from Mulekites. In Mormon's thematic parallels, Mulekites serve as stand-ins for the Gadiantons who later take over in the book of Helaman. The Mulekite and Gadianton stories thus form a double parallel to the Jaredites.

Given Mormon's possible manipulation of names,[27] it cannot be certain that the people he labeled Mulekites descended from a person with that name. *MLK* was a Hebrew root for "king,"[28] and thus the name Mulek carries with it the connotations of kingship. It is not only the Mulek name, but his declared heritage as the son of the king (Hel. 6:10) that conceptually ties the Mulekites to those who desired a king.

A possible manipulation of names seems the best explanation for multiple MLK-named persons in Mormon's account who advocate for a king. For example, Mormon introduces Amalickiah (AMaLicKiah) as one who was "desirious to be a king" (Alma 46:4). His revolt and subsequent coup over the Lamanites resulted in the longest accounts of warfare in Mormon's history (Alma 46–62). It is within that war that a renewed schism arises of men who sought to dethrone Pahoran and were "called king-men . . . [who] were desirous . . . to establish a king over the land"

---

25. See also Helaman 6:10: "Now the land south was called Lehi, and the land north was called Mulek, which was after the son of Zedekiah; for the Lord did bring Mulek into the land north, and Lehi into the land south."

26. "Behold, it came to pass that Mosiah discovered that the people of Zarahemla came out from Jerusalem at the time that Zedekiah, king of Judah, was carried away captive into Babylon" (Omni 1:15).

27. See Chapter 8.

28. John L. Sorenson, *Nephite Culture and Society: Collected Papers*, 110–11.

(51:5).[29] Without having the Nephite text, we can only assume that *kingmen* had a MLK root.

Furthermore, it is possible that an earlier Nephite dissenter whose followers wanted "to be a king over the people" (Alma 2:2) may have also had an MLK name. According to Royal Skousen, while the Printer's Manuscript consistently spells this person's name as "Amlici," the name of his followers is initially twice spelled "Amlikites."[30] There is some confusion about peoples named Amalekites and Amlicites in the Book of Mormon. Based on Mormon's use of names, a plausible reason for the confusion is that Mormon used the same MLK name to describe different groups.[31] For the purpose of his book, Mormon's concern was their status as dissenters who desired to be kings. He cared less about specific details that were tangential to this.

Antithetical Parallels and Repentance

Mormon predominantly used synonymous thematic parallels, where two elements are meant to be seen as replicating each other. When Mormon deviated from his predominant methodology, it is a signal that readers should pay attention. Thus, he tended to use the concept of reversals in antithetical thematic parallels to show repentance.[32] Although he had to write of apostasy and destruction, those were part of the historical backbone of his story. They were never its purpose. His message was not one of melancholy or defeat. It was (and is) a message of redemption through Jesus the Christ and the process of repentance.

A simple reversal is when we see a name that should have a pejorative connotation attached to one who is righteous. For example, Amulek (AMuLeK) has a MLK name. He lived in Ammonihah, a city that was

---

29. The king-men were likely the same who had earlier "been led by the flatteries of Amalickiah . . . that he would make them rulers over the people" (Alma 46:5).

30. Royal Skousen, *Analysis of Textual Variants of The Book of Mormon*, Vol. 4, Part 3, 1605–9.

31. For the controversy, see: Benjamin McMurtry, "The Amlicites and Amalekites: Are They the Same People?," 270–71. For the suggestion that they might be different people to whom Mormon gave the same name, see Brant A. Gardner, *Labor Diligently to Write*, 97–98.

32. There is one important case of an antithetical parallel that does not show repentance, but rather apostasy. Where Lehi$_1$'s people retain their language and religion, the Mulekites did not have a record and therefore lost both their language and religion.

antithetical to the Nephite religion. Nevertheless, he heeded an angel and sheltered Alma$_2$, soon becoming Alma$_2$'s stalwart missionary companion (Alma 8:16–32). The reversal in the expectation behind the MLK name juxtaposes the expectation against Amulek's transformation.

Likewise, Mormon used a Jaredite name to signal the thematic antithetical parallel embodied in one of Alma$_2$'s sons. When Mormon wrote about Alma$_2$ giving a final blessing to his sons, he spent time on Helaman$_1$ but gave a much shorter although similar blessing to Shiblon. Mormon's recounting of his blessings spends the most time with his third son, Corianton, whose name is similar to several Jaredite names—particularly Coriantumr, the last Jaredite king, who had been discovered by the people of Zarahemla (Omni 1:21) and whose name would be shared by another Nephite dissenter (Hel. 1:15). By using that name, Mormon may have intended to prime his readers for the story of an apostate. Indeed, that is the story Mormon told—at that point. However, we often miss Mormon's account of Corianton's repentance that allowed him to become a stalwart missionary.[33] Corianton's name was a juxtaposition of the assumption embedded in the name and the example of repentance. His story was not told to excoriate, but to encourage for change.

A more complex set of parallels occurs between Alma$_1$ and Alma$_2$. The men have the same name, which may have had a structural function to show prophetic continuity amidst political changes.[34] Although we remember both men for their righteous deeds, both had previously taught against the Nephite religion and had dramatic events that triggered their repentance process. Yet both became important to the development and

---

33. "Yea, and there was continual peace among them, and exceedingly great prosperity in the church because of their heed and diligence which they gave unto the word of God, which was declared unto them by Helaman, and Shiblon, and Corianton, and Ammon and his brethren, yea, and by all those who had been ordained by the holy order of God, being baptized unto repentance, and sent forth to preach among the people" (Alma 49:30).

34. "While each book in Mormon's history recounts a particular succession, each break between books also marks a succession. At the same time, Mormon softens the impact of these breaks by having all cross-book successions be those in which the successor shares his name with his father. . . That Mormon highlights dynastic continuity even at points of historical transition makes clear his interest in maintaining the essential progression of the trajectory of Christian preaching that underlies his history." Joseph Spencer, *An Other Testament; On Typology*, 111.

structure of Nephite government and religion.[35] Theirs was not a juxtaposition of names but a juxtaposition of their post-repentant lives, with their earlier position being antagonistic to the Nephite church.

Mormon's Message of Repentance

For Mormon, repentance meant returning to the covenant body of the house of Israel. It was at the heart of his message to the future Lamanites (and Gentiles). When he wrote, the Lamanites he knew had followed the traditions of their fathers for around a thousand years. They were long separated from the house of Israel. Nevertheless, Mormon showed that regardless of the time they might have spent away from the covenant, that covenant patiently awaited their repentance and return. He expressed his hope in a future reuniting with the covenant in his farewell contained in Mormon 7:

> And now, behold, I would speak somewhat unto the remnant of this people who are spared, if it so be that God may give unto them my words, that they may know of the things of their fathers; yea, I speak unto you, ye remnant of the house of Israel; and these are the words which I speak:
> Know ye that ye are of the house of Israel. Know ye that ye must come unto repentance, or ye cannot be saved. (Morm. 7:1–3)

Mormon's most dramatic showing of Lamanite repentance is embodied in two stories that occurred at different times, but which Mormon wrote as thematic parallels. The first was the conversion of the people who eventually took upon themselves the name Anti-Nephi-Lehies. Mormon told their story in detail, including the incident where they laid down their weapons of war and vowed not to take them up again (Alma 36:22). The Anti-Nephi-Lehies tragically demonstrated the power of that vow when the apostate Nephite-led Lamanites fell upon them and killed so many. We read this as a story of their great faith, and it is. However, if we focus too much on their faith, we miss the reason Mormon chose to focus on this story, which was to demonstrate that Lamanites were eminently redeemable (perhaps despite Nephite stereotypes). These Lamanites became at least as righteous as the Nephites; perhaps they were even more righteous. They had faith, and it was a faith that led to repentance and

---

35. $Alma_1$ created the concept of churches and established them in Zarahemla. He also plausibly influenced $Mosiah_2$'s change to judges, as $Mosiah_2$ uses language $Alma_1$ had used to refuse to be a king. $Alma_2$ is the first Chief Judge and High Priest over the Nephite churches.

acceptance of the covenant belonging to the house of Israel. Once part of the covenant, there was no difference between them and the Nephites.

The thematic parallel to that story is told in the book of Helaman. Just as the books of Mosiah and Alma tell of a set of brothers (the sons of Mosiah$_2$) who went to the Lamanite territory and converted the Anti-Nephi-Lehies, the book of Helaman tells of two brothers (Nephi$_2$ and Lehi$_2$, the sons of Helaman$_2$) who also go to the Lamanites and convert a body of people. The parallel to the Anti-Nephi-Lehies is explicit in Mormon's summary of their missionary efforts:

> And it came to pass that they did go forth, and did minister unto the people, declaring throughout all the regions round about all the things which they had heard and seen, insomuch that the more part of the Lamanites were convinced of them, because of the greatness of the evidences which they had received. And as many as were convinced did lay down their weapons of war, and also their hatred and the tradition of their fathers. (Hel. 5:50–51)

Given Mormon's penchant for using names to further his story, it is plausible that Mormon intended the name Anti-Nephi-Lehi as looking forward to the names of the later brothers, Nephi$_2$ and Lehi$_2$. The name would have thus been a signal to his readers that they should see the thematic parallel between the two stories.[36]

Mormon further demonstrated the ability of Lamanites to not only repent, but to become a very righteous people. They were sufficiently more righteous than the theoretically covenant-bound Nephites that they could send the prophet Samuel the Lamanite to them (Hel. 13–16). Interestingly, this is the only time that Mormon combines a name with this description. We never see "Nephi the prophet," "Alma the prophet," or any other "Nephite the prophet." Mormon could have given just his name, Samuel, but he seems to intentionally underscore the point that this was a Lamanite prophet. Thus, Samuel the Lamanite stands as a juxtaposition against the expected exclusivity of the Nephite prophets.

For both the Anti-Nephi-Lehies and those Nephi$_2$ and Lehi$_2$ converted, an important part of their repentance was to lay down their weapons of war. Mormon's expectation of cyclicality shows in his final plea to his future audience: "Know ye that *ye must lay down your weapons of war*, and delight no more in the shedding of blood, and take them not again, save

---

36. As pure speculation, it is possible that the scribes heard Joseph give the name, but their lack of consistent spelling gave the name Anti with an 'i' rather than Ante with an 'e'. Perhaps they were Ante-Nephi-Lehies, even more obviously tying the two groups together.

it be that God shall command you" (Morm. 7:4). The Lamanites that Mormon knew were immersed in a culture of war and bloodshed. He expected that the future Lamanites would be similar and would thus also need to lay down their weapons of war.[37] The two groups associated with the names Nephi$_2$ and Lehi$_2$ were part of history, but Mormon framed their histories as thematic parallels so that future readers might understand that what had already been repeated in the past could be expected in the future.

---

37. Mesoamerican cultures were not only warlike but developed war into a religious act associated with human sacrifice. The Anti-Nephi-Lehies were afraid that if "we should stain our swords again they can no more be washed bright through the blood of the Son of our great God" (Alma 24:13). That they were willing to take up arms to defend the Nephites only shows that it was not pacifism but a religious vow that kept them from taking up arms. The problem may have been related to the cult of war in Mesoamerican cultures, and culture to which they did not want to return.

Chapter Fifteen

Mormon's Appendix

After years of waiting to retrieve the plates, after wondering how they would be translated, after Martin Harris traveling to find a scholar who might translate them—after all of that, the translation began in the Spring of 1828.[1] By June, the book of Lehi and the beginning of the book of Mosiah had been translated.[2] And then the manuscript was lost. When Harris came to the Prophet to confess to the loss, he exclaimed: "Oh! I have lost my soul! I have lost my soul!" Joseph Smith's response was akin to despair. As his mother described it: "Oh! My God, my God, said Joseph clenching his hands together. All is lost, is lost! What shall I do? I have sinned."[3]

In July, God chastised Joseph, but yet promised that

> my work shall go forth, for inasmuch as the knowledge of a Savior has come unto the world, through the testimony of the Jews, even so shall the knowledge of a Savior come unto my people—and to the Nephites, and the Jacobites, and the Josephites, and the Zoramites, through the testimony of their fathers. (D&C 3:16–17)

Although it was comforting to know that all was not lost, the translation stopped, and the plates were taken from Joseph. However, with the assurance that the plates would only be taken for "a season" (v. 14), Joseph would soon receive a new revelation explaining how the lost content would be recovered:

> And now, verily I say unto you, that an account of those things that you have written, which have gone out of your hands, is engraven upon the plates of Nephi; Yea, and you remember it was said in those writings that a more particular account was given of these things upon the plates of Nephi.
>
> And now, because the account which is engraven upon the plates of Nephi is more particular concerning the things which, in my wisdom, I would bring to the knowledge of the people in this account.

---

1. Michael Hubbard MacKay and Gerrit J. Dirkmaat, *From Darkness unto Light: Joseph Smith's Translation and Publication of the Book of Mormon*, 91. The translation began after Martin Harris returned in early 1828. Emma scribed before Martin Harris and Martin Harris was scribing by April 1828.

2. MacKay and Dirkmaat, *From Darkness unto Light*, 93.

3. Lucy Mack Smith, *Lucy's Book. A Critical Edition of Lucy Mack Smith's Family Memoir*, 418; punctuation added.

Therefore, you shall translate the engravings which are on the plates of Nephi, down even till you come to the reign of king Benjamin, or until you come to that which you have translated, which you have retained;

And behold, you shall publish it as the record of Nephi; and thus I will confound those who have altered my words. (D&C 10:38–42)

The revelation indicates that there remained a source text that could be translated to replace the lost stories. However, it wasn't specific about what that source was, and the reference to the "plates of Nephi" may have led Joseph to assume that he would be given the large plates to translate and take the place of the portion of the abridged history that had been lost.[4] Thus, it may not have been until Joseph was translating 1 Nephi 9 that he realized that he was now translating from a completely separate record from the one Mormon had based his history on.

The plates were returned to Joseph on September 22, 1828,[5] but the translation would not fully resume until April 1829. Rather than starting over with the replacement text, Joseph began translating where they had left off in the early chapters of the book of Mosiah with Oliver Cowdery as the primary scribe. By May 31, he would have finished the translation of the book of Moroni and the Title Page,[6] the latter of which Joseph would later describe as "a literal translation, taken from the very last leaf, on the left hand side of the collection or book of plates, which contained the record which has been translated."[7] The Title Page therefore closed the set of plates that completed Mormon's intended Book of Mormon (including Moroni's additions). Only after completing the book Mormon intended did Joseph begin to translate the replacement text.

John Welch's timeline for the translation process has Joseph beginning with 1 Nephi on June 5, 1828. By June 28, he had finished with Omni and Words of Mormon.[8] Just as the Title Page introducing the Book of Mormon came at the end of Mormon's plates, so too did the Words of Mormon, which introduces the small plates, come at the end of that set, and there

---

4. Don Bradley, *The Lost 116 Pages: Reconstructing the Book of Mormon's Missing Stories*, 107–8.

5. Steven C. Harper, *Making Sense of the Doctrine & Covenants: A Guided Tour through Modern Revelations*, 46.

6. John W. Welch, "Timing the Translation of the Book of Mormon: 'Days [and Hours] Never to Be Forgotten,'" 48.

7. "History, 1838–1856, volume A-1 [23 December 1805–30 August 1834]," The Joseph Smith Papers, 34.

8. Welch, "Timing the Translation of the Book of Mormon," 48–49.

is internal evidence that Mormon wrote it soon after reading the end of Omni. When describing his discovery of the small plates, Mormon writes:

> [F]or after I had made an abridgment from the plates of Nephi, down to the reign of this King Benjamin, *of whom Amaleki spake*, I searched among the records which had been delivered into my hands, and I found these plates, which contained this small account of the prophets, from Jacob down to the reign of this King Benjamin, and also many of the words of Nephi. (W of M 1:3)

Here, Mormon seems to indicate that while abridging the large plates, he came upon something that referenced King Benjamin receiving the small plates from Amaleki.[9] This likely piqued Mormon's curiosity and led him to searching through the Nephite archive to find the plates that were mentioned. (Alternatively, he may have simply discovered the small plates while looking through the Nephi records for additional material.)

Regardless of how he discovered the small plates, the phrase "of whom Amaleki spake" must be referencing Amaleki's account of giving the plates to King Benjamin in Omni 1:25, as any account of this transfer of the small plates in the large plates, which recorded the deeds of the kings, would have been written from Benjamin's perspective rather than Amaleki's. This phrase, of course, would fit with Mormon reading some or all of the small plates just prior to writing his introduction to them.

One challenge that readers of the Book of Mormon today face with understanding Mormon's intent for his Words is that for nearly two centuries we have been reading it as a segue between the small plates and the book of Mosiah, due to Harris's loss of the early manuscript and the subsequent placement of the small plates in the published Book of Mormon. However, not only does Mormon never indicate any foreknowledge of the lost manuscript pages or how the small plates would eventually be used, he makes clear how he understood the relationship the small plates had to his own book: "But behold, I shall take these plates, which contain these prophesyings and revelations, and put them with the remainder of my

---

9. In a 2022 Facebook communication, Nathaniel Givens notes: "So Mormon is cruising along, abridging the large plates of Nephi (which ended up as the lost 116 pages) and he gets to Benjamin and all of a sudden decides to go search through his records? Obviously Benjamin must have mentioned receiving the small plates! This makes two things clear. First, Mormon wasn't randomly sifting through records. He was hunting for the small plates. Second, he didn't know the small plates existed. Because Amaleki gave the plates to Benjamin who ruled after his father, $Mosiah_1$, this information had to have been recorded in the lost chapters of the book of Mosiah." (Shared with permission.)

record, for they are choice unto me; and I know they will be choice unto my brethren" (W of M 1:6). Rather than intending to integrate the small plates into his own writings, he included them in addition to his record as what we would call an appendix today.

In fact, the first two sentences of Words make clear that Mormon wrote it after completing his writing in the Book of Mormon:

> And now I, Mormon, being about to deliver up the record which I have been making into the hands of my son Moroni, behold I have witnessed almost all the destruction of my people, the Nephites.
>
> And it is many hundred years after the coming of Christ that I deliver these records into the hands of my son; and it supposeth me that he will witness the entire destruction of my people. But may God grant that he may survive them, that he may write somewhat concerning them, and somewhat concerning Christ, that perhaps some day it may profit them. (1:1–2)

By this point Mormon had hidden up the entire Nephite archive, and the only records not in the hill Cumorah were the Book of Mormon plates he was about to give to Moroni and the small plates that he was now introducing. Because he said that he had witnessed "almost all the destruction of my people, the Nephites," he must have written Words after Mormon 6, which details those who fell in the battle. Thus, by the time Moroni wrote Mormon 8, both the plates of Mormon and the small plates were in Moroni's possession. Furthermore, parallel themes between Words of Mormon 1:8 and Mormon 7 suggest that both were written at a time when those ideas were most present in Mormon's mind.[10] Despite the dire times that Mormon was writing in, he remained hopeful that the small plates might benefit a future audience: "And my prayer to God is concerning my brethren, that they may once again come to the knowledge of God, yea, the redemption of Christ; that they may once again be a delightsome people" (W of M 1:8).

Having finished his abridged history of the Nephites, Mormon seemed acutely aware that his introduction to the small plates would be the last of his own writing: "And now I, Mormon, proceed to finish out my record, which I take from the plates of Nephi; and I make it according to the knowledge and the understanding which God has given me" (W of M 1:9). Beginning in verse 10, he realizes that while he had earlier indicated how he found the small plates, he had not explained the chain of custody that enabled him to acquire them. Although we have Amaleki's statement that he intended to

---

10. Eldin Ricks, "The Small Plates of Nephi and the Words of Mormon," 216, suggests that Words of Mormon was written in the Nephite year 385 when Mormon was 74.

give the plates to Benjamin in Omni 1:25, the account of Benjamin receiving and preserving them had to have come from the large plates:

> Wherefore, it came to pass that after Amaleki had delivered up these plates into the hands of king Benjamin, he took them and put them with the other plates, which contained records which had been handed down by the kings, from generation to generation until the days of king Benjamin.
>
> And they were handed down from king Benjamin, from generation to generation until they have fallen into my hands. And I, Mormon, pray to God that they may be preserved from this time henceforth. And I know that they will be preserved; for there are great things written upon them, out of which my people and their brethren shall be judged at the great and last day, according to the word of God which is written.
>
> And now, concerning this king Benjamin—he had somewhat of contentions among his own people. (W of M 1:10–12)

At this point in his introduction to the small plates, Mormon now makes mention of Benjamin five times despite the king only having a very brief and passing reference at the end of those plates. Thus, he concludes his introduction by highlighting King Benjamin's successes in defeating the Lamanites, countering wickedness from within the Nephites, and bringing peace—all of which stand in sharp contrast to the destruction of the Nephites that he opened Words with.

With the 1830 relocation of Words of Mormon from the end of the small plates to the beginning of the Book of Mormon, these reminiscent verses have for nearly two centuries been read as a bridge into the beginning of the book of Mosiah, and that context has colored the way they have been read.[11] The placement of Words of Mormon as the end of that appendix-like addition underscores Mormon's own intent that it and the small plates be read divorced from that context rather than defined by it.[12]

---

11. Jack M. Lyon and Kent R. Minson, "When Pages Collide: Dissecting the Words of Mormon," 121–36, argue that Words of Mormon 1:1–11 are the introduction and verses 12–18 are unrelated. They propose that verses 12–18 represent text that was retained when the 116 pages were lost. Clifford P. Jones, "That Which You Have Translated, Which You Have Retained," 1–64, argues that the whole of Words of Mormon was retained. Both of these solutions are interesting, but they both read Words of Mormon in the current textual position between Omni and Mosiah.

12. In *The Plates of Mormon*, The Words of Mormon has been relocated to the beginning of the small plates where its function as an introduction. That placement emphasizes the difficulty of seeing verses 12–18 connected to the book of Mosiah.

Bibliography

Abusch, I. Tzvi. "Maqlû III 1–30: Internal Analysis and Manuscript Evidence for the Revision of an Incantation." *Studia Orientalia* 106 (2009): 307–13.
Agar, Michael. *Language Shock: Understanding the Culture of Conversation.* New York: Perennial, 1994.
Alter, Robert. *The Art of Biblical Narrative.* New York: Basic Books, 2011.
———. *The Hebrew Bible: A Translation with Commentary: Prophets.* New York: W. W. Norton & Company, 2019.
Anderson, Lavina Fielding. "Mother Tongue: KJV Language in Smith Family Discourse." Paper presented at the Annual Meeting of the Mormon History Association, Springfield, Illinois, on May 22, 2009. Copy in author's possession.
Anderson, Ronald D. "Leitworter in Helaman and 3 Nephi." In *The Book of Mormon: Helaman Through 3 Nephi 8, According to Thy Word*, edited by Monte S. Nyman and Charles D. Tate, Jr., 241–49. Provo, UT: Religious Studies Center, Brigham Young University, 1992.
Ash, Michael R. *Rethinking Revelation and the Human Element in Scripture: The Prophet's Role as Creative Co-Author.* Redding, CA: FAIRLatterDaySaints.org, 2021.
Barlow, Philip L. *Mormons and the Bible: The Place of the Latter-day Saints in American Religion.* New York: Oxford University Press, 1991.
Barney, Kevin L. "Poetic Diction and Parallel Word Pairs in the Book of Mormon." *Journal of Book of Mormon Studies* 4, no. 2 (1995): 15–81.
Belnap, Daniel L. "The King James Bible and the Book of Mormon." In *The King James Bible and the Restoration*, edited by Kent P. Jackson, 162–81. Provo, UT: Religious Studies Center, Brigham Young University, 2011.
Bennett, Bob. *Leap of Faith: Confronting the Origins of the Book of Mormon.* Salt Lake City: Deseret Book, 2009.
Benson, Ezra Taft. "The Book of Mormon—Keystone of Our Religion." *Ensign*, November 1986. Available online at https://www.churchofjesuschrist.org/study/ensign/1986/11/the-book-of-mormon-keystone-of-our-religion.
Best, Karl F. "Changes in the Revelations, 1833 to 1835." *Dialogue: A Journal of Mormon Thought* 25, no. 1 (March 1992): 87–112.
Bierhorst, John, trans. *History and Mythology of the Aztecs: The Codex Chimalpopoca.* Tucson: University of Arizona Press, 1992.
Black, Sharon, and Brad Wilcox. "188 Unexplainable Names: Book of Mormon Names No Fiction Writer Would Choose." *Religious Educator* 12, no. 2 (2011): 119–33.
Bokovoy, David E., and John A. Tvedtnes. *Testaments: Links Between the Book of Mormon and the Hebrew Bible.* Tooele, UT: Heritage Press, 2003.
Bor, Daniel. *The Ravenous Brain: How the New Science of Consciousness Explains Our Insatiable Search For Meaning.* New York: Basic Books, 2012.
Bowen, Gregory A. "Sounding Sacred: The Adoption of Biblical Archaisms in the Book of Mormon and Other 19th Century Texts." PhD diss., Purdue University, 2016.
Bowen, Matthew L. *Name as Key-Word: Collected Essays on Onomastic Wordplay and the Temple in Mormon Scripture.* Orem, UT: The Interpreter Foundation; Salt Lake City: Eborn Books, 2018.

Bradley, Don. *The Lost 116 Pages: Reconstructing the Book of Mormon's Missing Stories*. Salt Lake City: Greg Kofford Books, 2019.

Brandt, Edward J. "The Name *Jesus Christ* Revealed to the Nephites." In *Second Nephi: The Doctrinal Structure*, edited by Monte S. Nyman and Charles D. Tate, Jr., 201–6. Provo, UT: Religious Studies Center, Brigham Young University, 1989.

Brown, Cecil H. *Lexical Acculturation in Native American Languages*. New York: Oxford University Press, 1999.

Brown, S. Kent. "The Exodus Pattern in the Book of Mormon." *BYU Studies* 30, no. 3 (Summer 1990): 111–26.

———. *From Jerusalem to Zarahemla: Literary and Historical Studies of the Book of Mormon*. Vol. 13 of Religious Studies Center Specialized Monograph Series. Provo, UT: Religious Studies Center, Brigham Young University, 1998.

Brown, Samuel Morris. *Joseph Smith's Translation: The Words and Worlds of Early Mormonism*. New York: Oxford University Press, 2020.

Bushman, Richard Lyman. *Joseph Smith: Rough Stone Rolling: A Cultural Biography of Mormonism's Founder*. New York: Vintage Books, 2005.

Campbell, Alexander. "Delusions." *Millennial Harbinger* 2, no. 1 (January 3, 1831): 85–100.

Cantor, Norman F. *In the Wake of the Plague: The Black Death and the World It Made*. New York: Simon and Schuster, 2001.

Carmack, Stanford. "Joseph Smith Read the Words." *Interpreter: A Journal of Latter-day Saint Faith and Scholarship* 18 (2016): 41–64.

Carson, D. A. "The Limits of Functional Equivalence in Bible Translation—and Other Limits, Too." In *The Challenge of Bible Translation: Communicating God's Word to the World*, edited by Glen G. Scorgie, Mark L. Strauss, and Steven M. Voth, 65–113. Grand Rapids, MI: Zondervan, 2003.

Childs, Larry G. "Epanalepsis in the Book of Mormon." *Deseret Language and Linguistic Society Symposium* 12, no. 1 (1986): 154–63.

Chonay, Dionisio José, and Delia Goetz, trans. *Annals of the Cakchiquels and Title of the Lords of Totonicapan*. Norman: University of Oklahoma Press, 1974.

Christenson, Allen J. *Popol Vuh: Literal Poetic Version, Transcription and Translation*. New York: O Books, 2007.

———. *Popol Vuh, the Sacred Book of the Maya: The Great Classic of Central American Spirituality, Translated from the Original Maya Text*. Norman: University of Oklahoma Press, 2003.

———. "The Use of Chiasmus by the Ancient K'iche' Maya." In *Parallel Worlds: Genre, Discourse, and Poetics in Contemporary, Colonial, and Classic Maya Literature*, edited by Kerry M. Hull and Michael D. Carrasco, 311–36. Boulder: University Press of Colorado, 2012.

Coe, Michael D. and Mark Van Stone. *Reading the Maya Glyphs*. London: Thames & Hudson, 2001.

Conkling, J. Christopher. "Alma's Enemies: The Case of the Lamanites, Amlicites, and Mysterious Amalekites." *Journal of Book of Mormon Studies* 14, no. 1 (2005): 108–17, 130–32.

Davis, Garold N. "Pattern and Purpose of the Isaiah Commentaries in the Book of Mormon." In *Mormons, Scripture, and the Ancient World: Studies in Honor of John L. Sorenson*, edited by Davis Bitton, 277–303. Provo, UT: Foundation for Ancient Research and Mormon Studies, 1998.

Davis, Ossie. "The English Language is My Enemy!" In *Language: Introductory Readings*, edited by Virginia P. Clark, Paul A. Eschholz, and Alfred F. Rosa, 242–43. New York: St. Martin's Press, 1966.

Bibliography

Davis, Randall C. "Early Anglo-American Attitudes to Native American Languages." In *Travel and Translation in the Early Modern Period*, edited by Carmine G. Di Biase, 229–38. Amsterdam: Editions Rodopi B. V., 1994.

Davis, William L. *Visions in a Seer Stone: Joseph Smith and the Making of the Book of Mormon*. Chapel Hill: University of North Carolina Press, 2020.

Douglas, Kate. "How Powerful is the Subconscious?" *New Scientist*, April 3–9, 2010, 32.

———. "The Subconscious Mind: Your Unsung Hero." *New Scientist*, December 1, 2007. http://www.newscientist.com/article/mg19626321.400-the-subconscious-mind-your-unsung-hero.html?full=true.

Eggington, William G. *"Our Weakness in Writing": Oral and Literate Culture in the Book of Mormon*. Provo, UT: Foundation for Ancient Research and Mormon Studies, 1992.

Eisenman, Robert. *James the Brother of Jesus*. New York: Penguin Books, 1997.

Evans, Paul S. "Creating a New 'Great Divide': The Exoticization of Ancient Culture in Some Recent Applications of Orality Studies to the Bible." *Journal of Biblical Literature* 136, no. 4 (Winter 2017): 749–64.

Faulring, Scott H., Kent P. Jackson, and Robert J. Matthews, eds. *Joseph Smith's New Translation of the Bible: Original Manuscripts*. Provo, UT: BYU Religious Studies Center, 2004.

Flake, Kathleen. "Translating Time: The Nature and Function of Joseph Smith's Narrative Canon." *The Journal of Religion* 87, no. 4 (October 2007): 497–527.

Frederick, Nicholas J. *The Bible, Mormon Scripture, and the Rhetoric of Allusivity*. Madison, NJ: Fairleigh Dickinson University Press, 2016.

———. "The Book of Mormon and Its Redaction of the King James New Testament: A Further Evaluation of the Interaction between the New Testament and the Book of Mormon." *Journal of Book of Mormon Studies* 27 (2018): 44–87.

———. "The Language of Paul in the Book of Mormon." In *They Shall Grow Together: The Bible in the Book of Mormon*, edited by Charles Swift and Nicholas J. Frederick, 205–34. Provo, UT: Religious Studies Center, Brigham Young University; Salt Lake City: Deseret Book, 2022.

French, Christopher, and Krissy Wilson. "Cognitive Factors Underlying Paranormal Beliefs and Experiences." In *Tall Tales About the Mind and Brain: Separating Fact from Fiction*, edited by S. Della Sala, 3–22. New York: Oxford University Press, 2007.

Gardner, Brant A. *The Gift and Power: Translating the Book of Mormon*. Salt Lake City: Greg Kofford Books, 2011.

———. *Labor Diligently to Write: The Ancient Making of a Modern Book*. Orem, UT: Interpreter Foundation, 2020.

———. "Literacy and Orality in the Book of Mormon." *Interpreter: A Journal of Latter-day Saint Faith and Scholarship* 9 (2014): 29–85.

———. "Nephi as Scribe." *Mormon Studies Review* 23, no. 1 (2011): 45–55.

———. *Second Witness: Analytical and Contextual Commentary on the Book of Mormon*. 6 vols. Salt Lake City: Greg Kofford Books, 2007.

———. *Traditions of the Fathers: The Book of Mormon as History*. Salt Lake City: Greg Kofford Books, 2015.

———. "When Hypotheses Collide: Responding to Lyon and Minson's 'When Pages Collide.'" *Interpreter: A Journal of Latter-day Faith and Scholarship* 5 (2013): 105–19.

Gee, John. "'Choose the Things That Please Me': On the Selection of the Isaiah Sections in the Book of Mormon." In *Isaiah in the Book of Mormon*, edited by Donald W. Parry and John W. Welch, 67–91. Provo, UT: Foundation for Ancient Research and Mormon Studies, 1998.

———. "Verbal Punctuation in the Book of Mormon I: (And) Now." *Interpreter: A Journal of Latter-day Saint Faith and Scholarship* 50 (2022): 33–50.

———. "The Wrong Type of Book." In *Echoes and Evidences of the Book of Mormon*, edited by Donald W. Parry, Daniel C. Peterson, and John W. Welch, 307–29. Provo, UT: Foundation for Ancient Research and Mormon Studies, 2002.

Givens, Terryl, with Brian M. Hauglid. *The Pearl of Greatest Price: Mormonism's Most Controversial Scripture*. New York: Oxford University Press, 2019.

Grey, Matthew J. "Approaching Egyptian Papyri through Biblical Language: Joseph Smith's Use of Hebrew in His Translation of the Book of Abraham." In *Producing Ancient Scripture: Joseph Smith's Translation Projects in the Development of Mormon Christianity*, edited by Michal Hubbard MacKay, Mark Ashurst-McGee, and Brian M. Hauglid, 390–451. Salt Lake City: University of Utah Press, 2020.

Grover, Jerry. *Ziff, Magic Goggles, and Golden Plates: Etymology of Zyf and a Metallurgical Analysis of the Book of Mormon Plates*. Provo, UT: Grover Publishing, 2015.

Gutjahr, Paul C. *The Book of Mormon: A Biography*. Princeton: Princeton University Press, 2012.

Hardy, Grant, ed. *The Book of Mormon: Another Testament of Jesus Christ*. Maxwell Institute Study Edition. Provo, UT, and Salt Lake City: Maxwell Institute for Religious Scholarship and Religious Studies Center and Deseret Book, 2018.

———. "Mormon as Editor." In *Rediscovering the Book of Mormon*, edited by John L. Sorenson and Melvin J. Thorne, 15–28. Provo, UT: Foundation for Ancient Research and Mormon Studies; Salt Lake City: Deseret Book, 1991.

———. *Understanding the Book of Mormon: A Reader's Guide*. New York: Oxford University Press, 2010.

Harper, Steven C. *First Vision: Memory and Mormon Origins*. New York: Oxford University Press, 2019.

"History, 1838–1856, volume A-1 [23 December 1805–30 August 1834]." The Joseph Smith Papers, accessed September 11, 2023. https://www.josephsmithpapers.org/paper-summary/history-1838-1856-volume-a-1-23-december-1805-30-august-1834/.

"History, 1838–1856, volume E-1 [1 July 1843–30 April 1844]." The Joseph Smith Papers, accessed August 28, 2022. https://www.josephsmithpapers.org/paper-summary/history-1838-1856-volume-e-1-1-july-1843-30-april-1844/.

"History, circa June–October 1839 [Draft 1]." The Joseph Smith Papers, accessed September 29, 2023. https://www.josephsmithpapers.org/paper-summary/history-circa-june-october-1839-draft-1/.

"History, circa Summer 1832." The Joseph Smith Papers, accessed March 17, 2023. https://www.josephsmithpapers.org/paper-summary/history-circa-summer-1832/4.

Hofstadter, Douglas R. *Le Ton Beau de Marot: In Praise of the Music of Language*. New York: Basic Books, 1997.

Holzapfel, Richard Neitzel. "Mormon, the Man and the Message." In *The Book of Mormon: Fourth Nephi Through Moroni, From Zion to Destruction*, edited by Monte S. Nyman and Charles D. Tate, Jr., 117–31. Provo, UT: Religious Studies Center, Brigham Young University, 1995.

Honey, David B. "The Secular as Sacred: The Historiography of the Title Page." *Journal of Book of Mormon Studies* 3, no. 1 (Spring 1994): 94–103.

Hopkins, Nicholas A., and J. Kathryn Josserand. "The Narrative Structure of Chol Folktales: One Thousand Years of Literary Tradition." In *Parallel Worlds: Genre, Discourse, and Poetics in Contemporary, Colonial, and Classic Maya Literature*, edited by Kerry M. Hull and Michael D. Carrasco, 21–42. Boulder: University Press of Colorado, 2012.

Hull, Kerry M. "Poetic Tenacity: A Diachronic Study of Kennings in Mayan Languages." In *Parallel Worlds: Genre, Discourse, and Poetics in Contemporary, Colonial, and Classic*

Maya Literature, edited by Kerry M. Hull and Michael D. Carrasco, 73–122. Boulder: University Press of Colorado, 2012.

Jackson, Kent P. *Understanding Joseph Smith's Translation of the Bible*. Provo, UT: Religious Studies Center, Brigham Young University; Salt Lake City: Deseret Book, 2022.

Jackson, Kent P., and Peter M. Jasinski. "The Process of Inspired Translation: Two Passages Translated Twice in the Joseph Smith Translation of the Bible." *BYU Studies* 42, no. 2 (Summer 2003): 35–64.

Johnson, Janiece. "Becoming a People of the Books: Toward an Understanding of Early Mormon Converts and the New Word of the Lord." *Journal of Book of Mormon Studies* 27 (2018): 1–43.

Jones, Clifford P. "That Which You Have Translated, Which You Have Retained." *Interpreter: A Journal of Latter-day Saint Faith and Scholarship* 43 (2021): 1–64.

Journal of Discourses. 26 vols. London and Liverpool: LDS Booksellers Depot, 1854–86.

Kelber, Werner H. *The Oral and the Written Gospel: The Hermeneutics of Speaking and Writing in the Synoptic Tradition, Mark, Paul, and Q*. Bloomington: Indiana University Press, 1997.

Knight, Joseph, Sr., "Reminiscence, Circa 1835–1847." In *Early Mormon Documents*, edited by Dan Vogel, 4:12–24. Salt Lake City: Signature Books, 1996–2003.

Lamb, Martin Thomas. *The Golden Bible; Or, The Book of Mormon. Is It from God?* New York: Ward & Drummond, 1887.

Ludlow, Daniel H. "The Book of Mormon Was Written for Our Day." *The Instructor*, July 1966, 265–67.

———. *Unlocking Isaiah in the Book of Mormon*. Salt Lake City: Deseret Book, 2003.

Lundbom, Jack R. *Biblical Rhetoric and Rhetorical Criticism*. Hebrew Bible Monographs 45. Sheffield, UK: Sheffield Phoenix Press, 2015.

Lyon, Jack M., ed. *The Readable Scriptures: The Book of Mormon: The Standard Works Reformatted for Clarity and Structure*. West Jordan, UT: Temple Hill Books, 2015.

Lyon, Jack M. and Kent R. Minson. "When Pages Collide: Dissecting the Words of Mormon." *BYU Studies* 51, no. 4 (2012): 121–36.

MacKay, Michael Hubbard. "The Secular Binary of Joseph Smith's Translations." *Dialogue: A Journal of Mormon Thought* 54, no. 3 (Fall 2021): 1–39.

MacKay, Michael Hubbard, and Gerrit J. Dirkmaat. *From Darkness unto Light: Joseph Smith's Translation and Publication of the Book of Mormon*. Provo, UT: Religious Studies Center, Brigham Young University; Salt Lake City: Deseret Book, 2015.

Mackay, Thomas W. "Mormon as Editor: A Study in Colophons, Headers, and Source Indicators." *Journal of Book of Mormon Studies* 2, no. 2 (Fall 1993): 90–109.

Mandler, George. "Organization and Memory." In *Human Memory: Basic Processes*, edited by Gordon Bower, 310–54. New York: Academic Press, 1977.

Matthews, Robert J. *"A Plainer Translation": Joseph Smith's Translation of the Bible: A History and Commentary*. Provo, UT: Brigham Young University Press, 1975.

McKinlay, Daniel B. "Amen." In *Encyclopedia of Mormonism*, 4 vols., 1:38. New York: Macmillan Publishing Company, 1991.

McMurtry, Benjamin. "The Amlicites and Amalekites: Are They the Same People?" *Interpreter: A Journal of Mormon Scripture* 25 (2017): 269–76.

Miller, Wade E. "Animals in the Book of Mormon: Challenges and Perspectives," Interpreter Foundation Blog, April 21, 2014. https://journal.interpreterfoundation.org/blog-animals-in-the-book-of-mormon-challenges-and-perspectives/

Miller-Naudé, Cynthia L., and Jacobus A. Naudé. "The Intersection of Orality and Style in Biblical Hebrew: Metapragmatic Representations of Dialogue in Genesis 34." In *Doubling and Duplicating in the Book of Genesis: Literary and Stylistic Approaches to the*

Text, edited by Elizabeth R. Hayes and Karolien Vermeulen, 57–77. Winona Lake, IN: Eisenbrauns, 2016.

Morley, Sylvanus Griswold. "The Hotun as the Principal Chronological Unit of the Old Maya Empire." In *Proceedings of the Nineteenth International Congress of Americanists: Held at Washington, December 27–31, 1915*, edited by Frederick Webb Hodge, 195–201. Washington, DC: International Congress of Americanists, 1917.

Morris, Larry E., ed. *A Documentary History of the Book of Mormon*. New York: Oxford University Press, 2019.

Moskowitz, Racheli, Moriyah Schick, and Joshua Waxman. "*Leitwort* Detection, Quantification and Discernment." In *La Svolta Inevitabile: Sfide e Prospettive per l'Informatica Umanistica*. Atti del IX Convegno Annuale dell'Associazione per l'Informatica Umanistica e la Cultural Digitale, edited by C. Marras, M. C. Passarotti, G. Franzini, E. M. G. Litta Modignani Picozzi. Milán: Universita Cattolicà a del Sacro Cuore, 2020.

Newberg, Andrew, and Mark Robert Waldman. *Born to Believe: God, Science, and the Origin of Ordinary and Extraordinary Beliefs*. New York: Free Press, 2006.

Nida, Eugene A. "The Role of Contexts in Translating." In *Word, Text, Translation: Liber Amicorum for Peter Newmark*, edited by Gunilla J. Anderman and Margaret Rogers, 195–201. Clevedon, UK: Multilingual Matters, 1999.

Ong, Walter J. *Orality and Literacy*. London: Routledge, 2002.

Oregon Department of Transportation Research Section. "Guide to Transcribing and Summarizing Oral Histories." Historic Columbia River Highway Oral History Project (n.p.: March 2010). Accessed March 22, 2022. https://www.oregon.gov/ODOT/Programs/ResearchDocuments/guide_to_transcribing_and_summarizing_oral_histories.pdf.

Parry, Donald W. *Poetic Parallelisms in the Book of Mormon: The Complete Text Reformatted*. Provo, UT: Neal Maxwell Institute for Religious Scholarship, Brigham Young University, 2007.

———. *Preserved in Translation: Hebrew and Other Ancient Literary Forms in the Book of Mormon*. Provo, UT: Religious Studies Center, Brigham Young University; Salt Lake City: Deseret Book Company, 2020.

———. "Why is the Phrase 'and it came to pass' so Prevalent in the Book of Mormon?" *Ensign*, December 1992. Available online at https://www.lds.org/ensign/1992/12/i-have-a-question/why-is-the-phrase-and-it-came-to-pass-so-prevalent-in-the-book-of-mormon.

Perry, Seth. *Bible Culture and Authority in the Early United States*. Princeton: Princeton University Press, 2018.

Person, Jr., Raymond F. "The Role of Memory in the Tradition Represented by the Deuteronomic History and the Book of Chronicles." *Oral Tradition* 26, no. 2 (October 2011): 547–50.

Pinker, Steven. *How the Mind Works*. New York: W. W. Norton & Company, 1997.

———. *The Language Instinct: How the Mind Creates Language*. New York: Viking, 2002.

Pinnock, Hugh W. *Finding Biblical Hebrew and Other Ancient Literary Forms in the Book of Mormon*. Provo, UT: Foundation for Ancient Research and Mormon Studies, 1999.

Pioske, Daniel. "Prose Writing in an Age of Orality: A Study of 2 Sam 5:6–9." *Vetus Testamentum* 66 (2016): 251–79.

Postal, Paul M. "Transformational Grammar: An Introduction." In *Language: Introductory Readings*, edited by Virginia P. Clark, Paul A. Eschholz and Alfred F. Rosa, 149–71. New York: St. Martin's Press, 1972.

Pratt, Parley P. *Autobiography of Parley P. Pratt*. 3rd ed. Salt Lake City: Deseret Book, 1938.

"Revelation Book 1." The Joseph Smith Papers., accessed March 13, 2022. https://www.josephsmithpapers.org/paper-summary/revelation-book-1/.

Reynolds, Noel B. "Lehi and Nephi as Trained Manassite Scribes." *Interpreter: A Journal of Latter-day Saint Faith and Scholarship* 50 (2022): 161–216.

———. "The Political Dimension in Nephi's Small Plates." *BYU Studies* 27, no. 4 (1987): 15–37.

Ricks, Eldin. "The Small Plates of Nephi and Words of Mormon." In *The Book of Mormon: Jacob Through Words of Mormon, To Learn with Joy*, edited by Monte S. Nyman and Charles D. Tate, Jr., 209–19. Provo, UT: Religious Studies Center, Brigham Young University, 1990.

Roberts, Brigham H. *New Witnesses for God, Volume 1*. Salt Lake City: Deseret Book, 1909.

———. *New Witnesses for God, Volume 2: The Book of Mormon*. Salt Lake City: Deseret News, 1920.

Rojo, Ana, and Iraide Ibarretxe-Antuñano. "Cognitive Linguistics and Translation Studies: Past, Present and Future." In *Cognitive Linguistics and Translation: Advances in Some Theoretical Models and Applications*, edited by Ana Rojo and Iraide Ibarretxe-Antuñano, 3–30. Vol. 23 of Applications of Cognitive Linguistics. Berlin: DeGruyter Moulton, 2013.

Rosenvall, Lynn A., and David L. Rosenvall, eds. *A New Approach to Studying the Book of Mormon*. Np: The Olive Leaf Foundation, 2017.

Rust, Richard Dilworth. *Feasting on the Word. The Literary Testimony of the Book of Mormon*. Salt Lake City: Deseret Book; Provo, UT: FARMS, 1997.

———. "Poetry in the Book of Mormon." In *Rediscovering the Book of Mormon: Insights You May Have Missed Before*, edited by John L. Sorenson and Melvin J. Thorne, 100–113. Provo, UT: Foundation for Ancient Research and Mormon Studies; Salt Lake City: Deseret Book Company, 1991.

Schniedewind, William M. *How the Bible Became a Book*. New York: Cambridge University Press, 2004.

Scodel, Ruth. "Self-Correction, Spontaneity, and Orality in Archaic Poetry." In *Voice into Text: Orality and Literacy in Ancient Greece*, edited by Ian Worthington, 59–79. Leiden, Netherlands: E.J. Brill, 1996.

Séguinot, Candace. "Translation Theory, Translating Theory and the Sentence." In *Word, Text, Translation: Liber Amicorum for Peter Newmark*, edited by Gunilla J. Anderman and Margaret Rogers, 84–94. Clevedon, UK: Multilingual Matters, 1999.

Shalev, Eran. "An American Book of Chronicles, Pseudo-Biblicism and the Cultural Origins of the Book of Mormon." In *American Approaches to the Book of Mormon*, edited by Elizabeth Fenton and Jared Hickman, 136–58. Oxford: Oxford University Press, 2019.

———. *American Zion: The Old Testament as a Political Text from the Revolution to the Civil War*. New Haven: Yale University Press, 2013.

Shannon, Thora Florence, and Avram R. Shannon. "'I Am the Law.' Jesus Christ and the Law of Moses in the Book of Mormon." In *I Glory in My Jesus. Understanding Christ in the Book of Mormon*, edited by John Hilton III et al., 145–67. Provo: BYU Religious Studies Center, 2023.

Shaw, Julia. *The Memory Illusion: Remembering, Forgetting and the Science of False Memory*. London: Random House Books, 2016.

Shermer, Michael. *The Believing Brain: From Ghosts and Gods to Politics and Conspiracies—How We Construct Beliefs and Reinforce Them as Truths*. New York: Times Books, 2011.

Skousen, Royal. *Analysis of Textual Variants of the Book of Mormon*. Vol. 4 of *The Book of Mormon Critical Text Project*. 6 parts. Provo, UT: Foundation for Ancient Research and Mormon Studies, 2007.

———. "Critical Methodology and the Text of the Book of Mormon." *Review of Books on the Book of Mormon* 6, no. 1 (1994): 121–44.

———. "How Joseph Smith Translated the Book of Mormon: Evidence From the Original Manuscript." *Journal of Book of Mormon Studies* 7, no. 1 (1998): 22–31.

———. "Translating the Book of Mormon: Evidence from the Original Manuscript." In *Book of Mormon Authorship Revisited: The Evidence for Ancient Origins*, edited by Noel B. Reynolds, 61–93. Provo, UT: Foundation for Ancient Research and Mormon Studies, 1997.

Skousen, Royal, and Robin Scott Jensen, eds. *Revelations and Translations, Volume 3: Printer's Manuscript of the Book of Mormon*. Facsimile edition. Part 1s and 2 of Vol. 3 of the Revelations and Translations series of The Joseph Smith Papers, edited by Ronald J. Esplin and Matthew J. Grow. Salt Lake City: Church Historian's Press, 2015.

———, eds. *Revelations and Translations, Volume 5: Original Manuscript of the Book of Mormon*. Facsimile edition. Vol. 5 of the Revelations and Translations series of *The Joseph Smith Papers*, edited by Matthew C. Godfrey, R. Eric Smith, Matthew J. Grow, and Ronald J. Esplin. Salt Lake City: Church Historian's Press, 2021.

Skousen, Royal, with Stanford Carmack. *The History of the Text of the Book of Mormon: Grammatical Variation*. Part 2 of Vol. 3 of The Book of Mormon Critical Text Project. Provo, UT: Foundation for Ancient Research and Mormon Studies, Brigham Young University Studies, 2016.

———. *The History of the Text of the Book of Mormon: The Nature of the Original Language*. Part 3 of vol. 3 of The Book of Mormon Critical Text Project. Provo, UT: Foundation for Ancient Research and Mormon Studies, Brigham Young University, 2018.

———. *The History of the Text of the Book of Mormon: The King James Quotations in the Book of Mormon*. Part 5 of vol. 3 of The Book of Mormon Critical Text Project. Provo, UT: Foundation for Ancient Research and Mormon Studies, Brigham Young University, 2019.

Sloan, David E. "The Anthon Transcripts and the Translation of the Book of Mormon: Studying It Out in the Mind of Joseph Smith." *Journal of Book of Mormon Studies* 5, no. 2 (1996): 57–81.

Smith, Gerald E. "Improvisation and Extemporaneous Change in the Book of Mormon, Part 1: Evidence of an Imperfect, Authentic, Ancient Work of Scripture." *Interpreter: A Journal of Mormon Scripture* 23 (2017): 1–44.

———. "Improvisation and Extemporaneous Change in the Book of Mormon, Part 2: Structural Evidences of Earlier Ancient versus Later Modern Constructions." *Interpreter: A Journal of Mormon Scripture* 23 (2017): 53–90.

Smith, Joseph. "Preface." In *The Book of Mormon*. Facsimile reprint of the 1830 edition. Independence, MO: Herald House, 1970.

Smith, Lucy Mack. *Lucy's Book. A Critical Edition of Lucy Mack Smith's Family Memoir*, edited by Lavina Fielding Anderson. Salt Lake City: Signature Books, 2001.

Smith, Robert F. *Egyptianisms in the Book of Mormon and Other Studies*. Provo, UT: Deep Forest Green Books, 2020.

Snow, Marcellus S. "Translating Mormon Thought." *Dialogue: A Journal of Mormon Thought* 2, no. 2 (Summer 1967): 49–62.

Sorenson, John L. *An Ancient American Setting for the Book of Mormon*. Provo, UT, and Salt Lake City: Foundation for Ancient Research and Mormon Studies and Deseret Book, 1985.

———. "Mormon's Sources." *Journal of the Book of Mormon and Other Restoration Scripture* 20, no. 2 (2011): 2–15.

———. *Nephite Culture and Society: Collected Paper*. Salt Lake City: New Sage Books, 1997.

Spackman, Randall P. "The Jewish/Nephite Lunar Calendar." *Journal of Book of Mormon Studies* 7, no. 1 (1998): 48–59.

Spencer, Joseph M. *An Other Testament: On Typology*. Np: Salt Press, 2012.

———. *The Vision of All: Twenty-five Lectures on Isaiah in Nephi's Record*. Salt Lake City: Greg Kofford Books, 2016.

Spencer, Stan. "Missing Words: King James Bible Italics, the Translation of the Book of Mormon, and Joseph Smith as an Unlearned Reader and Editor of a Visioned Text." *Interpreter: A Journal of Latter-day Saint Faith and Scholarship* 38 (2020): 45–106.

Stuart, David. *The Order of Days: The Maya World and the Truth about 2012*. New York: Three Rivers Press, 2011.

Szink, Terrence L. "Nephi and the Exodus." In *Rediscovering the Book of Mormon*, edited by John L. Sorenson and Melvin J. Thorne, 39–42. Provo, UT: Foundation for Ancient Research and Mormon Studies, 1991.

Tavris, Carol, and Elliot Aronson. *Mistakes Were Made (But Not by Me): Why We Justify Foolish Beliefs, Bad Decisions, and Hurtful Acts*. Boston: Mariner Books, 2015.

Thomas, Mark D. *Digging in Cumorah. Reclaiming Book of Mormon Narratives*. Salt Lake City: Signature Books, 2000.

Thomas, Rosalind. *Literacy and Orality in Ancient Greece*. New York: Cambridge University Place, 1999.

Thomasson, Gordon C. "Mosiah: The Complex Symbolism and Symbolic Complex of Kingship in the Book of Mormon." *Journal of Book of Mormon Studies* 2, no. 1 (1993): 21–38.

———. "What's in a Name? Book of Mormon Language, Names, and [Metonymic] Naming." *Journal of Book of Mormon Studies* 3, no. 1 (Spring 1994): 1–27.

Treat, Mary Lee. "No Erasers." In *Recent Book of Mormon Developments: Articles From the Zarahemla Record*, 1:54. Independence, MO: Zarahemla Research Foundation, 1984.

Underwood, Grant. "Relishing the Revisions: Joseph Smith and the Revelatory Process." Devotional address given at Brigham Young University–Hawaii, October 13, 2009' accessed March 9, 2022. https://speeches.byuh.edu/devotionals/relishing-the-revisions-joseph-smith-and-the-revelatory-process.

Valletta, Thomas R. "The Exodus: Prophetic Type and the Plan of Redemption." In *Thy People Shall be My People and Thy God My God: The 22nd Annual Sidney B. Sperry Symposium*, 178–90. Salt Lake City: Deseret Book, 1994.

Van der Toorn, Karel. *Scribal Culture and the Making of the Hebrew Bible*. Cambridge: Harvard University Press, 2007.

Vansina, Jan. *Oral Tradition as History*. Madison: University of Wisconsin Press, 1985.

Webster, Noah. *Webster's 1823 Dictionary*. https://webstersdictionary1828.com.

Welch, John W. "Chiasmus in the Book of Mormon." *BYU Studies Quarterly* 10, no. 1 (1969): 69–84.

———. "Timing the Translation of the Book of Mormon: 'Days [and Hours] Never to Be Forgotten.'" *BYU Studies Quarterly* 57, no. 4 (2018): 10–50.

Welch, John W., with Erick B. Carlson, eds. "Emma Smith Bidamon, as interviewed by Joseph Smith III (1879)." In *Opening the Heavens: Accounts of Divine Manifestations, 1820–1844*, 130–31. Provo, UT: Religious Studies Center, Brigham Young University; Salt Lake City: Deseret Book, 2005.

———, eds. "Joseph Smith to the *Times and* Seasons (1843)." In *Opening the Heavens: Accounts of Divine Manifestations, 1820–1844*, 127. Provo, UT: Religious Studies Center, Brigham Young University; Salt Lake City: Deseret Book, 2005.

Wendland, Ernst R. "Orality and Its Implications for the Analysis, Translation, and Transmission of Scripture." Unpublished manuscript, 2013, accessed April 5, 2022. https://www.academia.edu/3657392/Orality_and_the_Scriptures_Composition_Translation_and_Transmission.

Wessel, Walter W. "A Translator's Perspective on Alister McGrath's History of the King James Version." In *The Challenge of Bible Translation: Communicating God's Word to the World*, edited by Glen G. Scorgie, Mark L. Strauss, and Steven M. Voth, 199–211. Grand Rapids, MI: Zondervan, 2003.

"When Lehi's Party Arrived in the Land, Did they Find Horses There?," Book of Mormon Central, October 17, 2022. https://knowhy.bookofmormoncentral.org/knowhy/when-lehis-party-arrived-in-the-land-did-they-find-horses-there.

Wright, David P. "Isaiah in the Book of Mormon: Or Joseph Smith in Isaiah." In *American Apocrypha*, edited by Dan Vogel and Brent Lee Metcalfe, 157–234. Salt Lake City: Signature Books, 2002.

Wright, Mark A. "Axes Mundi: Ritual Complexes in Mesoamerica and the Book of Mormon." *Interpreter: A Journal of Mormon Scripture* 12 (2014): 79–96.

———. "Nephite Daykeepers: Ritual Specialists in Mesoamerica and the Book of Mormon." In *Ancient Temple Worship: Proceedings of the Expound Symposium 14 May 2011*, edited by Matthew B. Brown, Jeffrey M. Bradshaw, Stephen D. Ricks, and John S. Thompson, 243–57. Salt Lake City: The Interpreter Foundation and Eborn books, 2014.

Scripture Index

Old Testament

Genesis
Gen. 2:7 — 113
Gen. 3:20 — 113

Exodus
Ex. 16:7–8 — 139

Deuteronomy
Deut. 27:14–26 — 83n10

2 Samuel
2 Sam. 5:6–9 — 146

1 Chronicles
1 Chron. 16:36 — 83n10

Nehemiah
Neh. 5:121 — 126n11

Psalms
Ps. 106:48 — 83n10

Isaiah
Isa. 5:25 — 10
Isa. 6:3 — 132
Isa. 7:14 — 44, 45n18
Isa. 9:12 — 10
Isa. 9:17 — 10
Isa. 10:4 — 10
Isa. 25:8 — 30
Isa. 29:7–14 — 43
Isa. 40:3–4 — 27
Isa. 48:1 — 82
Isa. 49:22 — 81
Isa. 49:24 — 49
Isa. 50:1 — 50, 81–82
Isa. 51:22 — 81

Hosea
Hosea 13:14 — 30

Micah
Micah 5:8–15 — 87
Micah 5:19–20 — 87

New Testament

Matthew
Matt. 1:20–23 — 45
Matt. 3:4 — 29
Matt. 5:15 — 38
Matt. 5:26 — 25
Matt. 6:24–25 — 26
Matt. 8:29 — 29
Matt. 11:5 — 29
Matt. 13:6 — 32
Matt. 26:1–71 — 11
Matt. 29:27 — 51

Mark
Mark 1:2 — 27
Mark 1:7 — 27
Mark 1:24 — 29
Mark 10:44 — 51n29, 151

Luke
Luke 1:35 — 29
Luke 2:10 — 29
Luke 3:16 — 27
Luke 24:39–40 — 200

John
John 1:4–5 — 30
John 1:11 — 29
John 1:27 — 27
John 10:16 — 37

Acts
Acts 3:210 — 29
Acts 4:12 — 40–41
Acts 9 — xiii
Acts 22:26 — 29

Romans
Rom. 11:36 — 83n10

1 Corinthians
1 Cor. 13:47 — 31
1 Cor. 15:14 — 30
1 Cor. 15:54–55 — 30
1 Cor. 15:58 — 29

Philemon

Phil. 2:6–7 — 29

Hebrews
Heb. 4:12 — 29
Heb. 7:3 — 32
Heb. 9:27 — 31

James
James 3:25 — 30

1 Peter
1 Pet. 4:11 — 83n10

2 Peter
2 Pet. 3:4–6 — 11
2 Pet. 3:16 — 31

Revelation
Rev. 14:10–11 — 29, 31
Rev. 16:219 — 29
Rev. 19:6 — 29
Rev. 20:6 — 30
Rev. 20:10 — 29
Rev. 20:13 — 29
Rev. 22:13 — 31

Book of Mormon

1 Nephi
1 Ne. Header — 89–90
1 Ne. 1:1–3 — 185
1 Ne. 1:4 — 55, 185, 203
1 Ne. 1:4–15 — 185–86
1 Ne. 1:7–8 — 133
1 Ne. 1:14–18 — 131
1 Ne. 1:16–17 — 186
1 Ne. 1:20 — 203
1 Ne. 2:1–4 — 203
1 Ne. 2:8–9 — 133
1 Ne. 2:11–12 — 139
1 Ne. 2:13–16 — 97
1 Ne. 2:22 — xv, 180
1 Ne. 3:1 — 97
1 Ne. 3:9–10 — 133
1 Ne. 3:16 — 152n58

1 Ne. 3:31 — 139
1 Ne. 4:2–3 — 187
1 Ne. 4:18–19 — 133
1 Ne. 4:38 — 98
1 Ne. 5:16 — 98
1 Ne. 6:7 — 131
1 Ne. 7:4–6 — 98
1 Ne. 7:13 — 133
1 Ne. 7:20–8:1 — 98–99
1 Ne. 8:38–9:2 — 99
1 Ne. 9:1 — 99, 104
1 Ne. 9:2 — 80n3
1 Ne. 9:2–5 — 105, 168
1 Ne. 9:3–4 — 179–80
1 Ne. 10:3–10 — 188
1 Ne. 10:7–8 — 27
1 Ne. 10:12–14 — 188
1 Ne. 10:15–17 — 100
1 Ne. 10:17 — 188
1 Ne. 10:20 — 188
1 Ne. 11:8 — 132
1 Ne. 11:10 — 134
1 Ne. 11–16 — 25
1 Ne. 11:12 — 134
1 Ne. 11:21 — 114
1 Ne. 11:24 — 134
1 Ne. 11:33–35 — 26
1 Ne. 12:1–4 — 95–96
1 Ne. 12:2 — 134
1 Ne. 12:4–6 — 26
1 Ne. 12:12–20 — 26
1 Ne. 12:21–23 — 163
1 Ne. 13:7 — 152n58
1 Ne. 13:14–15 — 26
1 Ne. 13:29 — 58
1 Ne. 13:34–36 — 26
1 Ne. 14:4–10 — 100–101
1 Ne. 14:7 — 26
1 Ne. 14:21–25 — 26
1 Ne. 14:30—15:2 — 100
1 Ne. 14:39–41 — 26
1 Ne. 15:1 — 188
1 Ne. 15:7 — 188
1 Ne. 15:13 — 188
1 Ne. 16:3 — 139
1 Ne. 16:20 — 139–40
1 Ne. 16:35–36 — 140
1 Ne. 17:17 — 140
1 Ne. 17:22 — 140
1 Ne. 17:45 — 143

1 Ne. 17:47 — 153
1 Ne. 17:49 — 140
1 Ne. 17:52 — 96
1 Ne. 18:16 — 140
1 Ne. 18:20–21 — 58
1 Ne. 18:23–24 — 203
1 Ne. 18:25—19:1 — 105, 152n59
1 Ne. 19:1–5 — 106
1 Ne. 19:4 — 48
1 Ne. 19:7 — 49
1 Ne. 19:23 — 188
1 Ne. 20:21 — 82
1 Ne. 21:24 — 49
1 Ne. 23:29 — 56

2 Nephi
2 Ne. 1:21 — 153
2 Ne. 1:27–30 — 92
2 Ne. 2:20 — 40n11
2 Ne. 3:14–15 — 45
2 Ne. 3:17 — 126
2 Ne. 4:10 — 108
2 Ne. 4:13–15 — 106–7
2 Ne. 4:15–35 — 144–46
2 Ne. 4:17 — 142
2 Ne. 5:3 — 140
2 Ne. 5:5–6 — xv
2 Ne. 5:18 — 203
2 Ne. 5:24 — 148
2 Ne. 5:28–33 — 107
2 Ne. 6:2 — 58n52
2 Ne. 6:3–8 — 93
2 Ne. 6:6 — 81
2 Ne. 6:13 — 94
2 Ne. 6:17 — 81
2 Ne. 6:17–18 — 94
2 Ne. 6:26–30 — 94
2 Ne. 7:1 — 50, 81
2 Ne. 8:22 — 81
2 Ne. 9:30–54 — 134–35
2 Ne. 9:39 — 143
2 Ne. 9:52 — 143
2 Ne. 15:25 — 10
2 Ne. 17:1 — 81, 94n26
2 Ne. 19:12 — 10
2 Ne. 19:17 — 10
2 Ne. 21:4 — 10
2 Ne. 25:1–8 — 190–91
2 Ne. 25:2 — 143

2 Ne. 25:11–13 — 26
2 Ne. 25:12–13 — 192
2 Ne. 25:16–18 — 26
2 Ne. 25:19 — 41
2 Ne. 25:20 — 40
2 Ne. 25:29 — 39
2 Ne. 26:1–2 — 26
2 Ne. 26:4 — 192
2 Ne. 26:9–10 — 26
2 Ne. 26:10 — 190
2 Ne. 26:14 — 26
2 Ne. 26:17 — 26
2 Ne. 26:21 — 26
2 Ne. 28:18 — 26
2 Ne. 27:3 — 42
2 Ne. 27:15–20 — 44
2 Ne. 29:3 — 111
2 Ne. 31:1–4 — 193
2 Ne. 31:20–21 — 40n11
2 Ne. 33:1 — 125
2 Ne. 33:2 — xv

Jacob
Jacob 1:1–3 — 169
Jacob 1:8–9 — 96
Jacob 1:9 — 182
Jacob 1:11 — 152, 182
Jacob 1:15 — 152n58
Jacob 3:13 — 126
Jacob 4:1 — 58n52
Jacob 4:2 — 110
Jacob 5:18 — 96
Jacob 5:21 — 48

Jarom
Jarom 1:14 — 48

Omni
Omni 1:12–17 — 203
Omni 1:15 — 209n26
Omni 1:18 114n4
Omni 1:19 — 203, 205
Omni 1:20 — 51 fn. 30
Omni 1:20–22 — 205
Omni 1:21 — 118, 211
Omni 1:25 — 169, 179, 217–19
Omni 1:27–30 — 206
Omni 1:30 — 169–70

Words of Mormon
W of M 1:1–2 — 218

Scripture Index

W of M 1:3 — 178, 180, 217
W of M 1:4–5 — 173
W of M 1:5 — 126
W of M 1:6–9 — 218–19
W of M 1:10 — 208n23
W of M 1:10–12 — 219
W of M 1:11 — 220n11
W of M 1:12–18 — 220n11

Mosiah
Mosiah 1:2 — 120
Mosiah 1:16 — 170
Mosiah 2:5–6 — 142
Mosiah 2:13 — 153
Mosiah 2:36–37 — 56
Mosiah 3:3–9 — 29
Mosiah 3:17 — 40n11
Mosiah 3:21 — 29
Mosiah 3:24–27 — 29
Mosiah 3:27 — 31
Mosiah 4:11 — 29
Mosiah 5:1–2 — 205
Mosiah 5:8 — 40n11
Mosiah 5:13 — 29
Mosiah 5:15 — 29
Mosiah 6:3–4 — 205
Mosiah 7:1–2 — 206–7
Mosiah 7:21–22 — 58n52
Mosiah 7:27–28 — 56
Mosiah 8:13 — 51n30, 207
Mosiah 8:17 — 51
Mosiah 9:1 — 148n52
Mosiah 9:11—12 — 148
Mosiah 9:21 — 203
Mosiah 10:7 — 58n52
Mosiah 10:8 — 29
Mosiah 10:12 — 148
Mosiah 10:17 — 58, 153
Mosiah 10:22 — 85
Mosiah 11:9 — 152n58
Mosiah 12:1 — 151
Mosiah 13:1 — 29
Mosiah 13:8 — 29
Mosiah 13:11 — 129
Mosiah 13:24 — 29
Mosiah 13:24–26 — 86
Mosiah 13:33 — 199
Mosiah 15:1 — 199
Mosiah 15:2 — 29
Mosiah 15:21 — 40
Mosiah 15:25 — 30
Mosiah 16:3 — 30
Mosiah 16:8–9 — 30
Mosiah 16:15 — 85
Mosiah 21:6 — 140 n34
Mosiah 21:20 — 174
Mosiah 21:25–28 — 208
Mosiah 22:12 — 152n58
Mosiah 23:10 — 151
Mosiah 23:19–20 — xii
Mosiah 25:5–6 — xii, 171
Mosiah 25:7 — 29
Mosiah 26:3 — 30
Mosiah 27:1 — 140n34
Mosiah 28:10–11 — 170
Mosiah 27:11 — xiii
Mosiah 27:19 — xiii
Mosiah 28:11–13 — 205
Mosiah 28:11–20 — 170
Mosiah 29:6–11 — xiv
Mosiah 29:38–41 — 205

Alma
Alma Header — 182
Alma 1:21 — 174
Alma 1:25 — 29
Alma 2:1 — 117
Alma 2:2 — 210
Alma 2:11 — 117
Alma 2:11–12 — 116
Alma 4:16–17 — 182
Alma 4:20 — 1 71
Alma 5:16–20 — xiv
Alma 7:27 — 84
Alma 7:27–8:3 — 158–59
Alma 8:1–3 — 84
Alma 8:29 — 151
Alma 9:12 — 151
Alma 9:13 — 146
Alma 9:26 — 151
Alma 10:32–11:20 — 77–78
Alma 11:4–19 — 114
Alma 11:6 — 115
Alma 11:12 — 115
Alma 11:15 — 121
Alma 11:19 — 115
Alma 11:39 — 31
Alma 12:7 — 29
Alma 12:20 — 115
Alma 12:27 — 31
Alma 13:4 — 58n52
Alma 13:9 — 32
Alma 13:20 — 31
Alma 13:22 — 29
Alma 13:25 — 86
Alma 13:31 — 115
Alma 15:11 — 152
Alma 15:16 — 152n58
Alma 15:19–16:1 — 159
Alma 15:21 — 58n52
Alma 16:18 — 149
Alma 16:21 — 159
Alma 17:2 — xii
Alma 17:6 — 117
Alma 17:14 — 148, 152n58
Alma 17:14–15 — 149
Alma 17:18 — 50
Alma 17:28 — 140n34
Alma 18:5 — 113
Alma 18:32 — 29
Alma 19:13 — 114
Alma 19:16 — 113
Alma 19:19 — 140n34
Alma 21:1–2 — 117
Alma 21:6 — 29
Alma 22:12–13 — 128
Alma 22:22–30 — 209
Alma 22:28 — 149
Alma 23:3 — 153
Alma 24:13 — 214n37
Alma 24:19 — 47
Alma 27:7–9 — 159–60
Alma 29:17–30:6 — 160
Alma 30:6–12 — 75
Alma 30:56–58 — 75
Alma 32:4–7 — 104
Alma 32:38 — 32
Alma 34:10 — 199
Alma 34:14 — 199
Alma 35:15 — 48
Alma 36:4 — 143
Alma 36:22 — 213
Alma 37:1–2 — 182
Alma 37:21–32 — 121
Alma 38:11 — 121
Alma 39:2 — 121
Alma 42:10 — 30
Alma 43:3 — 174
Alma 43:4–6 — 117
Alma 45:22–23 — xiii

Alma 46:3–4 — 116
Alma 46:4 — 210
Alma 47:36 — 149
Alma 49:29–30 — 160
Alma 49:30 — 211n33
Alma 50:38 — 171
Alma 50:40 — 161
Alma 51:1 — 161
Alma 51:5 — 210
Alma 51:5–6 — 118
Alma 51:37 — 161
Alma 52:1 — 161
Alma 53:13 — xiii
Alma 53:23 — 161
Alma 54:5–24 — 82n8
Alma 55:35 — 161
Alma 56:2–58:41 — 82n8
Alma 58:35 — 140n34
Alma 60:1–36 — 82n8
Alma 60:4 — 140n34
Alma 61:2–21 — 82n8
Alma 62:52 — 161
Alma 63:1 — 161
Alma 63:11 — xiii
Alma 63:16–17 — 161

Helaman
Hel. 1:15 — 118, 121, 211
Hel. 1:21 — 161
Hel. 2:1–2 — 161
Hel. 2:12–14 — 206
Hel. 2:23 — 183
Hel. 3:3–19 — 77
Hel. 3:13–16 — 167, 195
Hel. 3:14 — 126
Hel. 3:16 — 149
Hel. 3:20 — xiii
Hel. 3:33 — 49
Hel. 3:37 — xiii, xv
Hel. 5:1–5 — xv
Hel. 5:5–15 — 137–38
Hel. 5:6 — 146
Hel. 5:6–7 — 138
Hel. 5:16 — xv
Hel. 5:49 — xv
Hel. 5:50–51 — 213
Hel. 6:10 — 209n25, 210
Hel. 6:15 — 175

Hel. 7:21 — 152n58
Hel. 10:2–3 — 133
Hel. 11:3–4, 9–16 — 130–31
Hel. 13:1–2 — xv
Hel. 13:5 — 163
Hel. 14:2 — 161
Hel. 16:14 — 29
Hel. 16:25 — 183

3 Nephi
3 Ne. Header — 183
3 Ne. 1:9–14 — xv
3 Ne. 1:12–22 — 155
3 Ne. 1:24 — 29
3 Ne. 2:4–8 — 162
3 Ne. 2:7–8 — 175
3 Ne. 3:2–10 — 82n8
3 Ne. 4:5 — 153
3 Ne. 5:8 — 125
3 Ne. 5:9 — xvi, 172
3 Ne. 7:1–4 — 183–84
3 Ne. 7:14 — 204
3 Ne. 8:1 — 172
3 Ne. 11:1–2 — 200
3 Ne. 11:8 — 200
3 Ne. 11:14 — 200
3 Ne. 11:18–41 — 25
3 Ne. 11:25 — 84
3 Ne. 12:26 — 25
3 Ne. 13:13 — 84
3 Ne. 13:24–35 — 26
3 Ne. 15:17 — 37
3 Ne. 19:4 — xvi
3 Ne. 19:19 — 201
3 Ne. 21:20 — 146
3 Ne. 21:21–23 — 87
3 Ne. 24:3 — 152n58
3 Ne. 26:6 — 125
3 Ne. 27:4 — 140n34
3 Ne. 27:22–23 — 87

4 Nephi
4 Ne. 1:6 — 175
4 Ne. 1:16–17 — 204
4 Ne. 1:17 — 120, 184
4 Ne. 1:21 — 175
4 Ne. 1:46 — 152n58
4 Ne. 1:48 — 167

Mormon
Morm. 1:4 — 167, 196
Morm. 2:17–18 — 195
Morm. 4:23 — 169
Morm. 5:16 — 37
Morm. 7:1–3 — 212
Morm. 7:1–5 — 108–9
Morm. 7:4 — 214
Morm. 7:8–9 — 197
Morm. 9:33 — 114

Ether
Ether 1:6–7 — 121
Ether 1:11–12 — 121
Ether 1:33 — 73
Ether 6:27 — 73
Ether 7:3 — 73
Ether 7:7 — 73
Ether 8:1 — 71
Ether 9:14–11:23 — 73
Ether 9:19 — 38
Ether 9:21 — 71
Ether 10:12 — 152n58
Ether 10:23 — 152n58
Ether 11:4–9 — 121
Ether 12:1 — 105, 121
Ether 12:23–24 — 126
Ether 12:26–27 — 125
Ether 15:11 — 206

Moroni
Moroni 7:45 — 31
Moroni 8–9 — 82n8

Doctrine and Covenants

D&C 3:12 — 3n2
D&C 3:14 — 215
D&C 3:16–17 — 215
D&C 10:38–42 — 216
D&C 10:45 — 3n3
D&C 18:23 — 40n11
D&C 20:8–9 — 3n4
D&C 45:60 — 3n5

Pearl of Great Price

Moses
Moses 6:52 — 40n11
Moses 6:57 — 40n11

Subject Index

#

1 Nephi, book of
  header, 89
  political justification for, 107n4, 180
3 Nephi, book of
  dissolution of Nephite government in, 183
  header, 183
  name of, 172, 184

A

Aaron, 117, 128–29
Abinadi, 49, 85–86, 128–129, 171, 199, 208
Abish, 113
Abraham, book of, 12
Abusch, Tzvi, 74
Agar, Michael, 35
Alma, book of
  begins annalist history, 157
  two record keepers, 182
Alma$_1$, 50, 116, 119, 171, 207–8, 211–12
  record of, 171, 196
Alma$_2$, 82–83, 86, 103–4, 114, 119–22, 130, 146, 160, 170–74, 182–83, 196, 211–12
  record of, 171–72
Alter, Robert, 45, 129
Amaleki, 116–17, 169, 179, 206–10, 217–19
Amalekites, 116–17, 210
Amalickiah, 210
"amen," 83–85
Ammaron, 167, 169
Ammon, 37, 50, 76, 117, 159–160, 207–8, 211
Amulek, 78, 83, 86, 115, 130, 137, 152, 199, 211
anachronisms, 35, 39n8
"and," 95–96
"and it came to pass," 91–94
"and now", 91–94
Anderson, Lavina Fielding, 32
Anderson, Ronald D., 137
animals, 37n5, 38
Annals of Cuauhtitlan, 175–76
Annals of the Cakchiquels, 176–77
Anthon Transcript, 42
Anti-Nephi-Lehies, 212–14
antithetical parallels, 210–12
Antionah, 115, 120
Antionum, 75, 103, 115
Anthon, Charles, 42, 44
antithetical parallels, 210–12
Aronson, Elliot, 147
Ash, Michael R. Ash, 61n3
asses, 38

B

backlooping, 46
baktun, 156, 161, 163
Barlow, Philip L., 20
Barney, Kevin L., 150–51
base–20 system, 156–57
Benjamin, 116, 120, 169, 173, 179–80, 196, 199, 217, 219, 253
  sermon of, 173, 196
Bennett, Bob, 18n4
Best, Karl F., 14n38
Bidamon, Emma Smith, 42
blindsight, 63
Bokovoy, David E., 74
book headers, 21, 88–90, 183
book names, 178
Book of Commandments and Revelations, 14
Book of Covenants, 20
Book of Mormon
  animals, 38
  audiences of, 18, 103–4
  chapters, 80–88
  chronological organization, 174–78
  influenced by cultural expectations, 23
  modern elements, 8
  named books, 79–80, 178–84
  and Nephite literacy, 123
  oral culture of, 123
  and parallel biblical stories, 20
  printed book, 20

style of, 21
unique names in, 113
Bor, Daniel, 52, 63n6
Bountiful, 24, 120, 184, 200–201
Bowen, Matthew L., 113
Bradley, Don, 79, 170, 204
brain functions, 64
Brandt, Edward J., 40, 199
brass plates, 86, 130, 186
   model for Nephi$_1$, 168n1
Brown, Cecil H., 38
Brown, S. Kent, 185
Brown, Samuel M., 4
Bushman, Richard Lyman, 15

C

calendars, 155–56
   birth of Christ, 162–63
Campbell, Alexander, 21
candles, 38
Cantor, Norman F., 198n8
Carmack Stanford, 8, 61
Carson, D. A., 16
chapter breaks, 85–88, 178
   on five-year intervals, 157–61
chapter headings, 88–90
Cherokee war song, 216
Christenson, Allen J., 65, 131, 142
cognitive linguistics, 16
Columbus, 38
Corianton, 121–22, 141–42, 211
Coriantumr, 118, 211
Cowdery, Oliver, 9, 88, 178–79, 216
crucifixion, 201
Cumorah, 206
cyclical history, 201–2

D

Davis, Garold N., 188
Davis, Ossie, 63
Davis, Randall C., 16
Davis, William L. 71, 72
Dead Sea Scrolls, 187
Decalogue, 86
dialogue form, 120, 129–32
diphrastic kennings, 152–54
dyadic pairs, 150–51
dynastic record, 105, 107, 119–20, 169, 171, 183, 212n34

E

E. B. Grandin Publisher, 9
Eggington, William, 123, 125
Eichrodt, Walther, 40
elephants, 38–39
Ether, book of, 208
   genealogy list, 72–73, 78
   and memory tax, 72, 78,
Ether, plates of, 170
extemporaneous speech, 71

F–G

Flake, Kathleen, 11–12
Frederick Nicholas J., 23–25, 27
freemen, 118
French, Christopher C., 64
Gadianton Robbers, 130, 153, 204–9
Gee, John, 81–82, 91, 95–96
genealogy list, 72–73, 78
Gideon (people of), 84, 172
Gideon (place), 84
gift and power of God, 3, 5, 61, 180n9, 204
Gilbert, Eli, 20
Gilbert, John H., 89–90, 183
Givens, Nathaniel, 217n9
Glynn, Ian, 63
Grandin, E. B., 9

H

Hardy, Grant, 189, 196n4, 197n5
Harris, Martin, 6, 42, 44, 181, 215, 217
Haven, Charlotte, 19
Hebrew, 114
Helaman$_1$, 119–21, 171, 182, 211
Helaman$_2$, 119, 137–38, 146–47, 161, 167, 182–83, 213
Helaman, book of, 182
Herodotus, 127
Hofstadter, Douglas R., 66
Holzapfel, Richard Neitzel, 195n2
Hopkins, Nicholas A., 150n54
horses, 38
hotun, 157–61
House of Israel, 212
Hull, Kerry M., 152

I

Ibarretxe-Antuñano, Iraide, 216
incantations, 74

inquit statements, 81–82
Isaiah chapters, 10, 24–25
    Nephi$_1$ and Jacob use of, 48–49, 188
    reason for, 109–11
    recut, 81
Itzá, 161

J

Jackson, Kent P., 11
Jacob, 5, 25, 79–81, 93–96, 110, 120, 130, 134, 152, 168–69, 182, 186–94, 199, 217
    sources used, 193–94
Jaredites, 114, 205
Jasinski, Peter M., 11
Jesus Christ, 19, 21, 25–26, 35–41, 44–45, 56, 75, 96, 108, 113, 115, 119–20, 128, 137, 155–56, 160–63, 173, 177, 184, 193, 197–201, 204, 211, 218
    Christ/Messiah, 39
    God, 198
    prayed to, 201
    shows wounds, 200–201
John the Baptist, 27
Johnson, Janiece, 19
Jones, Clifford P., 220n11
Joseph Smith Translation of the Bible, 9
Josserand, J. Kathryn, 150n54

K

katun, 156, 161
Kelber, Werner, 59, 78, 91, 103, 125
King James Bible
    allusion to, 27
    edition quoted, 24
    italicized words, 10–11
    in Joseph's family, 32
    quotations in Book of Mormon, 28
king-men, 118
Knight, Joseph, 6
Korihor, 75, 76

L

Lamanites, 213
Lamb, Reverend M. T., 35, 36
large plates, 85, 88, 105–7, 168–70, 202, 207
    book divisions on, 179
    difference from small, 169
    made by commandment, 106
    Mormon's main source, 173, 195
    named for quantity, 168
    organized as annals, 174–75
    "plates of Nephi," 168
Law of Moses, 199
Lehi, book of, 180–85
Lehi$_1$, 92, 96–100, 185, 193, 198–199, 203–4, 211
    record of, 185
    tent of, 95–101
    plates of, 180n9
Lehi$_2$, 137–38, 182, 213–14
leitmotif, 143–46
leitwort, 136–40
literacy, 46
    co-exists with orality, 126
    culture of, 20, 111, 123
    error correction, 47
    mentality, 59
    and oral elements, 127
lost 116 pages, 79
    actual size, 79n2
    Coriantumr, 118
    history in, 204
    Joseph Smith's reaction to, 215
Lyon, Jack M., 220n11

M

Mackay, Michael Hubbard, 50
Mackay, Thomas W., 195
Marot, Clémont, 66
Matthew Grey, 12–13
Mayan literature, 131
Mayan long count, 177
Mayan prophecy, 162
McKinlay, Danel B. 83n10
memorized texts, 127–29
memory
    chunks, 53–54
    high tax in Ether, 72, 78
    intervening clauses, 59
    limitations of, 52
    production of language, 52
    sentences starting with "having," 58
    short term, 52, 59
    and top-heavy sentences, 57
memory tax, 72, 78
mentalese, 62–67
Mesoamerica
    animals, 37n5
    literacy of, 123

and war, 214n37
Miller, George, 52
Minson, Kent R., 220n11
Morley, Sylvanus Griswold, 158n6
Mormon, 3–5, 11, 15, 20, 25, 37, 77–97, 104, 107–9, 113–22, 126–30, 155–63, 167–86, 195–220
  copies text, 82
  differs from Nephi$_1$, 25
  envisioned audience of, 108–9, 214
  final farewell, 108
  geographic insertions, 76–77
  hides Nephite archive, 218
  as historian, 195–96
  hope of, 211
  inserts flashback, 207
  inserts text, 74, 115
  and Jaredite/Gadianton parallel, 205–8
  metonymic naming, 115–22
  purposes for writing, 197–214
  repeats narrative, 208n24
  and repentance, 212–14
  and simultaneous stories, 207
  and small plates, 173, 218
  and sourcing, 173–74, 195–97
  and two Mosiahs, 205n18
  use of dynastic names, 183
  use of five-year intervals, 157–61
  writing style, 83
  writing on plates, 195
Moroni, 5, 21, 39, 49, 82, 85, 88, 108, 114, 116, 125–27, 167, 170, 197–98, 205–6, 216–18
  envisioned audience of, 108
  finishes Mormon's record, 108
Mosiah$_1$, 182–83, 203–5, 208–9, 217
Mosiah$_2$, 76, 116, 128, 150, 163, 169–73, 182, 196, 204–8, 212–13
Mosiah, book of
  calendar, 177
  lost chapters, 79
  three kings in the book, 182
Mulek/Mulekites, 114, 114n4, 116, 208
murmuring, 138–40

N

names
  Adam, 113
  Eve, 113
  father and son share, 119
  MLK, 116–18, 208–11

Nephi, 184
Nephi$_1$, 5, 25–26, 42–44, 79–83, 90, 93–100, 103–10, 125–27, 130–34, 138–39, 142–43, 148, 163, 168, 174, 179–82, 185–89, 192–94, 198–99, 203–4,
  audience, 104–8, 189
  delights in plainness, 192
  introduces Isaiah, 189–93
  narrative demarcation of, 96–101
  psalm of, 143, 144–46
  and record keeping, 104
  reports making plates, 104–7
  on scattered Israel, 189
  scribal training, 187
  and Tree of Life, 26, 193
  use of Isaiah 48–49, 188
  use of pesher, 193
  use of scripture, 187–89
Nephi$_1$, books of, 179–80
Nephi$_2$, 119–20, 137–38, 182, 213–14
Nephi$_3$, 82, 87, 119–20, 130, 152, 172, 184, 196, 204,
  4 Nephi named for, 120
  disciple of Christ, 120
  record of, 172
Nephi$_3$, books of, 183–84
Nephihah, 182
Nephite archive, 167, 177–78, 218
Nephite governmental collapse, 120
Nephite twelve disciples, 25–26
Nephite understanding of God, 198–99
New Testament
  in Book of Mormon, 27–29
  quotations imprecise, 30
  "virgin," 44
Nida, Eugene A., 28
Noah (king), 129, 208
"now," 95–96
"nu," 95

O

Ong, Walter, 46, 59, 104, 125, 129, 132, 141
"or", 47–50
oral culture, 32, 78, 110, 123, 125, 127, 130, 132, 141, 146
orality, 46–7, 59, 91, 103–4, 110, 124–33, 138, 143, 146
  among Nephites, 126
  co-exists with literacy, 127
  conventions of, 91

corrective "or," 47, 50
error correction, 46–47
importance of memorization, 128
and incomplete sentences, 51, 59
increases memory load, 53
influence on New Testament, 103
lack of trust in writing, 124
memory use, 59
redundancy in, 132–36
repetition in, 132
Original Manuscript, 3, 22, 54, 55, 80, 88–89, 208n2
line separating headers, 88
no punctuation, 90

P

parallelisms, 142–46
Parry, Donald, 141n35, 142
Pea, Sarah DeArmon, 19
Perry, Seth, 28
Person, Raymond F., Jr., 109–10
pesher, 187, 189
Peter, 40
Pinker, Steven, 53, 57, 62, 64
Pinnock, Hugh W. 141n35, 142
Pioske, Daniel, 146
Plates of Nephi, 3, 167
in D&C 10, 216
political reasons for, 181n10
transmission lines, 169
Pliny the Elder, 124
Popol Vuh, 65–66
Postal, Paul, 53n37
Pratt, Orson, 78, 81, 86–87
Pratt, Parley P., 13
Printer's Manuscript, 21–22, 54–55, 80, 89, 179
line separating headers, 89
lacks punctuation, 90
prophecy, 3, 41–43, 201
600-year, 161
Mayan, 162
time sets, 161–63
pseudo-biblical language, 23

Q–R

Quiché, 65–66
Ramah, 206
reign of the judges, 157, 162
reigns of kings and judges, 180–84

"remember," 137–38
repetitive resumption, 55–57, 74–78
Richards, Samuel W., 6
Ricks, Eldin, 218n10
Rigdon, Sidney, 12
Roberts, B. H., 1–15
Rojo, Ana, 16
Rust, Richard Dilworth, 143, 198, 202

S

Scodel, Ruth, 46
sentences
in Hebrew, 95
incomplete, 51, 57
Sermon on the Mount in, 24, 26, 87
Shiblon, 121
Shim, 167–68, 178
small plates, 168–70
as appendix, 218
books of, 179–80
"plates of Nephi," 168
Smith, Emma, 42
Smith, Joseph
agent of translation, 8–16, 86
in translations and revelations, 12–16

T

Tavris, Carol, 147
Ten Commandments, 86
"tent of my father," 95–101
textual markers in lieu of punctuation, 90–96
thematic parallels, 202–3
Jaredites and Gadianton Robbers, 205, 208
in lost pages, 203–4
in Mosiah, 204–8
Nephite nations, 204–5
Ramah and Cumorah, 206
Thomas, Rosalind, 127–28
Thomasson, Gordon C., 114–15, 170
Timberlake, Henry, 16
Title Page, 41, 216
and two purposes for Mormon's book, 197
translation
1830 reception audience, 18
agent of, 5, 8–16, 61
anachronisms, 38–39
animals, 37
and archaic endings, 22
B. H. Roberts on, 15

of Bible by Joseph Smith, 9
Brigham Young on, 15, 23
of Cherokee war song, 17–18
cross-cultural translation, 35
differences in, 18, 66
divine translator theory, 5, 7–8
extemporaneous speech, 71
and fulfilled prophecy, 42–45
infallible, 6–7
intended audience, 16
iron-clad, 4
loose control, 4, 6
mentalese, 62–67
of Native American text, 18
quotations not verbatim, 20
relationship to Nephite text, 61
revelatory, 11, 12
Richard Bushman on, 15
tight control, 4, 6
Urim and Thummim, 6
use of New Testament, 27, 29–30
use of seer stone, 9, 42, 51, 53
of "virgin," 44
Western agricultural background of, 36
Treat, Mary Lee, 47
Tree of Life vision, 26, 95, 193
tun, 156
Tvedtnes, John A., 74
twelve Nephite disciples, 25–26

U–Z

Underwood, Grant, 14
Urim and Thummim, 6
Van der Toorn, Karl, 129
vigesimal system, 156–57
weapons of peace, 47
weapons of war, 47, 213–14
weights and measures, 77–78, 115
Welch, Jeannie, 54
Welch, John W., 5, 141–42, 188, 216
Wendland, Ernst, 92, 124n5, 128n19
Wessel, Walter W., 28
Whitmer, David, 6, 53–54
Wilson, Krissy, 64
Wiseman, Robert, 187
Words of Mormon, The, 79, 217–19
Wright, Mark A. 163, 284
    meaning of showing wounds, 200
    Mormon sensitive to units of five, 157
    on year counts, 177
Young, Brigham, 15, 23
Zarahemla, 116, 180, 182
Zeezrom, 115, 120
Zeniff, 83
    record of, 171, 196, 207–8

Also available from
Greg Kofford Books

See more Book of Mormon resources at
https://gregkofford.com/collections/bofm

The Gift and Power: Translating the Book of Mormon

Brant A. Gardner

Hardcover, ISBN: 978-1-58958-131-9

From Brant A. Gardner, the author of the highly praised *Second Witness* commentaries on the Book of Mormon, comes *The Gift and Power: Translating the Book of Mormon*. In this first book-length treatment of the translation process, Gardner closely examines the accounts surrounding Joseph Smith's translation of the Book of Mormon to answer a wide spectrum of questions about the process, including: Did the Prophet use seerstones common to folk magicians of his time? How did he use them? And, what is the relationship to the golden plates and the printed text?

Approaching the topic in three sections, part 1 examines the stories told about Joseph, folk magic, and the translation. Part 2 examines the available evidence to determine how closely the English text replicates the original plate text. And part 3 seeks to explain how seer stones worked, why they no longer work, and how Joseph Smith could have produced a translation with them.

Second Witness: Analytical and Contextual Commentary on the Book of Mormon

Brant A. Gardner

Second Witness, a new six-volume series from Greg Kofford Books, takes a detailed, verse-by-verse look at the Book of Mormon. It marshals the best of modern scholarship and new insights into a consistent picture of the Book of Mormon as a historical document. Taking a faithful but scholarly approach to the text and reading it through the insights of linguistics, anthropology, and ethnohistory, the commentary approaches the text from a variety of perspectives: how it was created, how it relates to history and culture, and what religious insights it provides.

The commentary accepts the best modern scholarship, which focuses on a particular region of Mesoamerica as the most plausible location for the Book of Mormon's setting. For the first time, that location—its peoples, cultures, and historical trends—are used as the backdrop for reading the text. The historical background is not presented as proof, but rather as an explanatory context.

The commentary does not forget Mormon's purpose in writing. It discusses the doctrinal and theological aspects of the text and highlights the way in which Mormon created it to meet his goal of "convincing . . . the Jew and Gentile that Jesus is the Christ, the Eternal God."

Praise for the *Second Witness* series:

"Gardner not only provides a unique tool for understanding the Book of Mormon as an ancient document written by real, living prophets, but he sets a standard for Latter-day Saint thinking and writing about scripture, providing a model for all who follow. . . . No other reference source will prove as thorough and valuable for serious readers of the Book of Mormon."
      -Neal A. Maxwell Institute, Brigham Young University

1. 1st Nephi: 978-1-58958-041-1
2. 2nd Nephi–Jacob: 978-1-58958-042-8
3. Enos–Mosiah: 978-1-58958-043-5
4. Alma: 978-1-58958-044-2
5. Helaman–3rd Nephi: 978-1-58958-045-9
6. 4th Nephi–Moroni: 978-1-58958-046-6

Traditions of the Fathers: The Book of Mormon as History

Brant A. Gardner

ISBN: 978-1-58958-665-9

**2015 Best Religious Non-fiction Award
by the Association for Mormon Letters**

"In the study of historical texts, context is king. Traditions of the Fathers masterfully contextualizes the diverse peoples of the Book of Mormon as they move, merge, and multiply across the Mesoamerican landscape. More than a simple lens, Gardner's multidisciplinary approach provides readers with illuminating, prismatic views of the Book of Mormon." — Mark Alan Wright, Assistant Professor of Ancient Scripture at Brigham Young University and Associate Editor of the *Journal of Book of Mormon Studies*

"The work he has done is rich, thorough, provocative. Like all Kofford books, this one is attractively produced, easy to hold in the hands and easy on the eyes. But best of all, it's informative, cogent, and altogether worth reading. I recommend it." — Julie J. Nichols, Association for Mormon Letters

Beholding the Tree of Life: A Rabbinic Approach to the Book of Mormon

Bradley J. Kramer

Paperback, ISBN: 978-1-58958-701-4
Hardcover, ISBN: 978-1-58958-702-1

Too often readers approach the Book of Mormon simply as a collection of quotations, an inspired anthology to be scanned quickly and routinely recited. In Beholding the Tree of Life Bradley J. Kramer encourages his readers to slow down, to step back, and to contemplate the literary qualities of the Book of Mormon using interpretive techniques developed by Talmudic and post-Talmudic rabbis. Specifically, Kramer shows how to read the Book of Mormon closely, in levels, paying attention to the details of its expression as well as to its overall connection to the Hebrew Scriptures—all in order to better appreciate the beauty of the Book of Mormon and its limitless capacity to convey divine meaning.

Praise for *Authoring the Old Testament*:

"Latter-day Saints have claimed the Book of Mormon as the keystone of their religion, but it presents itself first and foremost as a Jewish narrative. *Beholding the Tree of Life* is the first book I have seen that attempts to situate the Book of Mormon by paying serious attention to its Jewish literary precedents and ways of reading scripture. It breaks fresh ground in numerous ways that enrich an LDS understanding of the scriptures and that builds bridges to a potential Jewish readership." — Terryl L. Givens, author of *By the Hand of Mormon: The American Scripture that Launched a New World Religion*

"Bradley Kramer has done what someone ought to have done long ago, used the methods of Jewish scripture interpretation to look closely at the Book of Mormon. Kramer has taken the time and put in the effort required to learn those methods from Jewish teachers. He explains what he has learned clearly and carefully. And then he shows us the fruit of that learning by applying it to the Book of Mormon. The results are not only interesting, they are inspiring. This is one of those books that, on reading it, I thought 'I wish I'd written that!'" — James E. Faulconer, author of *The Book of Mormon Made Harder* and *Faith, Philosophy, Scripture*

The Vision of All: Twenty-five Lectures on Isaiah in Nephi's Record

Joseph M. Spencer

Paperback, ISBN: 978-1-58958-632-1
Hardcover, ISBN: 978-1-58958-633-8

In *The Vision of All*, Joseph Spencer draws on the best of biblical and Latter-day Saint scholarship to make sense of the so-called "Isaiah chapters" in the first two books of the Book of Mormon. Arguing that Isaiah lies at the very heart of Nephi's project, Spencer insists on demystifying the writings of Isaiah while nonetheless refusing to pretend that Isaiah is in any way easy to grasp. Presented as a series of down-to-earth lectures, *The Vision of All* outlines a comprehensive answer to the question of why Nephi was interested in Isaiah in the first place. Along the way, the book presents both a general approach to reading Isaiah in the Book of Mormon and a set of specific tactics for making sense of Isaiah's writings. For anyone interested in understanding what Isaiah is doing in the Book of Mormon, this is the place to start.

Praise for *Gathered in One*:

"With this book, Joseph M. Spencer has accomplished a remarkable feat. He has produced a reader-friendly, engaging study of the writings of Isaiah in the Book of Mormon that makes Isaiah accessible without overly-simplifying his theology and message." — Nicholas J. Frederick, Assistant Professor of Ancient Scripture, Brigham Young University, author of *The Bible, Mormon Scripture, and the "Rhetoric of Allusivity"*

"Spencer has produced by far the most helpful examination of the theological significance of Isaiah within the Book of Mormon. . . . In the emerging field of distinctively theological readings of the Book of Mormon, Joseph Spencer has made a major contribution, suggesting that conversations about the Book of Mormon are far from over." — John Christopher Thomas, *Journal of Book of Mormon Studies*

The 1920 Edition of the Book of Mormon: A Centennial Adventure in Latter-day Saint Book History

Richard L. Saunders

Hardcover, ISBN: 978-1-58958-775-5

Members of The Church of Jesus Christ of Latter-day Saints tend to see the Book of Mormon through the lens of personal use, as a single textual and scriptural monolith—*the* Book of Mormon. That is somewhat natural, since we tend to have at hand and in-use, only the copy or version in our language needed to study it for inspiration. In the process, the point tends to get overlooked that while we may accept the text as inspired, the physical embodiment of that text—the Book of Mormon—is a mortal reality. The *Book* of Mormon, while it has a "spirit," also has a mortal "body" (or rather, bodies) existing in space and time. As such, it has a history—and because it comes to us in the form of a book, it also has a book history.

This study is divided into three parts. The first part is a straightforward history of the edition's editing, production, and manufacturing processes. It examines key points in the reprint history of the book, following important factors in the subsequent impressions of the work across nearly thirty years of re-impressions, corrections, transfers, and one new format. The narrative crowded into chapters one through four together leave Part II to catalogue the bibliographic minutia that is the beating heart of analytic book history and which provides entertainment for true-blooded bibliophiles. The details contained in the production and manufacturing contracts and coupled to the typographical evidence explained in Part III, together resolve once and for all the question of what constitutes the 1920 edition and what does not.

Praise for *The 1920 Edition of the Book of Mormon*:

"This is both the definitive history of the 1920 edition of the Book of Mormon and a peek into how decisions were made at the highest levels of Church leadership at the time. A priceless work for bibliophiles and a great read for anyone interested in the history of The Church of Jesus Christ of Latter-day Saints in the twentieth century." — Gregory Seppi, Curator, L. Tom Perry Special Collections, Brigham Young University

The Lost 116 Pages: Reconstructing the Book of Mormon's Missing Stories

Don Bradley

Paperback, ISBN: 978-1-58958-760-1
Hardcover, ISBN: 978-1-58958-040-4

On a summer day in 1828, Book of Mormon scribe and witness Martin Harris was emptying drawers, upending furniture, and ripping apart mattresses as he desperately looked for a stack of papers he had sworn to God to protect. Those pages containing the only copy of the first three months of Joseph Smith's translation of the golden plates were forever lost, and the detailed stories they held forgotten over the ensuing years—until now.

In this highly anticipated work, author Don Bradley presents over a decade of historical and scriptural research to not only tell the story of the lost pages but to reconstruct many of the detailed stories written on them. Questions explored and answered include:

- Was the lost manuscript actually 116 pages?
- How did Mormon's abridgment of this period differ from the accounts in Nephi's small plates?
- Where did the brass plates and Laban's sword come from?
- How did Lehi's family and their descendants live the Law of Moses without the temple and Aaronic priesthood?
- How did the Liahona operate?
- Why is Joseph of Egypt emphasized so much in the Book of Mormon?
- How were the first Nephites similar to the very last?
- What message did God write on the temple wall for Aminadi to translate?
- How did the Jaredite interpreters come into the hands of the Nephite kings?
- Why was King Benjamin so beloved by his people?

Despite the likely demise of those pages to the sands of time, the answers to these questions and many more are now available for the first time in nearly two centuries in *The Lost 116 Pages: Reconstructing the Book of Mormon's Missing Stories*.

Gathered in One: How the Book of Mormon Counters Anti-Semitism in the New Testament

Bradley J. Kramer

Paperback, ISBN: 978-1-58958-709-0
Hardcover, ISBN: 978-1-58958-710-6

Since the Holocaust, a growing consensus of biblical scholars have come to recognize the unfair and misleading anti-Semitic rhetoric in the New Testament—language that has arguably contributed to centuries of violence and persecution against the Jewish people.

In *Gathered in One*, Bradley J. Kramer shows how the Book of Mormon counters anti-Semitism in the New Testament by approaching this most Christian of books on its own turf and on its own terms: literarily, by providing numerous pro-Jewish statements, portrayals, settings, and structuring devices in opposition to similar anti-Semitic elements in the New Testament; and scripturally, by connecting with it as a peer, as a divine document of equal value and authority, which can add these elements to the Christian canon (as the Gospel of John can add elements to the Gospel of Matthew) without undermining its authority or dependability.

In this way, the Book of Mormon effectively "detoxifies" the New Testament of its anti-Semitic poison without weakening its status as scripture and goes far in encouraging Christians to relate to Jews respectfully, not as enemies or opponents, but as allies, people of equal worth, importance, and value before God.

Praise for *Gathered in One*:

"His thesis is fresh, provocative, and rigorously argued. A signal contribution to Book of Mormon studies." — Terryl L. Givens, author of *By the Hand of Mormon: The American Scripture that Launched a New World Religion*

"Impressed by the book and its scholarship and attitude, I recommend it to all who are interested in the history of Christian attitudes towards the Jews, as well as those working towards interfaith reconciliation and mutual respect'" — Yaakov Ariel, professor of religious studies at the University of North Carolina at Chapel Hill and author of *Evangelizing the Chosen People: Missions to the Jews in America, 1880–2000*

Authoring the Old Testament: Genesis–Deuteronomy

David Bokovoy

Paperback, ISBN: 978-1-58958-588-1
Hardcover, ISBN: 978-1-58958-675-8

For the last two centuries, biblical scholars have made discoveries and insights about the Old Testament that have greatly changed the way in which the authorship of these ancient scriptures has been understood. In the first of three volumes spanning the entire Hebrew Bible, David Bokovoy dives into the Pentateuch, showing how and why textual criticism has led biblical scholars today to understand the first five books of the Bible as an amalgamation of multiple texts into a single, though often complicated narrative; and he discusses what implications those have for Latter-day Saint understandings of the Bible and modern scripture.

Praise for *Authoring the Old Testament*:

"*Authoring the Old Testament* is a welcome introduction, from a faithful Latter-day Saint perspective, to the academic world of Higher Criticism of the Hebrew Bible. . . . [R]eaders will be positively served and firmly impressed by the many strengths of this book, coupled with Bokovoy's genuine dedication to learning by study and also by faith." — John W. Welch, editor, *BYU Studies Quarterly*

"Bokovoy provides a lucid, insightful lens through which disciple-students can study intelligently LDS scripture. This is first rate scholarship made accessible to a broad audience—nourishing to the heart and mind alike." — Fiona Givens, co-author, *The God Who Weeps: How Mormonism Makes Sense of Life*

"I repeat: this is one of the most important books on Mormon scripture to be published recently. . . . [*Authoring the Old Testament*] has the potential to radically expand understanding and appreciation for not only the Old Testament, but scripture in general. It's really that good. Read it. Share it with your friends. Discuss it." — David Tayman, The Improvement Era: A Mormon Blog

Textual Studies of the Doctrine and Covenants: The Plural Marriage Revelation

William Victor Smith

Paperback, ISBN: 978-1-58958-690-1
Hardcover, ISBN: 978-1-58958-691-8

Joseph Smith's July 12, 1843, revelation on plural marriage was the last of his formal written revelations and a transformational moment in Mormonism. While acting today as the basis for the doctrine of eternal nuclear families, the revelation came forth during a period of theological expansion as Smith was in the midst of introducing new temple rituals, radical doctrines on God and humanity, a restructured priesthood and ecclesiastical hierarchy, and, of course, the practice of plural marriage.

In this volume, author William V. Smith examines the text of this complicated and rough revelation to explore the motivation for its existence, how it reflects this dynamic theology of the Nauvoo period, and how the revelation was utilized and reinterpreted as Mormonism fully embraced and later abandoned polygamy.

Praise for *Textual Studies*:

"No Mormon text is as ritually important and as fundamentally mysterious as Doctrine and Covenants 132. William V. Smith's work is a fine example of what a serious-minded and meticulous blend of source and redaction critical methods can tell us about the revelations produced by Joseph Smith. This is a model of what the future of Mormon scriptural studies should be."
— Stephen C. Taysom, author of *Shakers, Mormons, and Religious Worlds: Conflicting Visions, Contested Boundaries*

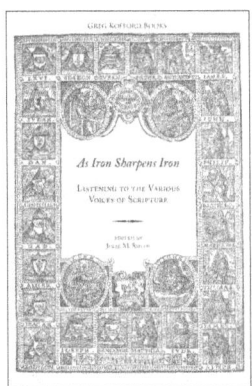

As Iron Sharpens Iron: Listening to the Various Voices of Scripture

Julie M. Smith

Paperback, ISBN: 978-1-58958-501-0

2016 Best Religious Non-fiction Award, Association for Mormon Letters

Our scripture study and reading often assume that the prophetic figures within the texts are in complete agreement with each other. Because of this we can fail to recognize that those authors and personalities frequently have different—and sometimes competing—views on some of the most important doctrines of the Gospel, including the nature of God, the roles of scripture and prophecy, and the Atonement.

In this unique volume, fictionalized dialogues between the various voices of scripture illustrate how these differences and disagreements are not flaws of the texts but are rather essential features of the canon. These creative dialogues include Abraham and Job debating the utility of suffering and our submission to God, Alma and Abinidi disagreeing on the place of justice in the Atonement, and the authors Mark and Luke discussing the role of women in Jesus's ministry. It is by examining and embracing the different perspectives within the canon that readers are able to discover just how rich and invigorating the scriptures can be. The dialogues within this volume show how just as "iron sharpeneth iron," so can we sharpen our own thoughts and beliefs as we engage not just the various voices in the scriptures but also the various voices within our community (Proverbs 27:17).

Hugh Nibley: A Consecrated Life

Boyd Jay Petersen

Hardcover, ISBN: 978-1-58958-019-0

Winner of the Mormon History Association's Best Biography Award

As one of the LDS Church's most widely recognized scholars, Hugh Nibley is both an icon and an enigma. Through complete access to Nibley's correspondence, journals, notes, and papers, Petersen has painted a portrait that reveals the man behind the legend.

Starting with a foreword written by Zina Nibley Petersen and finishing with appendices that include some of the best of Nibley's personal correspondence, the biography reveals aspects of the tapestry of the life of one who has truly consecrated his life to the service of the Lord.

Praise for *A Consecrated Life*:

"Hugh Nibley is generally touted as one of Mormonism's greatest minds and perhaps its most prolific scholarly apologist. Just as hefty as some of Nibley's largest tomes, this authorized biography is delightfully accessible and full of the scholar's delicious wordplay and wit, not to mention some astonishing war stories and insights into Nibley's phenomenal acquisition of languages. Introduced by a personable foreword from the author's wife (who is Nibley's daughter), the book is written with enthusiasm, respect and insight. . . . On the whole, Petersen is a careful scholar who provides helpful historical context. . . . This project is far from hagiography. It fills an important gap in LDS history and will appeal to a wide Mormon audience."
—Publishers Weekly

"Well written and thoroughly researched, Petersen's biography is a must-have for anyone struggling to reconcile faith and reason."
—Greg Taggart, Association for Mormon Letters

Joseph Smith's Polygamy: Toward a Better Understanding

Brian C. Hales
and Laura H. Hales

Paperback, ISBN: 978-1-58958-723-6

In the last several years a wealth of information has been published on Joseph Smith's practice of polygamy. For some who were already well aware of this aspect of early Mormon history, the availability of new research and discovered documents has been a wellspring of further insight and knowledge into this topic. For others who are learning of Joseph's marriages to other women for the first time, these books and online publications (including the LDS Church's recent Gospel Topics essays on the subject) can be both an information overload and a challenge to one's faith.

In this short volume, Brian C. Hales (author of the 3-volume Joseph Smith's Polygamy set) and Laura H. Hales wade through the murky waters of history to help bring some clarity to this episode of Mormonism's past, examining both the theological explanations of the practice and the accounts of those who experienced it first hand. As this episode of Mormon history involved more than just Joseph and his first wife Emma, this volume also includes short biographies of the 36 women who were married to the Prophet but whose stories of faith, struggle, and courage have been largely forgotten and ignored over time. While we may never fully understand the details and reasons surrounding this practice, Brian and Laura Hales provide readers with an accessible, forthright, and faithful look into this challenging topic so that we can at least come toward a better understanding.

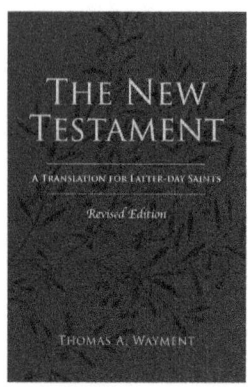

The New Testament: A Translation for Latter-day Saints, Revised Edition

Thomas A. Wayment

Paperback, ISBN: 978-1-58958-786-1

The language of the King James Bible will always be part of the Latter-day Saint cultural fabric in English. It is woven into our hymns, our ordinances, and our scriptural canon, and it has been one of the primary vehicles through which we encounter the word of God. However, when the language of translation becomes too foreign, too distant from the present age, it is time to consider the possibility of another translation. The four-hundred-year-old King James Bible in use by English speaking Latter-day Saints is an artifact of the seventeenth century and is no longer a living and breathing text. The New Testament was written by the marginalized and impoverished; its language is that of common people and not the educated elites.

The New Testament: A Translation for Latter-day Saints is an invitation to engage again the meaning of the text for a new and more diverse English readership by rendering the New Testament into modern language in a way that will help a reader more fully understand the teachings of Jesus, his disciples, and his followers.

This new revised edition is an effort to correct the first edition—in nearly two hundred instances—both in the notes and less frequently in the text. In addition, the introductory material has been expanded to include discussions of the Joseph Smith Translation and on reading scripture, and appendices have been added detailing the many instances in which the language of the New Testament appears in other Latter-day Saint scripture.

Praise for *The New Testament: A Translation for Latter-day Saints*:

"Wayment's volume is uneclipsed by any other available Latter-day Saint presentation of the New Testament." — Philip L. Barlow, *BYU Studies Quarterly*